THE MEDIEVAL READER

STUDIES IN MEDIEVAL AND RENAISSANCE HISTORY

Third Series

Volume I

(Old Series Vol. XXVI,
New Series, Vol XVI)

THE MEDIEVAL READER

Reception and Cultural History in the Late Medieval Manuscript

Edited by

Kathryn Kerby-Fulton and Maidie Hilmo

AMS PRESS
New York

AMS PRESS INC.

ISSN 0081-8224
ISBN 0-404-62850-8 (Set)
ISBN 0-404-64551-8 (Third Series, Vol. 1)

Library of Congress Catalog Card Number 63-22098

All AMS books are printed on acid-free paper that meets the guidelines for performance and durability of the Committee on Production Guidelines for Book Longevity of the Council on Library Resources.

Manufactured in the United States of America

Contents

The Vernacular Reader

We dedicate this volume to our mothers
Doreen Kerby and Magdalena Benesch

Introduction

Despite the best efforts of recent scholarship, medieval reading habits and interpretive responses remain among the most elusive aspects of the cultural history of the Middle Ages. It is a subject, we believe, that is best treated as a problem of cultural history, and not merely of literary criticism, where to date it has been only partially addressed as an aspect of literary theory. Although there have been some excellent attempts to reconstruct and recover medieval reading methods from what has come to be known today as medieval literary theory, the limitations of this approach have become increasingly apparent, and not only in relation to vernacular texts. The reason for this lack of success may be owing to the fact that just as the medieval period tolerated an astonishingly wide chasm between theory and practice in fields like medicine, law (especially civil law), and natural history (the bestiary being a striking case in point), so they did in interpretive disciplines as well. The literary theory that emerges in learned prologues of biblical exegetes and early humanists is, therefore, however illuminating as a system of thought, of limited use in the actual understanding and cultural construction of medieval texts. This, it has been recently argued, is especially true in relation to the vernacular. In an essay entitled "The Notion of the Vernacular," Ruth Evans, Andrew Taylor, Nicholas Watson and Jocelyn Wogan-Browne have somewhat provocatively declared:

> The term "theory" cannot be used in relation to Middle English literature . . . without considerable historical and critical negotiation. The term "medieval literary theory" is a modern one, and the appearance of Minnis and Scott's book of that title (1988) coincided with the rise within the academy of a strong interest in something called literary theory . . . However, although there is now a consensus that Latin scholastic culture of the Middle Ages had a body of writings that can be grouped under the rubric of "medieval literary theory," it must be understood that the category, as well as the term, is modern, not medieval. One effect of the field's focus on an exclusively Latin corpus has been the delineation of a theoretical field rooted in academic origins and spheres of influence.[1]

Vernacular prologues, as they go on to argue, have more of a pragmatic nature to offer, owing to their cultural "situatedness," but, on closer inspection even these are rarely about *actual* reading. The prologues are especially helpful on issues of authorial intention, authorial inspiration, and even, on occasion, authorial embarrassment. Thus we have, for instance, the evident concern at being involved in the lowly task of vernacularization expressed by learned friar, Osbern Bokenham, whose prologue quips that if anyone asks who wrote his book, they should be told it came from a horse-dealer.[2] The vernacular prologues can also be a rich source for authorial modelling of how reading *should* proceed: "when ye rede by yourself alone, ye oughte not to be hasty to rede moche at ones, but ye oughte to abyde therupon, and som tyme rede a thynge ageyne twyes, or thryes, or oftener."[3] Thus the advice of the *Mirror of Our Lady*, which contains one of the most explicit of extant Middle English prologues on the subject of reading. What is still missing, however, is the other half of the equation: reception.

We are left, then, with the question: how did medieval people read? How did they use the physical page? How did what they read affect them historically and culturally? And, perhaps, most importantly, why does it matter? It matters because the evidence, when we bother to stop and collect it, can be so revealing as to be disturbing to established modern constructions of major texts and historical documents.[4] It can add whole new layers to our awareness of how medieval texts functioned culturally. To take but one example from the present volume, as Maidie Hilmo's essay demonstrates, the cycle of illustrations added to the *Pearl* manuscript by an insightful contemporary reader creates virtually a parallel meta-narrative, linking its four poems on radically diverse subjects in an over-arching visual allegory of the journey towards the celestial Jerusalem—an interpretation and a linkage we would never likely make without the help of this unknown reader. Medieval reading practices can be uncovered from codicological or iconographic analysis of the manuscripts themselves (as in Olson's, Schaap's or Hilmo's pieces), or from the process of text translation, bowdlerization or political appropriation (as in Voaden and Jönsson's or Kerby-Fulton and Horie's), or from evidence of audience literacy or provenance (as Patricia Baer's and Tanya Schaap's essays both show). The essays here are grouped according to two kinds of reader: the professional and the vernacular. Each group contains three case studies, and has been introduced by a leading scholar in the field, and so there is little need for detailed comment here, except perhaps to explain our definition of the "professional reader": in a related but more specific usage than Malcolm Parkes made of the term in his classic essay on "The Literacy of the Laity,"[5] for us a "professional reader" is someone whose job is the preparation of a text for the reading public, whether as supervisory scribe, corrector, annotator, editor, or illustrator. Such readers usually felt it was incumbent upon them not only to prepare, but also to *adapt* the text for presentation to the patron or reading community. Their impact was enormous, and this is why understanding their habits of reading is important for cultural history.

All the essays published here, then, address some aspect of the medieval reading process, either through manuscript study, or by exploring questions of audience, literacy, vernacularity, book ownership and social class, medieval libraries, transmission of texts, translation, use of text and image, or some other aspect of medieval reading and response. Together the essays collectively demonstrate not only the activities of two kinds of readers (not, by the way, mutually exclusive), but also five types or functions of medieval reading which, as Denise Despres and I have suggested elsewhere, are especially characteristic of approaches to texts in the later Middle Ages.[6] In addition to the many functions of reading moderns share with medieval readers, and, indeed, readers of other historical periods, late medieval reading was particularly likely to emphasise, we suggest, the following five processes: mnemonic retention, meditative analysis, self-reflection, performative functions, and dissenting perspectives. This last requires elaboration: dissent, whether religious, political, moral, interpretive or aesthetic, is endemic to reading experience in all ages. What sets medieval reader response apart on this score is the instability of manuscript culture (in which any text can be altered with each new copy), the degree of power exerted by "professional readers" in textual production, and the widespread cultural assumption that "correction" (by annotation, erasure or expunction) was the duty of all good readers. Under such circumstances reader dissent becomes a force to be reckoned with.

To give a few brief instances of each of these five from the present volume: there is the *meditative* function of pictorial reader response in the *Pearl* Manuscript, in this case metatextually realized by a professional reader working just slightly later than the original was produced. His cycle suggests an equal concern with *self-reflection,* prompted, in part, by the role of the dreamer in *Pearl* itself. Other papers in the collection also demonstrate the extraordinary concern medieval readers seem to have had with self-reflection: Linda Olson's essay, for instance, shows how the professional reader who abridged the *Confessions* was preoccupied "with the interiority of Augustine's progressive conversion process," even as he "eliminated aspects which might be theologically or philosophically dangerous." Nor is he the only *dissenting* reader discussed in the volume: as Rosalynn Voaden and Arne Jönsson suggest, the professional reader who translated the "Epistola solitarii" (Alphonse of Jaén's remarkable defence of Bridget of Sweden's visions) excised passages in order to suppress vernacular access to material which might over-encourage visionary experience, or even authorship, especially in female readers. Kerby-Fulton and Horie introduce an even more literal instance of attempted textual subversion, in relation to the political history of the French translation of the *Modus tenendi parliamentum,* a translation that made an ideologically idealised Latin text widely available to a class of people with both the means and motivation to manipulate parliamentary procedures. The evidence for the audience of *Piers Plowman,* as illuminated in the articles by Tanya Schaap and Patricia Baer, raises important issues of vernacularity and literacy relative to a host of readership hermeneutics. The annotations transcribed or otherwise consulted by Schaap supply a wealth of data about *mnemonics* for reader guidance (e.g., in notes like "diuisiones graciarum," Bodleian Library, MS Digby 102, fol. 88r), or subjects for *meditation* ("Jhesus A carpenters sonn ye Judge of all justices in this worlde," British Library, MS. Add. 35157, fol. 94v).[7] These *Piers Plowman* annotators also signal *performative* moments in the text (e.g., "Concyence spake of criste *and* of the crosse," Digby 102, fol. 87v), as does the Norwich annotator of Augustine ("Oratio Augustini," 10.13) in one of his rare appearances. And these readers, too, sometimes dissent ("an Vnsownd opynion", Add. 35157, fol. 91v).

All contributors of essays were trained in part or in whole at University of Victoria. There are still far too few universities in North America where a student can get training in paleography and codicology: our hope is that this volume will encourage more scholars to do such work, to mount such programmes, and, most important, to *become* (now in a different sense) "professional readers" of the Middle Ages themselves.

Maidie Hilmo and I would like to thank the following people for their help and patience: Derek Pearsall and Nicholas Watson for their willingness to introduce the essays and work with each contributor during the revision process, Jack Hopper at AMS Press, for his patience and enthusiasm, Lyman Robinson, of the University of Victoria, for his wisdom, kindness and support during the volume's darkest hours, Darlene Hollingsworth for her meticulous and dedicated work on the copy-edited manuscript, Kelly Parsons for her cheerful work on the Index, and most especially the contributors themselves, whose friendship and faith in us sustained our spirits through the worst and most unexpected tribulations of publication.

Kathryn Kerby-Fulton, Yale University/University of Victoria

Notes

1. Jocelyn Wogan-Browne, Nicholas Watson, Andrew Taylor and Ruth Evans, *The Idea of the Vernacular: An Anthology of Middle English Literary Theory, 1280–1520* (Exeter, 1999), p. 315. They cite the important collection by Alastair J. Minnis and A. B. Scott (with the assistance of David Wallace), *Medieval Literary Theory and Criticism, c. 1100 - c. 1375: The Commentary Tradition* (Oxford, 1988).
2. "Be not aknowe whom it comyth fro, / But seyth, . . . From a frend of yourys that usyth to selle/ Goode hors at feyrys," *The Idea of the Vernacular*, ed. Wogan-Browne et al., p. 70, lines 214–18.
3. Cited from the prologue to "The Mirror of Our Lady," *The Idea of the Vernacular*, ed. Wogan-Browne et al., p. 262, lines 121–22.
4. For specific instances, see Kathryn Kerby-Fulton and Denise Despres, Introduction, *Iconography and the Professional Reader: The Politics of Book Production in the Douce Piers Plowman* (Minneapolis, 1999).
5. For Parkes, "the literacy of the professional reader" is that of "the scholar or professional man of letters," which he distinguished from the cultivated reader and the pragmatic reader; see, "The Literacy of the Laity," in *The Medieval World*, ed. David Daiches and A. Thorlby (London, 1973), p. 555.
6. *Iconography and the Professional Reader.*

7. For the instances from Digby 102, see Schaap's article, for the instances from Add. 35157, see the article by Carl Grindley she cites, "Reading *Piers Plowman* C-text Annotations: Notes Toward the Classification of Printed and Written Marginalia in Texts from the British Isles 1300–1641," K. Kerby-Fulton and M. Hilmo, *The Middle English Professional Reader at Work* (forthcoming in *English Literary Studies* 85, 2001).

The Professional Reader: Scribes, Illustrators, and Workshop Reading Strategies

Introduction by Derek Pearsall

The analogy between codicological and archaeological investigation is one that has often been drawn, from the time of the pioneering essay of Leopold Delaissé in 1967, "Towards a History of the Medieval Book,"[1] and not least effectively in a review by Tom Shippey of the facsimile of Oxford, Bodleian Library, MS Fairfax 16,[2] in which he spoke of the value of such a manuscript miscellany to the literary scholar as comparable to that of a midden to the archaeologist. The analogy is indeed a very useful one. When one thinks, for instance, of how archaeological sites were plundered in the nineteenth century for museum-loot, whole strata of material evidence for past civilisations laid waste in the pursuit of objects relating to cultures that were then currently fashionable—Roman, Trojan, Carthaginian—one is irresistibly reminded of the plundering of literary manuscripts by nineteenth-century scholars for texts of works by currently fashionable major writers, and of the discarding upon the rubbish-heap of history of those manuscripts that contained texts that were not useful in the construction of critical editions. Of course, an archaeological site can be irrecoverably destroyed by brutal and historically insensitive excavation, where a manuscript remains intact—unless indeed it has been dismembered or mutilated by connoisseurs of illumination.

But the modern archaeologist, like the modern codicologist, having acquired this sensitivity, is aware of the many ways in which a site, or a manuscript, may yield up evidences through which we may understand, in depth and to some extent at first hand, the mentalities of a past culture. Like the archaeologist, too, the modern codicologist must have a theory of what he or she may expect to find: not a demand that the site, or manuscript, should surrender what a modern expectation requires that it should have, but a series of working hypotheses for the interpretation of material evidence. For the archaeologist, what is not there—a space, a hole, an imprint can be as important as what is there, but only if there is a structure of understanding in place for evaluating its significance. For the codicologist, every mark on every page is significant, but there must also be deep-structured understanding of what the absence of particular marks—line-ruling, text-divisions, capitalization—might mean. The development of modern theories of reception and reader-response, and the more flexible approach to questions of text-production, have helped to provide, in supplement to the older disciplines of palaeography and analytic bibliography, the needed structures of understanding.

There are various particular ways in which manuscripts can be persuaded to yield up their secrets, to reveal their secret entrance-ways into the cultural mentalities of the people who made and read them. It can happen, for instance, with the actual copying of the text. Scribes make "mistakes," but mistakes may be of many kinds: there are some that the scribe would obviously wish that he had not made, and be pleased to have corrected for him, but some scribal variants may provide evidence of ways of thinking that we want to know about almost as much as we want to know about the original author's intentions, and some may be creative miswritings that the author himself might well have preferred. Scribes, it has been said, are a medieval author's earliest critics, the first whose critical response to a text, intelligent or otherwise, we get to hear about.

Pictures in a manuscript, likewise, sometimes provide nothing other than a glimpse of the monotonies and repetitions of workshop practice; but they can equally give us insight into the way in which an informed early reader understood a text. An artist may "misunderstand" a text, but his misunderstanding will be as informative as any understanding that might be found more acceptable to modern tastes, and may lead us to an enlightened revision of our own view. In one of the essays below, Maidie Hilmo speaks of another way in which pictures can disclose hidden meanings. She reads the miniatures in the *Pearl* manuscript not so much as evidence of the responses of an early reader as evidence of their role as an aspect of text-production. For her, they function in important ways as a visual guide to the reading process.

Manuscript annotations and marginalia can also show us how a text was prepared for the reader—what parts were thought to need special elucidation or commentary, what parts were thought worth signaling with a *nota bene.* Such marks in the manuscript may point backward, enigmatically, to the author: some authors, such as Gower, clearly had a part in the preparation of the text for the reader, but with others (Chaucer, Langland) it is quite hard to say. But reception-theory does not have to confess itself defeated if authorial intention cannot be proved: the way a text was understood, the way it came to be understood, are all part of the complexly incremental process of interpretation that we inherit, add to, and hand on. No text is clean of these processes, except one that has never been read. The study of Oxford, Bodleian Library, MS Digby 102, below, by Tanya Schaap, is interesting as showing two layers in this process: a mid-fifteenth century layer of marginal annotation, contemporary with the making of the manuscript (the work of what is called here a "professional reader") and giving us clear indications of the ways in which the poem was intended to be read and understood; and an early sixteenth-century layer, through which we can perceive something of the partiality of interpretation, on the part of an "enthusiastic and concerned reader," and something too of the inevitability of that partiality.

Readers who left the evidence of their reading in marginalia of this kind may be a century or more distanced from the making of the manuscript, but they belong to essentially the same culture. Linda Olson's study of a fourteenth-century abridgement of Augustine's *Confessions* is specially interesting as an example of a reader who was by no means contemporary with the making of the work—indeed, he was a thousand years later—but who can still claim to be a "professional reader" in a special way. Here is someone who participated fully in the mental activity of the original author's work, so much so that he sets out deliberately to remodel it as what he conceives it essentially to be, that is, a unique stimulus to confessional interiority. Augustine's text is abridged and reshaped so that it becomes primarily, and perhaps more than Augustine himself would have approved, a narrative of personal spiritual growth and development. There is less emphasis on philosophical and theological issues, and the author, who was a member of the Benedictine house at Norwich, may well have intended the work as an introduction to the spiritual life for younger members of his community. A single manuscript thus opens up a world of change.

It is clear from these three essays, with the meticulousness of their close work on the manuscripts, and the sophistication of their theoretical equipment, that the codicological excavation is proceeding busily and productively.

Harvard University

Notes

1. L. M. J. Delaissé, "Towards a History of the Medieval Book," *Divinitas* 11 (1967), 423–36.
2. T. A. Shippey, review of Bodleian Library, MS Fairfax 16, facsimile with introduction by John Norton-Smith (London, 1979), in *Times Literary Supplement* (March 7, 1980), 272.

The Image Controversies in Late Medieval England and the Visual Prefaces and Epilogues in the *Pearl* Manuscript: Creating a Meta-Narrative of the Spiritual Journey to the New Jerusalem

Maidie Hilmo

And again the kingdom of heaven is like to a merchant seeking good pearls. Who when he had found one pearl of great price, went his way and sold all that he had and bought it. (Matt. 13.45–46)[1]

And the twelve gates are twelve pearls, one to each . . . (Apoc. 21.21)

The *Pearl* Manuscript (London, British Library, MS Cotton Nero A. x, Article 3)

The modest size of the *Pearl* Manuscript of 90 vellum leaves, about 4 3/4 by 6 3/4 inches,[2] makes it easily portable and so particularly suitable for private reading. It is the antithesis of the Vernon Manuscript, the largest extant Middle English work, which is about four times as long and as big.[3] Both are literary manuscripts, but their respective measurements signal what their illustrations manifest: diametrically opposed influences with respect to the image controversies that disturbed as they stimulated the cultural productions of the late fourteenth century in England.

Before I discuss the twelve miniatures in the *Pearl* Manuscript, it is best to consider when the illustrations were made in relation to the copying of the text and why this matters. On the basis that the first folio of the *Pearl* poem looks worn, as if it had lain unprotected for a time before the bifolium of pictures was added in front of it, the miniatures were thought to have been executed sometime after the scribe had finished the text. As late as 1996 Kathleen Scott stated in her catalogue that the poems in this manuscript were composed after about 1360, copied between 1375–1400, and illustrated about 1400–1410.[4] In the following year, the hiatus in time between the copying of the script and the making of the miniatures was challenged by Paul Reichardt, who observed that the first of the pictures preceding the text, especially the lower right quadrant, looks just as worn.[5] This, among other reasons concerning their quality (discussed below), means that the *Pearl* Manuscript illustrations could have been made shortly after the script, that is, around the last decade of the fourteenth century when the Vernon Manuscript was made. Such a date for their composition makes all the more informative any differences in content and style in the illustrations of these two manuscripts. These differences are telling with respect to the *Pearl* Manuscript illustrations which, seen in isolation from their historical context, have been much maligned.

Extensive literary attention has been paid to the poems in the *Pearl* Manuscript—*Pearl, Cleanness, Patience,* and *Sir Gawain and the Green Knight*—which are extant only in this small, unpretentious book. Except for the pioneering work of Israel Gollancz,[6] there was little interest in the miniatures until they were taken somewhat more seriously by Jennifer Lee who saw them as an early form of audience response, although she thought that the artist was "neither a skilled illuminator nor an able literary critic."[7] Close to a decade later, Sarah Horrall considered that "in a simplified form" the artist presents "the main elements of the stories" (the criticism about their lack of adaptation to the stories being "much exaggerated").[8] Within another decade Kathleen Scott accorded the artist professional status, although she disagreed with Lee about him as a critic or interpreter of the poems because of his "lack of attention" to them.[9] Around the same time, Blanch and Wasserman made a detailed study of the hand imagery in the poems which, in the context of the iconography of the the *dextra Domini* in art, provided a useful context for the writing Hand in the miniature of Belshazzar's Feast.[10] Previous to this study by Blanch and Wasserman, who observe in passing that the illuminations "have been consistently described as 'crude',"[11] almost all of the modern critics who have mentioned them at all have given, at best, only a lukewarm assessment concerning their quality and their relevance to the text.

It is this very issue which Reichardt takes up, quoting Sir Frederic Madden's words in his title: "'Several Illuminations, Coarsely Executed': The Illustrations of the *Pearl* Manuscript"[12] and makes the real basis for his re-evaluation of the date of the miniatures. He sees the common scholarly assumptions that the texts and illustrations were "produced in isolation from each other" as "a variation on the old theme of the disparity between the excellence of the poems and the ineptness of the pictures bound with them," a preconception based on Madden's pronouncement about their inferiority and extraneous character.[13] Reichardt argues that the repetitive nature of the illustrations, one of the criticisms of them by Horrall, actually contributes to the impression that the four texts form part of an integrated and consistent literary vision.[14] To this end he discusses the numerical resonances of the twelve miniatures, which I will not elaborate upon; instead, I take up where he leaves off to show the sort of continuity the illustrations provide.

In the section immediately following, I consider the relevance of the image controversies of the times with respect to their style and content, both features which appear to have misled critics questioning their quality and relevance. Then I demonstrate that these miniatures provide a spiritual "reading" integrating all four poems within a liturgical and apocalyptic discourse. In the process I show, for the first time and with the aid of modern technology, what is revealed underneath the dark wavy "spot" of the first miniature. I also explore the implications, in terms of design and significance, of the presently misaligned worm holes and repairs along the spine, previously unnoticed, in the miniatures preceding the *Pearl* poem.

The Image Controversy in England

To understand the nature and purpose of the *Pearl* Manuscript illustrations, given their extreme plainness and the absence of holy images, it is useful to see them in the context of the images debates sparked in the late fourteenth century by Wyclif and the Lollard movement. The miniatures of the *Pearl* Manuscript deal not only with the dangers of idolatry but strictly avoid occasions for it. Yet they do not avoid featuring orthodox views about the Eucharist and utilizing conventional iconographic expectations in relation, for instance, to the Noah and Jonah cycles. In this section, I will present the iconodule position favoring the use of holy images as argued by Walter Hilton, along with a visual example from the Vernon Manuscript which includes two of Hilton works.[15] Following this I will refer briefly to iconomachic views about the dangers of images as expressed by Wyclif and the Lollards.

Part IV of the Vernon Manuscript includes the first book of the *Scale of Perfection*, composed in the 1380s by Walter Hilton.[16] He is also associated with *De Adoracione Ymaginum*, a tract on the defence of images which is not included in the Vernon but demonstrates significant parallels in content and phraseology to the *Scale*.[17] By illustrating the efficacy of devotion to images of the Virgin in the miniatures for the *Miracles of Our Lady*[18] (the sort of subject avoided in the *Pearl* Manuscript) and in its inclusion of texts such as the *Scale*, the Vernon Manuscript, in effect, becomes a participant in the debate, manifestly documenting the orthodox position on images. N. F. Blake considers it possible that the onset of the Lollard heresy prompted the Vernon collection.[19]

The Vernon Manuscript demonstrates, in a particularly interesting way, the orthodox view on representing, for example, the Trinity. This subject in enclosed within the "þ" beginning the *Prick of Conscience* (fig.1). The initial is superimposed on a rectangular panel just below the intriguing instruction: "Hose wole mai rede and look." The most immediate subject for looking is, of course, the historiated initial leading into the text. The dove is absent in this representation of the Mercy Seat, a configuration of the Trinity usually showing a seated God the Father holding the crucified Christ while the dove, representing the Holy Ghost, descends from above. The third person of the Trinity is alluded to by the red cross-nimbus around God the Father and is everywhere implied in the triplicate forms inside and outside the historiated initial. These include the three black spikes which pierce the hands and

Fig.1 Historiated initial of the Trinity at the beginning of the *Prick of Conscience.* The Vernon Manuscript, Oxford, Bodleian Library, MS Eng. Poet. a. 1, fol. 265r. (By permission of the Bodleian Library, University of Oxford.)

feet of Christ, the spray with three red buds, the black outlines of three plants with trefoil tops, and the three notches in the gold frame. All these visualizations reflect the triple emphasis on the Trinity in the introductory lines to the poem beside and below the pictorial panel. In his tract on images Hilton argues in favor of the legitimacy of representations of the Trinity, a practice the Lollards condemned (see the discussion following shortly). Hilton excuses simple folk who might think the three persons in the Trinity are separate persons because they think of divine things in bodily terms and would do better if they could.[20]

Although Hilton condones the use of corporeal analogies by the uneducated, he also discusses the more sophisticated use of images by the literate who kneel before images that serve as a reminder, whereupon they forget them and pray to God and the saints.[21] In the bottom right corner of the Vernon depiction of the Trinity, just such a literate figure is represented. He holds a scroll inscribed with the first verse of the Psalm 50: *miserere mei deus s(e)c(un)d(u)m magna(m) mi(sericordi)am.*[22] These words from the fourth penitential psalm, "Have mercy on me, O God, according to thy great mercy," are appropriate to the subject of the *Prick of Conscience* and also to the illustrated subject of the Mercy Seat within the "þ." The descending curve of the thorn forms a boundary separating the kneeling figure outside from the spiritual dimension showing the object of his contemplation inside the letter. As it ascends, the prayer scroll crosses over the boundary of the letter into the space within, while the bottom of the cross breaches this same boundary as it descends into the monk's earthly realm.[23] The reader of this manuscript can also perceive the Trinity in abstract form in the way the letter "þ" is composed of three strands, purple, blue and red, which join at the descending curve and the vertical bar to enclose the scene within. These three strands are interwoven, interlaced, and interlocked as they combine, separate, and recombine, only to start all over again unendingly. This echoes the emphasis in the adjacent poem on the eternal existence of the Trinity. The invitation above the pictorial panel signals the reader to emulate the monk and to look and look until the Trinity is seen to be both incarnated and symbolized in the letter beginning the poem. This is a unique visualization of the idea of the Word being incarnated in the vernacular letter.[24] The emphasis on the bleeding gash in Christ's side within the historiated initial serves as a further reminder of this sort of corporeal analogy which, in turn, would lead the literate to a more abstract apprehension of the Trinity, as implied by the three interwoven strands that compose the letter itself. It is the Incarnation that justifies the making of holy images.[25] Because Christ became flesh, images could legitimately be made of him.

Within the framework of Hilton's *Scale* and his tract on images, the role of such an image can be seen to serve not only an aid for the simple to meditate upon the incarnate Christ, but by becoming more proficient in the spiritual life and exercising the imagination in a life of prayer, the spiritually advanced person can come to a vision of the divine. At the beginning of the second book of the *Scale,* reflecting his mature thought, Hilton speaks again of the process and the goal of contemplation:

> Gostly to oure purpos, Ierusalem is as mikel for seyen siȝht of pes, & bitokeneþ contemplacioun in perfit luf of God. For contemplacioun is not ellis bot a siȝht of Iesu, whilk is verrey pes. þan if þu coueite for to come to þis blessid siȝht of verrey pees & ben a trew pilgrym to Ierusalem-ward, þawȝ it be so þat I were neuer here, nerþeles as ferforþ as I kan I schal sette þe in þe weye þederward.[26]

What were the circumstances that may have stimulated Hilton's spiritual explorations regarding contemplation and such defences as the *De Adoracione Ymaginum* in late medieval England?[27] Anne Hudson observes that while several points go back to the earlier iconoclastic controversies in the East, the matter must have been debated in schools during the late fourteenth and early fifteenth centuries, Oxford scholars in particular being engaged in the subject.[28] Hilton and Wyclif both supported religious writings in English, but these contemporaries diverged on other issues. Wyclif himself did not originate opposition to images nor completely condemn them, as indicated in his treatise on the Ten Commandments.[29] Commenting on the first two Commandments, he admits that the prohibition against images predated the Incarnation and that they are justified as books for the unlearned, that they can excite religious devotion and raise the mind to God, but worship of the dead image itself is idolatry.[30] He considered that representations of the Trinity in the Mercy Seat configuration could lead mislead people into thinking God the Father and the Holy Spirit each have a separate physical existence because they are visually represented as an old man and as a dove respectively.[31] One of the "Twelve Conclusions of the Lollards" singles out this sort of image of the Trinity as the "most abhominable."[32] Seen in this context, the Vernon historiated initial of the Mercy Seat with a monk praying before it makes a twofold statement affirming the orthodox position on images and on the monastic life, both mistrusted by Wyclif and the Lollards.

The Lollards not only championed access to religious truths by lay folk but considered that both men and women who were worthy[33] could preach in the vernacular, a direct challenge to the ordained male priesthood. Connected with the issue of preaching was that of the status of the Eucharist. As early as 1382 one of Wyclif's propositions was that Christ is not present in the sacrament of the altar.[34] Associated with the dangers of idolatry attendant upon veneration of the man-made object was Wyclif's concern with the excessive materialism and sensuous indulgence provoked by the image delighted in for its beauty or costliness.[35] According to one of his sermons, worshipping images and the consecrated host is a twin transgression against the first commandment.[36] Wyclif considered that the sooner the accidentals or externals of images, rather than what they stood for, were left behind, the better.[37] The lavishness of scale, the gold leaf of the borders, and the ornamentation of the Vernon Manuscript would undoubtedly have represented everything that the Lollards found disturbing, and may even account for the surreptitious rubbing out of the faces of some of the images.[38] An early fifteenth-century text in an anthology of works mostly critical of the church reflects tolerance for images without wealthy adornments such as a "pore ymage stondyng in a symple kirk or chapel"[39]

The concept of humble images brings me to the illustrations of the *Pearl* Manuscript. W. R. Jones lucidly presents the main concerns of both sides of the image controversy in England at this time, but he concludes that the image debate "never attracted the attention of the medieval artist nor led to a reappraisal of the basic theory and practice of representing divinity in pigment and stone."[40] Referring to the "astringent effect" of the Lollard antipathy to images, in her introduction to her catalogue, Kathleen Scott says that it seems unlikely that opposition to images did not have an influence on the manner in which books were decorated.[41] Yet surprisingly, since she does consider the Lollard impact on art, she does not apply these theoretical observations in her catalogue entry for the *Pearl* Manuscript illustrations.

What I am proposing is that contemporary image controversies had a *profound* effect exactly in the contentious space where conflicting and overlapping currents met: illustrated vernacular literary manuscripts. The Vernon Manuscript emphatically manifests the orthodox position both visually and verbally. But why was the *Pearl* Manuscript illustrated in so plain a style, especially in view of its poetry which is a tour de force of verbal ornament and polished style, a rhetorical performance that draws upon the alliterative tradition of Anglo-Saxon poetry and exhibits no lack of confidence about the resources of the language—if it does not reflect a sensitivity to some of the image issues raised by the Lollards? It is unrealistic to expect that "the medieval artist" was unaffected and did not change "the practice of representing divinity in pigment and stone." The very absence of images of "divinity" in the *Pearl* Manuscript suggests that the contrary is true. While the illustrations do not identify the *Pearl* Manuscript as a Lollard product, it may be that they reflect to some extent an awareness of Lollard concerns either by the artist or by the intended readers. There may also have been an element of caution, for if people were being told that "false ymagys and bokis were worthi to be destroyed,"[42] then wise artists would not have wanted to provoke destruction of their labour. Aston gives three examples of the burning of images including one of St. Andrew, one of a cross, and one of the head of a Virgin, and one example of service books in which the Lollards destroyed the names and illuminated haloes of saints.[43] If, out of an appreciation of Lollard ideas about images, or out of caution, holy images were best avoided, what is left if an artist is restricted from direct illustration of many of a text's subjects? To do so indirectly is far more demanding and requires a more intimate knowledge of that very text.

When the subjects vary, as they do in the *Pearl* Manuscript, from elegy to heroic romance, the difficulty is increased. What a modern reader would naturally expect by way of illustration for *Sir Gawain and the Green Knight*, for instance, is not there. In none of the four miniatures for this poem is the famous pentangle shown on the front of Gawain's shield, nor an image of the Virgin on the inside. There is not even a green garter (1829–32, 2395–96; also described as a belt, 2485, and a "bende," 2517[44]). It is no wonder that modern critics have questioned the literacy of the artist or the relevance of the miniatures. Although Phillipa Hardman does not discuss the tokens in relation to the illustrations of the manuscript, she astutely points out that they would have been understood by pious medieval readers as having ambiguous overtones and might even have been viewed by some as idolatrous.[45] She argues that Lollard views on image worship might have provoked questioning of the courtly Gawain's religious practices while his reliance on tokens could have reminded medieval readers of the tensions between orthodox and irregular beliefs.[46]

The illustrator is also engaged in some of the current social issues alluded to by the poet including those involving images, the Eucharist, and preachers. Emphasis may be given by repetition of certain subjects, as in the recurrence of "preaching" figures, or by omission, as in the absence of the tokens mentioned in *Gawain*. In the visual prefaces and epilogues, it is the deeper spiritual meaning of the poems which the illustrator features to create an allegorical meta-narrative unifying and shaping reception. Whatever one may think of the purely aesthetic value of these images, the rest of my study will show that the artist demonstrates a comprehensive vision of the text and conveys it thoughtfully. The *Pearl* images do not invite worship nor do they illustrate miraculous powers, but perhaps, in the end, they do inspire contemplation of the celestial, the "vision of peace" that is Jerusalem, in the spiritual pilgrim who reads the manuscript.

Intimations of the New Jerusalem in the Miniatures of the **Pearl** *Manuscript*

It is as prefaces to *Pearl* that the first four miniatures function, preparing the viewer for a spiritual quest whose goal is not fully achieved until the very last miniature in the manuscript. This final illustration serves as an epilogue not only to *Sir Gawain and the Green Knight* but to the whole compilation as well, coming back full circle. Some of the intervening miniatures pick up on the sacramental emphasis of the last lines of the *Pearl* text relating to the priest's administration of the Eucharist, by means of which we can become the servants of God. Further, transforming two of the courtly feasts illustrated into liturgical events, they investigate the priestly and prophetic calling itself. What the artist has done is to create a visual allegory in which many of the biblical and romance incidents of the poems become a progressive series of variations on the pilgrimage to the court of heaven, ultimately seen in apocalyptic terms. In effect, the poems in this compilation have been linked by a visual program. The artist was faced by the same challenge as that which confronted the Ellesmere designer of the *Canterbury Tales* who decided to illustrate the pilgrim narrators beside the beginnings of their respective tales in order to strengthen the sense of coherence and unity of that compilation.[47] The *Pearl* Manuscript illustrator's manner of rendering the featured subjects of the four texts unites them. Even the principal characters look alike, as if this same cast were dramatically enacting the successive events, producing the sense of an autobiographical journey in which the viewer participates. The *Pearl* Manuscript avoids direct depictions of God, the Virgin, and the Saints, sensitive subjects for illustration in view of the iconophobic views of the followers of Wyclif, the Lollards, and various other reformist factions active during the this period—hence the exclusion of portraits of the celestial court where modern readers might expect them, and the visual substitution of indirect representations.

The first miniature in the manuscript establishes the visionary framework of what is to follow by showing the dreamer asleep on the side of a flowery hill with stylized trees (fig. 2). Like the illustration of the dreamer on the first folio of the Douce 104 manuscript of *Piers Plowman,* this figure functions as a kind of author portrait since the viewer follows his progress.[48] The dreamer's body parallels the lines of the undulating hillside above and of the dark green spot below him, inviting the viewer to allow the identification of the bereaved dreamer with the landscape. Upon first glance the "erber grene" (38) seems to be part of the typical sort of pleasure garden outside a castle enclosure (one can imagine a castle not too far distant) which could extend to several acres and include treed areas with streams, as indicated in the study on contemporary aristocratic gardens by Laura Howes.[49] What is intriguing about this visual representation is the prominent dark green spot below the dreamer towards which he reaches even in his sleep.

Since it is not obvious in looking at the original manuscript what the spot "contains"—whether it was meant to represent a spot within the earth or a pond of water—I was fortunate in having the opportunity to discuss the problem with Anthony Parker, the British Museum's Senior Conservation Officer in the Manuscripts Conservation Studio. By the application of sophisticated technology,[50] he was able photographically, as it were, to lift off the dark layer of paint to reveal what is underneath. Perhaps not surprisingly, there is just a continuation of the flowery meadow on the hillside (fig. 3). The dark paint was added later. It is the same streaky paint as that applied roughly to the streams in the other three *Pearl* miniatures (figs. 4–6). Because this blue paint was applied on top of the yellow grass at the center of the hill, consistent with dry spots in August, the wavy spot is of a darker aqua green color than the blue of the streams in the other three miniatures.

So what does the spot, which was deliberately colored in to complete this picture, signify? Clearly it was considered important to emphasize the multi-layered suggestiveness of the "spot." The possible

Fig. 2 *Pearl.* The dreamer/narrator falls asleep. London, British Library, MS Cotton Nero A. x, Article 3, fol. 41r. (By permission of the British Library.)

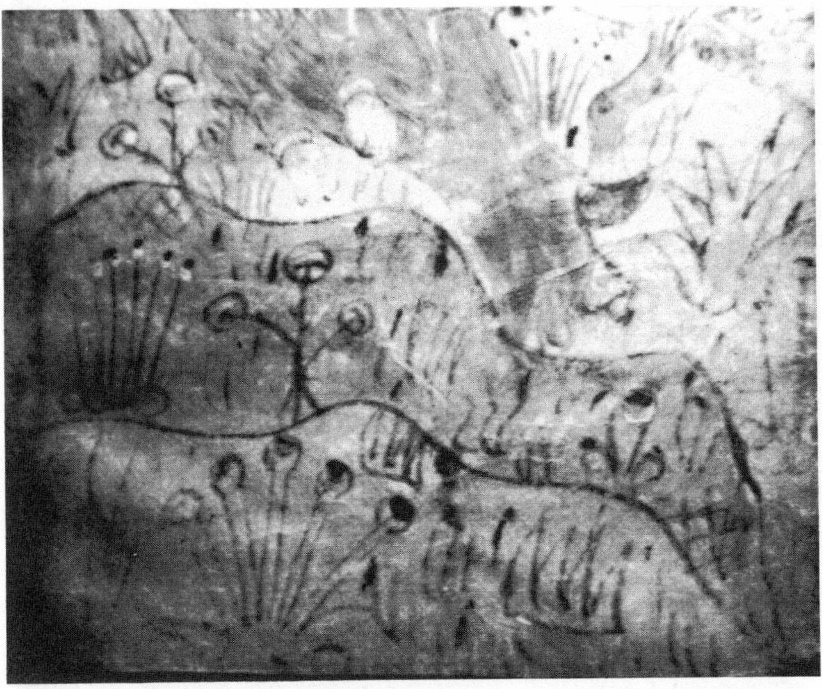

Fig. 3 *Pearl.* Under the dark spot. London, British Library, MS Cotton Nero A. x, Article 3, fol. 41r. (By permission of the British Library.)

Fig. 4 *Pearl.* The dreamer walks through a forest beside a stream he cannot cross. London, British Library, MS Cotton Nero A. x, Article 3, fol. 41v. (By permission of the British Library.)

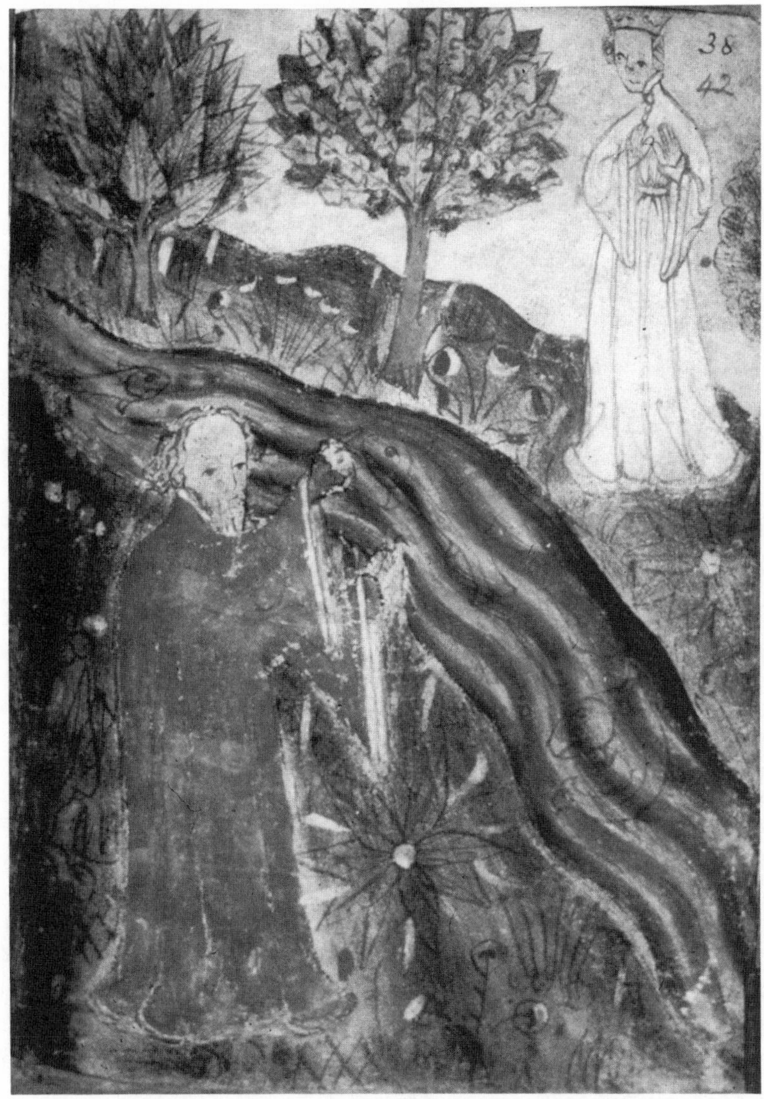

Fig. 5 *Pearl.* The dreamer chastised by the Pearl Maiden across the stream. London, British Library, MS Cotton Nero A. x, Article 3, fol. 42r. (By permission of the British Library.)

Fig. 6 *Pearl.* The dreamer looks across the stream at the Pearl Maiden within the New Jerusalem. London, British Library, MS Cotton Nero A. x, Article 3, fol. 42v. (By permission of the British Library.)

levels of signification include: **1**.The spot where, on a symbolic level, the pearl flowed through the grass to the ground (10). **2**. The flowery turf upon which he "felle" into a sudden sleep (57). **3**. His daughter's grave. **4**. The spot where the "sede" (34) will sprout into flower as the dreamer tries to console himself with the knowledge that his buried pearl, like a seed, will likewise come to life again. The seed image resonates with the parables of the mustard seed in which the "Kingdom of heaven is likened to a man that sowed good seed in his field" (Matt. 13.24), preparing the way for the rendition, in both the text and the last *Pearl* miniature, of paradise as a kingly estate. Further, it anticipates the grown-up version of the daughter he encounters later in the *Pearl* poem, in that it is "the least indeed of all seeds: but when it grows up, it is greater than all herbs and becomes a tree" (Matt. 13.32). This last adds an extra layer of meaning to the trees in the miniature. The "pearl of great price" later in the same chapter in Matthew (13. 45–46) links both seed and pearl images with the kingdom of heaven. The visual program intimates that this is the real goal of the quest. **5**. The stream, a little later in the vision, beside which "stroþe-men" sleep (115) and on the bottom of which stones shine like those that glint through glass, as the steaming stars glitter in the clouds in the winter night (113–16). The semi-translucence of the paint is particularly effective in conveying this in that some of the white and red spots of the flowers originally underneath are still visible, allowing for this conflated or alternate interpretation of them as luminous stones reflecting the stars above. In the poem, the jeweled stream reflecting the starry skies serves as an analogy of the subterranean or interior state from which the dreamer is transported to his vision of the New Jerusalem.[51] The gestures of the dreamer in the second *Pearl* miniature (fig. 4) appear to refer to this inversion. **6**. An anticipation, also, of the stream as a barrier preventing the dreamer from crossing over to the Pearl Maiden in the celestial realm. As prominently featured in the following miniatures in which it slashes obliquely across the visionary landscape (figs. 3–5), it becomes a river of death as indicated by the large sea-creatures (showing through the paint), not mentioned in the *Pearl* text but occupying the deep in the miniatures of Noah, as well as of Jonah and the Whale.[52] At the beginning of the *Pearl* poem the dreamer is likewise frustrated when he cannot grasp either the fallen pearl or, as the reader soon finds out, the dead child symbolized by the pearl, which in turn is seen to symbolize the kingdom of heaven from which man is excluded by sin. Thus, as Elizabeth Petroff Martin remarks in connection with both Dante's *Divine*

Comedy and *Pearl*, the introductory landscapes "are also the containers for the seeds of the future landscapes of the poem."[53]

In this first miniature, the dreamer is not wearing his chaperon with its scalloped liripipe which seems to have taken on a life of its own, as if lifted by a breeze.[54] In his dreamscape, represented in the second miniature on the verso folio (fig. 4), he walks hatless through a transfigured forest of trees: "As bornyst syluer þe lef on slydez,/þat þike con trylle on vch a tynde" (77–78). Since these trees occur in his dream, they are close replications of those in the landscape in which he fell asleep, as the miniaturist astutely implies not only by their similarity, but also by the compositional masses which occupy the same spaces on both the recto and verso sides, as does the hill side (even the dark wavy spot, located below the dreamer in the first, is replaced by the stream in the second). The miniatures indicate that it is the perception of the ecstatic dreamer that has changed. The sense of a disjunction of realities, however, is implied by the alteration of the dreamer's red houpelande, which in the four *Pearl* miniatures varies between two different shades of red (not to mention the loss of whatever cord was tying it in at the waist in his recumbent position) and different styles of sleeve, suggesting the time lapses and the unexplained shifts characteristic of dreams. Despite the artist's cautionary choice of subjects, the face of the dreamer in the second miniature appears to have been rubbed out, suggesting that the person responsible was unaware of the referent.

The standing dreamer points down to the stream he cannot cross with his left hand while beckoning with his right hand to the Pearl Maiden across from him in the facing, third miniature (fig. 5). This landscape seems an extension of that of the second miniature—but for a slight jog at the joining edges. While these *Pearl* miniatures are on a bifolium added to the text of *Pearl*, there is a circumstance that allows, among other things, for the possibility that these facing scenes were drawn continuously on the same sheet originally—namely, the presence of three worm holes which now do not quite line up but once obviously did.[55] Likewise previously unnoticed, there is evidence that this bifolium was expertly repaired along the spine with an added strip some time in the past, as Anthony Parker pointed out to me when we were discussing the problem of continuity. This, in addition to the non-alignment of the worm holes, means that each leaf of the bifolium was separated when the original fold along the spine was cut off, presumably because it was damaged, to be replaced by new backing to the remaining portion of each leaf to make a bifolium once again.[56] What this suggests even more strongly than at present is that the repetitiveness of the settings in these miniatures was intended to suggest the spatial paradoxes intimated by the poem—of continuous yet simultaneous realities and of passing from one to the other by visionary means. Petroff Martin describes this sort of relationship in geometrical terms: "the interrelationship of successive landscapes . . . is not only linear, but circular and reciprocal.[57]

The third miniature gives the first view of the Pearl Maiden herself, significantly displaying only three pearls, rather than the plethora described in the poem. This can only be an allusion to the Trinity, an early indication of her true significance. The Pearl Maiden herself looks across to the dreamer on the previous, facing miniature, repelling his summons with a gesture of reproach.[58] In the poem she chastises him for his own attempts to cross the stream. In the role of teacher, she reproaches him for seeking to recover that which is transitory and for failing to accept her transformed status from child to Queen. Like a preacher, she recounts to him, in the vernacular of course, the parable of the vineyard by way of explaining the doctrine of salvation by grace, exemplifying divine generosity at the court of heaven where all are equal.[59] As if to reinforce her message, the figure in the bottom left of the same miniature seems to function not merely as the dreamer but in the role of witnessing narrator, pointing to her with both hands the better to direct the viewer's gaze to the focus of the illustration.

In the last *Pearl* miniature (fig. 6), the dreamer likewise points up to the Pearl Maiden whose right hand is now held to her heart[60] as she holds out her left hand to him. They no longer seem as disconnected in relation to each other as in the previous miniatures. The dreamer's eyes appear to look at the viewer, inviting spiritual participation. The Pearl Maiden is revealed as Queen within the New Jerusalem, shown as a medieval fortified castle with crenellated walls and a crenellated tower, the openings in the shape of crosses helping to reinforce the transformed sense. By her position between the tower and a church-like structure, she can also be identified as the pearl gate of John's apocalyptic vision (21.21). Dressed in white she is the Bride of Christ at the celestial wedding feast referred to in the poem (although the bridal white can also serve as an allusion to her shroud). This multivalent image of the Pearl Maiden implies that the New Jerusalem is itself a body made up of the maidens within it, except that in the miniature their equality is indicated by the one who represents them all and in herself represents the mystical body of Christ. The mound on which the dreamer sleeps in the first *Pearl* miniature is also the mound upon which the New Jerusalem is located, the love garden having become a paradisal garden, supporting Petroff Martin's observation concerning the text that "the opening landscape is not fully understandable until we see its final transformation in the last landscape of the poem."[61]

What is of particular interest in the last of the *Pearl* miniatures is that, unlike the poem which ends abruptly with the narrator awakening back in the arbor where he fell asleep, seeking consolation in seeing, if not the Pearl, at least the Eucharist, here he is left in his dream, looking up beyond the stream but unable to enter the New Jerusalem. Likewise, in the miniature of the Flood, Noah is depicted in the Ark (fig. 7), but there is no corresponding scene of his safe landing. This sense of destination deferred is reinforced in the miniature of Jonah thrown to the whale (fig. 8), but his arrival on dry land is not shown.[62]

The subject of the Eucharist with which the *Pearl* poem ends resurfaces at the beginning of *Cleanness*, which comes next in the manuscript. The second prefatorial miniature for *Cleanness*, showing Daniel interpreting the handwriting on the wall at Belshazzar's Feast, contains some curious items among the Jewish holy vessels (fig. 9). Recalling the opening of the poem which mentions unclean priests who insincerely offer up the Mass, loathing God and his vessels, the illustrator has depicted the Jewish vessels as the Christian vessels of the Mass, a circumstance not noted by scholars before insofar as the miniatures are concerned. In his dissertation, however, Francis John Ingledew demonstrates that "the concept of cleanness proceeds unequivocally from the liturgical discourse of ordination and the eucharist, and that its use signals the poem's concern with the priesthood."[63] The stories of Noah's Flood, Sodom, and Belshazzar's Feast, he continues, deal with the means by which cleanness is urged and with the "conventions of prophetic discourse on the Last Things." He shows that the court of Babylon, a carnal court, is opposed to the divine court, described at the beginning of *Cleanness* in the scene of the eschatological Wedding Feast.[64]

In the miniature of Belshazzar's Feast, the vessels include a gold monstrance with the host of the Eucharist, a chalice, and a bishop's crozier. By this interpretation of the vessels seen in terms of those of the Mass, the artist is adhering to orthodox rather than Lollard ideas about the Transubstantiation. Such a visual reading was undoubtedly suggested by the mention of Belshezzar's blasphemous honoring of heathen idols with cups which had formerly been blessed by bishop's hands (1718, also 1445). The white table linen, referred to in connection with

Fig. 7 *Cleanness.* Noah afloat in the Ark. London, British Library, MS Cotton Nero A. x, Article 3, fol. 60r. (By permission of the British Library.)

Fig. 8 *Patience.* Jonah cast into the whale. London, British Library, MS Cotton Nero A. x, Article 3, fol. 86r. (By permission of the British Library.)

Fig. 9 *Cleanness.* Daniel interprets the handwriting on wall at Belshazzar's feast where the holy vessels are displayed. London, British Library, MS Cotton Nero A. x, Article 3, fol. 60v. (By permission of the British Library.)

the coverings upon which the treasures of Jerusalem were laid out (1440), suggests altar cloths, as well as the tablecloths shown in illustrations of courtly feasts, both of which the miniaturist exploits, the latter exemplified in the feast scene at King Arthur's court at Camelot (fig. 10). There the golden columned structure on the right of the bleeding blond head more closely resembles a ciborium used to house the Eucharist. Strangely configured in this scene is the placement of the Green Knight's decapitated head against the backdrop of the white tablecloth, like a head of John the Baptist. Certainly, there appear to be ritual sacrificial overtones in this layout, possibly supporting Ingledew's observations concerning the suggestions in the poem of the Circumcision, which was assimilated to the Passion in medieval homiletic literature about the Five Wounds of Christ.[65] This subject is also symbolized in the poem, as will be recalled, by the Pentangle. The feast of the Circumcision, the first wound Christ suffered, is celebrated on January 1, placing it within the Yuletide season when the events of the poem begin. Certainly any reference to the Circumcision, which became a common subject in fourteenth- and fifteenth-century art, gives quite another dimension to the sharp weapons dominating this miniature.[66] There is no biblical mention of where the Circumcision of Christ took place, but one late fourteenth-century half-page miniature for a "Poem on the Life of Christ" shows it taking place on a cloth-covered table or altar, with the Virgin and two figures shown behind it.[67] Since the Circumcision refers, like the Baptism, to cleansing, any such overtones in this miniature, along with its liturgical emphasis, place this last poem in the manuscript within the framework of Christian salvation history.[68]

The first prefatorial miniature for *Cleanness* features Noah and his family in the Ark (fig. 7). One of his sons stirs the waves of the Flood waters. The fish which swam in the river of death separating the dreamer from the Pearl Maiden have now increased in size, and one symbolically swallows another, anticipating the next miniature prefacing *Patience* showing the Whale swallowing Jonah (fig. 8). The spiritual significance of these sea creatures derives from the discussion of the sins in *Cleanness* where the proud are described as rushing "into þe deuelez þrote" (180). This image is no doubt derived from visual representations of the mouth of hell popular since late Anglo-Saxon times.[69] In the account of the Flood, there is only "deth in þe depe stremez" (374) and, at the end of forty days, there stirred no flesh that "þe flod nade al freten" (403–04).[70] Even though the text of *Patience* says that no tooth touched Jonah (252), in the miniature the artist couldn't resist following the

Fig. 10 *Sir Gawain and the Green Knight.* The Green Knight decapitated at the Yuletide feast at Camelot. London, British Library, MS Cotton Nero A. x, Article 3, fol. 94v. (By permission of the British Library.)

dramatic iconography of the mouth of hell by having the whale's sharp teeth closing over his head. That he has descended into hell is first implied by the analogies that the whale's stomach "stank as þe deuel" and "sauoured as helle," and then is specifically stated when Jonah says the Lord heard him from "hellen wombe" (274, 275, and 306). Just as the Pearl Maiden in her person is also the New Jerusalem, so the infernal counterpart is represented in the miniatures by the swallowing sea creature which is identified as the body of Satan who is also hell.

The account of Noah is but one in the series in *Cleanness* proving the might of God's Word, closely identified with the power of his hands, provoked to punish or to deliver, as when the Flood waters had washed away the filth of the earth and he bade the passengers in the Ark to go to the door (499–500). The story of the abominations of Belshazzar associates his lechery (he enjoys richly dressed concubines), his desecration of God's vessels, and his idolatry. Daniel tells Belshazzar that he has defiled the sacred vessels in which were served

> Wale wyne to þy wenches in waryed stoundes;
> Bifore þy borde hatz þou broȝt beuerage in þ'edé,
> Þat blyþely were fyrst blest with bischopes hondes,
> Louande þeron lese goddez þat lyf haden neuer,
> Made of stokkes and stonez þat neuer styry moȝt. (1716–20)

There are elaborate descriptions of the artfulness both of God's vessels and of the idols made of sticks and stones, both are gilded and adorned with silver, but they are differentiated by the fact that the former were consecrated as holy "in His presens" (1496). So while both the poem and the miniature (fig. 9) demonstrate an awareness of contemporary issues, they show support for the orthodox concept of the holiness of the vessels and there is no criticism of their material substance or beauty, as there might be if either were strictly Lollard endeavors. The miniature draws attention to the unclean priests who handle the Eucharist, as mentioned on the facing page where the poem begins. The visual lines of direction indicated by the hands of God, the king, and Belshazzar emphasize the "reading" process involved in the interpretation of God's Word.

The miniature conflates several stages of the process. In the upper left the Hand of God has just finished writing the three fateful words: *Mane Techal Phares.* Since the meaning of these mysterious "runisch sauez" (1545) is not given until after Daniel has read them (1727), they would initially have appeared as unintelligible letters. They are compared to the furrows cut by a ploughman into the earth (1547). Possibly the miniaturist portrayed the words on a scroll rather than directly on the wall because of the biblical associations of the description of them as "scrypture" (1546). It also recalls the earlier image of the clean soul of the penitent being brighter than pearls and as smooth as newly scraped parchment (1134). There the poet indicates that whether it be a man's soul or any kind of vessel that once served him, God forbids that it be made unclean on pain of his vengeance, as the story of Belshazzar proves. Here, however, God's engraved words feel to the terrified Belshazzar as if they are fraying his very "flesche" (1553). In the miniature the writing Hand is further emphasized by Belshazzar's right hand which is raised beside it (although palm out rather than turned like the Hand) as he looks at it. Beside him in the miniature is the Queen, who was not present during the writing episode, but who later counsels her husband to send for Daniel, infused with the spirit of God. Then in the lower left part of the miniature Daniel, whose position is almost a mirror image of the three-quarter profile of the King, looks off into the distance away from the letters to "read" their meaning. His gesture indicates that he is explaining them, but since his hands point down, their negative import is signaled: because of the King's sinfulness, God has reckoned his kingdom, his reign is in the balance and is found wanting, and so his kingdom will be taken from him and given to the Persians.

The other miniature which shares with the scene of Belshazzar's Feast the central position in the twelve miniatures in this manuscript is that of Jonah being thrown to the whale (fig. 8). This first prefatorial miniature for *Patience* is depicted in the space below the end of the text of *Cleanness,* as if in continuation of it, which in a sense it is because it also features the power of the Word. Jonah refused God's request to preach his words to the the people of Nineveh, so he was punished by being swallowed by the whale. The second prefatorial miniature on the verso depicts Jonah releasing God's words locked within him (350) by preaching at Nineveh as originally requested (fig. 11). This prophet is very like Daniel in dress. His gesture is also similar since he prophesizes God's vengeance against Nineveh, which will be swallowed by the deep abyss in forty days (359–64). His large size in relation to the audience to whom he preaches indicates his importance, just as the heroic axe-wielding King Richard, for example, is shown larger than his crew in the miniature preceding a vernacular romance

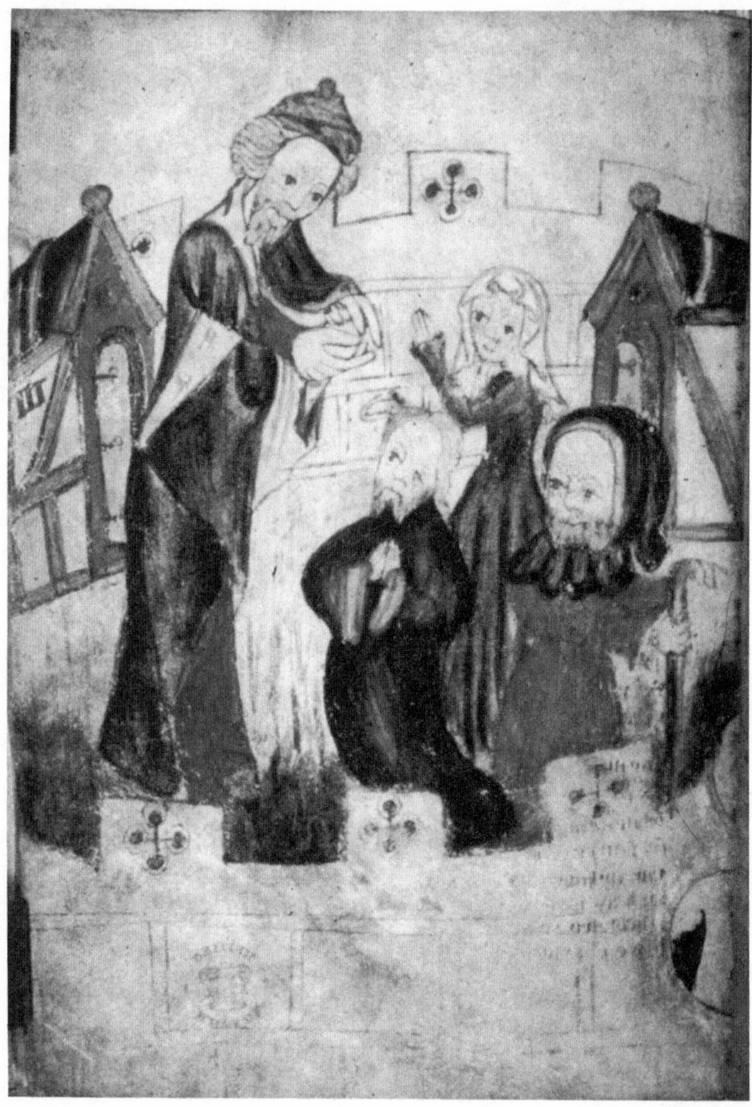

Fig. 11 *Patience.* Jonah preaching in Nineveh. London, British Library, MS Cotton Nero A. x, Article 3, fol. 86v. (By permission of the British Library.)

in the Auchinleck Manuscript.[71] But in the *Patience* illustration the ermine trim on his sleeve gives a further clue as to Jonah's typological significance. In Matthew 12.40 Christ speaks of his coming death and resurrection in terms of the story of Jonah who was in the whale's belly three days and nights. Following the Harrowing of Hell, Christ was thought to have preached to the captives in hell. Augustine considered that the spirits in prison to whom Christ preached (I Peter 3.18–19; 4.17) referred to the captives in hell and also to those "prisoners in the death of unbelief and wickedness."[72] In the poem, the people of Nineveh are referred to as accursed fiends engaged in villainy and venomous beliefs (82, 71). The *Patience* miniature contains elements both of the Harrowing and the Preaching iconographies, the former reflected in the large Christ-like figure bending over the smaller figures who are often led by Adam and Eve raising their hands to him, suggested here by the woman. Among the audience in the preaching miniature is a figure dressed in the same red houpelande and the blue chaperon with liripipe (which he is now wearing) as the dreamer in the first *Pearl* miniature (fig. 2), which gives the impression that the dreamer-narrator is on a spiritual pilgrimage and is taking part in the Old Testament incidents. Now he is more dwarf-like and shrunken with age as he leans on his cane, perhaps having become identified also with the poet narrator of *Patience* who twice describes himself as poor and patient (35–36, 528–31). He consoles himself with the thought that, like the first and last of the blessed, he too shall inherit the kingdom of heaven as described at the beginning of the poem when he hears Matthew 5.3–11 read at Mass. The idea of an internal journey is reinforced too by the portrayal earlier of Daniel, the interpreter of dreams. A spiritual or internal journey is often in itself, metaphorically, a descent.

Descent myths involving transformations, as explored by Northrop Frye, include not only descents into the subterranean or submarine world, but also metaphorically, into the forest, often conceived in terms of the hunt, which includes sexual overtones.[73] The first two visual epilogues of *Sir Gawain and the Green Knight* recapitulate the poem in just these terms. The first depicts the sexual temptation of Gawain by the Lady Bercilak (fig. 12). Like the Pearl dreamer whom he resembles, Gawain is asleep, in this case within "comly cortynes" (1732). She calls to him, rousing him from his dark dreams about his coming encounter at the Green Chapel. Instead of showing her kissing him, the artist has her chucking his chin in a courting gesture as shown, for instance, on the lid of a medieval ivory casket displaying amorous couples.[74] Although

Fig. 12 *Sir Gawain and the Green Knight.* The temptation of Gawain. London, British Library, MS Cotton Nero A. x, Article 3, fol. 129r. (By permission of the British Library.)

in the poem, the lady's fashionable gown is décoleté (1741), the prudish artist has given her a high-necked, albeit fashionable houpelande, yet the viewer does see the neck and shoulders of the sleeper instead! The fabric is gathered at her waist but there is no evidence of the green girdle she gives him at the end of this encounter, since that is not what the artist is featuring.

It is in the bedroom, as Phillipa Hardman argues, that the Virgin Mary's knight needs her protection from danger, as mentioned by the poet (1768–69). The artist's rendition is in accord with the issues raised in the preceding poems. According to *Cleanness*, the sins which most outrage God are the fleshly ones (202, 265–72), for which he caused not only the Flood but the destruction of Sodom and Gomorrah. Yet man appears to be repeatedly inclined to desecrate his own image by "harlottrye vnhonest, heþyng of seluen" (579). In the last part of *Patience* Jonah is annoyed because God saved the people of Nineveh, but God replies that naturally he would preserve his handiwork made in his own image; also, they were repentant (501–04). It is within this theological construct that the temptation of Gawain is seen. If he had allowed himself to be seduced, it would have been a sin not only against the lord of the castle, but against the Lord. It is after this episode that Gawain goes to make his confession in the castle chapel. Later Bercilak says that Gawain is to other knights as a pearl is to a white pea (2364–65).

The next *Gawain* miniature on the verso folio of the temptation scene depicts the armed Gawain riding to the dreaded Green Chapel at the appointed time on New Year's Day (fig. 13). Although this miniature is much faded, it is still possible to see the artist's imaginative recreation of Wirral in this eerie, unearthly landscape. In the bottom half the fully armed Gawain searches for the chapel, sees nothing resembling such a thing, but he comes to a barrow (2170–72). It is this that is portrayed on the bottom right. It does not appear to have been previously noticed, but there is the faint outline of a seated figure crouched forward inside the hollow of the cave. Perhaps the servant's earlier description of the inhabitant of that wasteland (2098–2109) influenced the artist, or perhaps the barrow suggested a burial mound. The Green Knight appears in the upper half of the miniature. Curiously, this standing figure holding a huge axe is an exact replica of Gawain in the prefatorial miniature (fig. 10), except that now he wears green instead of red. Gawain on his horse exactly duplicates the Green Knight on his horse in the earlier miniature (without loss of his head), except that he is now in red. What is one to make of this? The transposition of these

Fig. 13 *Sir Gawain and the Green Knight.* Gawain seeks the Green Chapel and comes to a barrow. British Library, MS Cotton Nero A. x, Article 3, fol. 129v. (By permission of the British Library.)

Fig. 14 *Sir Gawain and the Green Knight.* Gawain enters Camelot. London, British Library, MS Cotton Nero A. x, Article 3, fol. 130r. (By permission of the British Library.)

two figures, along with the hunched figure in the mouth of the cave, seems to imply a transformation of identity. This reinforces the presentation of the journey as a spiritual descent not unlike Jonah's into the whale.

Visually, the denied access to the New Jerusalem, in which the last of the *Pearl* miniatures left the dreamer, is resolved in the very last miniature in the manuscript in which Gawain is shown at the threshold of Camelot, being welcomed back by the regal figure of King Arthur (fig. 14). Arthur raises up Gawain, just as in the Harrowing of Hell iconography, a large figure of Christ, often raises by his hand the figure of Adam.[75] Gawain is received at the arched entranceway which, in the visual allegory created by the artist, becomes the gate of Eden (out of which Adam was first cast by Michael with his flaming sword), visually prefigured in this manuscript's miniatures by the Pearl Maiden in her symbolic role as gate of the New Jerusalem in John's apocalyptic vision. The Queen's presence in the last miniature recalls the crowned Pearl Maiden. The artist has finally allowed the hero, albeit of a different poem, to enter the court of heaven. *Sir Gawain and the Green Knight* ends with the prayer including the audience, drawing the connection between Camelot and the bliss of the celestial court

> Now þat bere þe croun of þorne
> He bryng vus to His blysse! (2529–30)

University of Victoria

Notes

1. The Holy Bible, trans. from the Latin Vulgate, Douai version (London, 1914). Subsequent references to the Bible will be from this version and enclosed within brackets following the quotation in my main text, as indicated in the inscription.
2. Or 171 by 123 mm, see Kathleen Scott, *Later Gothic Manuscripts: 1390–1490*, vol. II (London, 1996), pp. 66–68, cat. no. 12. See also the descriptions in A. S. G. Edwards, "The Manuscript: British Library MS Cotton Nero A.x," in *A Companion to the Gawain-Poet* (Cambridge, 1997), pp. 197–220. For the facsimile see Israel Gollancz, ed., *Pearl, Cleanness, Patience, and Sir Gawain: Reproduced in Facsimile from the Unique MS. Cotton Nero A.x in the British Museum*, Early English Text Society, os 162 (1923; repr. London, 1955).
3. The Vernon Manuscript measures about 393 x 544 mm (about 15 1/2 x 21 1/2 inches) and now has 350 out of an original 422 or 426 leaves, according to A. I.

Doyle, Introduction, *The Vernon Manuscript: A Facsimile of Bodleian Library, Oxford, Ms. Eng. Poet.a.1* (Cambridge, 1987), p. 1.

4. Scott, *Later Gothic Manuscripts* II, 62. This appears to be based on A. I. Doyle, "The Manuscripts," in *Middle English Alliterative Poetry and Its Literary Background*, ed. D. Lawton (Cambridge, 1982), pp. 92–93, who suggested it had been copied in two stages, the script in the last quarter of the fourteenth century, with the 12 miniatures added at the end of the fourteenth or early fifteenth centuries. The rest of the miniatures inserted into the body of the manuscript occur on the ruled, blank pages or spaces between the poems, suggesting that it was probably not planned for illustration initially.
5. Paul Reichardt, "'Several Illuminations, Coarsely Executed': The Illustrations of the *Pearl* Manuscript," *Studies in Iconography* 18 (1997), 137–38. That the pictures were likely made after the pages were assembled into gatherings is evident from the fact that the Jonah scene was painted over the two large holes in the vellum to show through to the folio underneath. Sarah M. Horrall, "Notes on British library, MS Cotton Nero A x," *Manuscripta* 30 (1986), 193–94, attributes the high belt on the women's gowns and the men's bag sleeves to the early fifteenth century. However, the women's belts are worn no higher than the one shown on the Virgin Mary in the Vernon Manuscript on fol. 126v. The Pearl dreamer's houpelande sleeve styles are similar to those of the bag-sleeves of the angel appearing to Zacharias and of the wide sleeves worn by the sleeping Joseph on fols. 105r and 105v respectively of the Vernon. See also Iris Brooke, *Western European Costume: Thirteenth to Seventeenth Century* (London, 1939), pp. 60–62. The blue chaperon with liripipe on fols. 41r and 86v is similar to the fourteenth-century example of fig. 32 A on p. 74 of Brooke.
6. Gollancz, The Illustrations, *Pearl, Cleanness, Patience and Sir Gawain*, pp. 9–11.
7. Jennifer Lee, "The Illuminating Critic: The Illustrator of Cotton Nero A.X," *Studies in Iconography* 3 (1977), 44.
8. Horrall, "Notes," 198 and 196 respectively.
9. Scott, Later Gothic Manuscripts II, 67.
10. Robert J. Blanch and Julian N. Wasserman, "Tools of the Trade: the Hand of God, the Hand of Man," *From Pearl to Gawain: Forme to Fynisment* (Gainsville,1995), pp. 65–110.
11. Blanch and Wasserman, "Tools of the Trade," p. 110. They are referring to the use of gestures.
12. This is, as previously noted, in *Studies in Iconography* 18 (1997), 119–42. For the quotation, see Sir Frederic Madden, ed., *Syr Gawayne: A Collection of Ancient Romance Poems, By Scottish and English Authors* (London, 1939), p. xlvii.
13. Reichardt, "'Several Illuminations, Coarsely Executed': The Illustrations of the *Pearl* Manuscript," 137–38.
14. Horrall, "Notes," 197. Reichardt, "'Several Illuminations, Coarsely Executed': The Illustrations of the *Pearl* Manuscript," 136.
15. These are the first book of the *Scale of Perfection* (see below) and *Letters to a Layman: On the Mixed Life.*
16. N. F. Blake, "Vernon Manuscript: Contents and Organisation," in *Studies in the Vernon Manuscript*, ed. Derek Pearsall (Cambridge, Eng., 1990), p. 55. David L. Jeffrey, Introduction, *Toward a Perfect Love: The Spiritual Counsel of Walter Hilton* (Portland, OR, 1985), p. xxii, mentions that there are twenty-five early manuscripts of Book I of the *Scale of Perfection* (which he refers to as *Coming to Perfection*), indicating its popularity.

Book II, written some time before Hilton's death in 1396, survives in fifteen manuscripts. Margery Kempe includes "Hylton's boke" as among the books of contemplation read to her by a priest. See "Margery Kempe, *The Book of Margery Kempe*: Book I, Chapters 58–59 (Extract)," *The Idea of the Vernacular: An Anthology of Middle English Literary Theory, 1280–1520*, eds. Jocelyn Wogan-Brown et al. (University Park, PA, 1999), p. 298.

17. Joy M. Russell-Smith, "Walter Hilton and a Tract in Defence of the Veneration of Images," *Dominican Studies* 7 (1954), 180–214. For *De Adoracione Ymaginum*, see John Clark and Cheryl Taylor, *Walter Hilton's Latin Writings*, 2 vols., Analecta Cartusiana 124 (Salzburg, 1987) 1, 179–214.
18. On fol. 125v, the prototype of the Virgin has come out of her statue to restore the amputated leg of a faithful man who had prayed many times before her image; on fol. 126r, a priest who had prayed before her statue on behalf of another priest who lay with a nun then administers the Eucharist to the former fornicator, attended by the prototype of the Virgin herself; and on fol. 126v, the prototype of the Virgin has again left her statue in the minster church to dispute with the devil about the fate of her sacristan who had always greeted her statue in passing (she also rescues the latter from drowning). These miniatures demonstrate that the honor accorded the image comes through to the original (although here the Virgin, not God, is shown to respond). It is the theological position articulated by Walter Hilton in the passage referring to John of Damascus, who quotes Basil; see *De Adoracione Ymagimum*, in *Walter Hilton's Latin Writings* 1, 194. For a translation of John of Damascus, *The Orthodox Faith* book 4.16 (but the reference in Hilton's medieval version, above, is to book 4.8), see *Saint John of Damascus: Writings*, trans. Frederick H. Chase, Jr. (1958: repr. Washington, D.C., 1970), pp. 370–73.
19. N. F. Blake, "Vernon Manuscript: Contents and Organisation," pp. 58–59.
20. London, British Library, MS Royal 2.B.x, fol. 180r, trans. By G. R. Owst, *Literature and the Pulpit in Medieval England* (Oxford, 1961), p. 138.
21. Owst, *Literature and the Pulpit*, p. 138. See also Russell-Smith, "Walter Hilton," 194, 197.
22. This is transcribed in Scott, *Later Gothic Manuscripts* II, 19. Since I am using italics for the Latin, I have placed the silent expansions in brackets. Psalm 50 is also included in the Vernon Mansucript with each Latin verse followed by an English translation and explanatory amplification. For the text see Carl Hosrtmann, ed., *The Minor Poems of the Vernon MS.*, part I, Early English Text Society, os 98 (1892; repr. New York, 1973), p. 12 ff.
23. I am grateful to Margot Louis for the observation that the scroll and the crucifix cross over the boundary.
24. See the discussion of this idea, though not with respect to the Vernon historiated initial, by Nicholas Watson, "Conceptions of the Word: The Mother Tongue and the Incarnation of God," in *New Medieval Literatures*, ed. Wendy Scase et al. (Oxford, 1997), pp. 87–124.
25. In the same chapter of John of Damascus from which Hilton quotes (see note 18 above), the former states that because God was made man in substance, the image of his crucifixion, for instance, reminds us of his saving Passion, and so we fall down and adore that which is represented.
26. Stanley Stewart Hussey, "An Edition, From the Manuscripts, of Book II of Walter Hilton's Scale of Perfection," PhD diss., U of London, 1962, p. 72. This passage from book 2.21 is from London, British Library, MS Harley 6579, fol. 85r.

27. In addition to the Augustinian Hilton, the defenders of holy images were to include the Dominican Roger Dymmock, Robert Rypon, Robert Alynton, the Franciscan William Woodford, the Carmelite Thomas Netter, and Reginald Pecock. Most of them were "Oxford-educated, first generation anti-Wyclifites," as observed by W. R. Jones, "Lollards and Images: The Defense of Religious Art in Later Medieval England," *JHI* (1973), 37. Anne Hudson also refers to John Deveros. See her Notes to "Images and Pilgrimages," *Selections from English Wycliffite Writings* (Cambridge, Eng., 1978), pp. 179–81.
28. Anne Hudson, Notes to "Images and Pilgrimages," pp. 179–81. She supports this by noting the use of scholastic terminology and of contemporary examples, as well as overlapping citations, suggesting they derive from a continuing debate. She also mentions that such associates of Wyclif as Robert Alynton later wrote against him.
29. Cistercians and Franciscans had questioned "conspicuous symbols of worldly success," as pointed out by Jones, "Lollards and Images," p. 27. Further, in 1356, Archbishop FitzRalph of Armagh warned of the idolatrous "danger from the veneration of images which some frequently and wrongfully call by the name of those they are intended to represent, such as St. Mary of Lincoln, St. Mary of Walsyngham, St. Mary of Newarke, and so forth." He denounces "the oblations which are offered to such images on account of the false and fabricated miracles wrought by their minsters." See Owst, *Literature and Pulpit*, pp. 140–41. Anne Hudson mentions that William Woodford, later an opponent of Wyclif, discusses the matter in 1372–73, clearly drawing on well-worn arguments; Notes to "Images and Pilgrimages," p. 179. For Wyclif's treatise see Johannis Wyclif, *Tractus de mandatis divinis*, ed. Johan Loserth and F. D. Matthew (London, 1922), p. 153 ff.
30. Wyclif, *Tractus*, p. 156.
31. Wyclif, *Tractus*, p. 156. See the discussions by Mary Aston, *Lollards and Reformers: Images and Literacy in Late Medieval England* (London, 1984), p. 139, and by Jones, "Lollards and Images," 29–30.
32. "Twelve Conclusions of the Lollards," in *Selections from English Wycliffite Writings*, p. 27.
33. Watson, "The Politics of Middle English Writing," *The Idea of the Vernacular*, p. 340–41.
34. For the "Wycliffe Propositions condemned at London, A. D. 1382," see Henry Gee and William John Hardy, *Documents Illustrative of English Church History* (London, 1910), pp. 108–09. Wyclif also proclaimed that formal confession is unncessary if a person is repentant.
35. Wyclif, *Tractus*, p. 156.
36. *Johannis Wyclif Sermones*, ed. J. Loserth (London, 1887–1890), p. 90. See the discussion in Aston, *Lollards and Reformers*, p. 141.
37. See the discussion by Aston, *Lollards and Reformers*, p. 139.
38. In the *La Estorie del Evangelie* or Gospel miniatures, the facial features of the Virgin and of the angel are obliterated in the Annunciation (fol. 105r), as are the faces of Mary and Zacharias in that of the birth of John the Baptist (fol. 105v), and the faces of the angel and of Zacharias in the temple scene (fol. 105r), and probably also the face of the angel in the scene of the Shepherds (fol. 105v). In the miniatures for the Miracles of Our Lady, the evil figures of the devil (fol. 126v) and the faces of the Vikings (fol. 124r) appear also to have been rubbed to rob them of their evil power. This combination of damage to holy and unholy figures also occurs in an illustrated

Piers Plowman manuscript where the face of Mercy (fol. 94r) and the figure of the devil (fol. 96r) have been rubbed and darkened. These may be seen in color in Derek Pearsall, ed., *Piers Plowman: A Facsimile of Bodleian Library, Oxford, MS Douce 104* (Cambridge, 1992).

39. "Images and Pilgrimages," *Selections from English Wycliffite Writings*, p. 84. The text is from London, British Library, MS Additional 24202, fols. 26r-28v, as mentioned by Hudson in her notes to "Images and Pilgrimages," p. 179.
40. Jones, "Lollards and Images," 50.
41. Scott, *Later Gothic Manuscripts* I, 43–47. The catalogue entry for the *Pearl* Manuscript is no. 12 in vol. II, published together with the first volume.
42. Jones, "Lollards and Images," 33, referring to *Select Works of John Wyclif*, vol. 3, ed. Thomas Arnold, (Oxford, 1869–71), p. 462.
43. Aston, *Lollards and Reformers*, pp. 171–73. These were the image of St. Andrew from the cemetery at the church of St. Andrew at Trowse Newton in 1427, the cross at Bromehold in 1424, and the image of the Virgin at the parish of Byfield in 1416. The incident of the service books occurred in 1417 when the abbot of St. Albans had a nocturnal search made. One of these defaced service books, as Aston mentions, "was sent to the king who passed it on to the archbishop of Canterbury to serve as an object-lesson for Londoners" (p. 173).
44. Malcolm Andrew and Ronald Waldron, eds. *The Poems of the Pearl Manuscript: Pearl, Cleanness, Patience, Sir Gawain and the Green Knight* (London, 1978), Subsequent line references to the poems will be from this edition and will be inserted in brackets following the quotations in my text.
45. Phillipa Hardman, "Gawain's Practice of Piety in *Sir Gawain and the Green Knight*," *Medium Ævum* 68.2 (1999), 247–67.
46. Hardman, "Gawain's Practice of Piety," 261.
47. See my forthcoming article on San Marino, Huntington Library, MS EL 26 C9, "Framing the Canterbury Pilgrims for the Aristocratic Audience of the Ellesmere Manuscript," *English Literary Studies.*
48. See Kathryn Kerby-Fulton and Denise L. Despres, *Iconography and the Professional Reader: the Politics of Book Production in the Douce "Piers Plowman"* (Minneapolis, 1999).
49. Laura L. Howes, *Chaucer's Gardens and the Language of Convention* (Gainesville, 1997).
50. He used a Video Spectral Comparator and an IC8 Integrator Comparator.
51. See the discussion in Denise Despres, "*Pearl*: Penance Through the Dream Vision," *Ghostly Sights: Visual Meditation in Late-Medieval Literature* (Norman, OK, 1989), pp. 89–118.
52. Fols. 60r and 86r respectively.
53. Elisabeth Petroff Martin, "Psychological Landscape in Fourteenth Century allegory and Painting: The *Pearl* and *La Divina Commedia*," PhD diss., U of California, 1972, pp. 368–69, as quoted in Kevin Douglas Marti, "The Figurative Use of the Body in *Pearl*," PhD diss., Cornell U, 1988, p. 193. See also Petroff (Martin), "Landscape in *Pearl*: The Transformation of Nature," *The Chaucer Review* 16.2 (1981): 180–93.
54. Gollancz, "The Illustrations," p. 9, thought this might be a "metaphorical idea" indicating the dreamer's spirit has sped forth. A similar chaperon can be seen on the man leaning on a cane in the miniature of Jonah preaching in Nineveh, fol. 86v. See my subsequent discussion.
55. One of them is just visible as a white dot on the top left tree (fig. 2) of the first miniature. In the manuscript itself it measures 1.4 cm. from the top and 3 cm. from

the inner edge. On the third miniature, visible as a black dot in the middle of the top left tree (fig. 5), it measures 1.3 cm. from the top and 2.3 cm. from the inner edge in the manuscript.

56. Of course, this does not exclude the possibility that there may have been more folios between the pictures and the text.
57. Elisabeth Petroff Martin, "Psychological Landscape," pp. 368–69.
58. Compare Canon XXXV, illustrated as "W" in the Chirogrammatic Plate D and Gestus XXXIV illustrated as Chirogrammatic Plate B in John Bulwer's mid-seventeenth-century *Chirologia: or the Natural Language of the Hand and Chironomia: or the Art of Manual Rhetoric*, ed. James W. Cleary (Carbondale and Edwardsville, 1974), pp. 186, 193, 64 and 117. In speaking of the chastising hand of God, he refers the signification of Isaiah 11.15 when he prophesies that "the Lord . . . shall lift up his hand over the river" (Douai version), a consideration that may not have been far from the mind of the designer of these miniatures.
59. This is in contrast to William Langland's portrayal of the hierarchy in heaven, according to merit, as pictured by the marginal illustration of the saved thief on fol. 65r of the Douce Manuscript. See my discussion in "Retributive Violence and the Reformist Agenda in the Illustrated Douce 104 MS of *Piers Plowman*," *Fifteenth-Century Studies* 23 (1997), 26.
60. Marti, in the chapter on "*Interior Intimo Meo*: The Spatiality of the Heart," in his dissertation, "The Figurative Use of the Body in *Pearl*," pp. 206–48, develops the significance of the pearl at the center of the Pearl Maiden's breast, corresponding with the location of the heart, connecting it with the rose and the Eucharist.
61. Elisabeth Petroff Martin, "Psychological Landscape," 368–69.
62. See, for instance, the miniature of Jonah being cast up at the gate of a city, very like the New Jerusalem in the *Pearl* miniature. Oxford, Bodleian Library, MS Liturg.198, 1350–60, fol. 60r, is reproduced in Lucy Freeman Sandler, *Gothic Manuscripts 1285–1385*, vol. I (London, 1986), Ills. 320.
63. "Jerusalem, Babylon, Camelot: the concept of the court in the 'Pearl'-poet," PhD diss., Washington U, 1989, p. 62.
64. John Ingledew, "Jerusalem, Babylon, Camelot," pp. 63–64.
65. Ingledew, "Jerusalem, Babylon, Camelot," p. 162.
66. See, for instance, the large sharp knife used in the Circumcision in such miniatures as Oxford, Bodleian Library, MS Hatton 1, fol. 24v, reproduced in Scott, *Later Gothic Manuscripts* I, as Ills. 21. On the Circumcision in art, see Gertrud Schiller, *Iconography of Christian Art* I, trans. Janet Seligman (Greenwich, CT, 1971), pp. 88–90. Schiller, p. 88, points out that the knife used is included among the Instruments of the Passion and that the Circumcision itself is one of the Seven Sorrows of Mary.
67. See Cambridge, Trinity College, MS B.10.15, fol. 7v, reproduced in Sandler, *Gothic Manuscripts* I, Ills. 323.
68. Cf. Ingledew, "Jerusalem, Babylon, Camelot," p. 122.
69. See, for instance, the hell mounth in the scene of the Fall of the Rebel Angels in Oxford, Bodleian Library, Junius 11, p. 3 which also contains several elements the poet describes in *Cleanness*. Perhaps this manuscript, or one very like it, was familiar.
70. On the human level, the swords of the evil Babylonians "swolwed" the Israelites (1268; also, 1253).
71. See fol. 326r as reproduced in the facsimile, *The Auchinleck Manuscript: National Library of Scotland Advocates' MS. 19.2.1*, ed. Derek Pearsall and I. C. Cunningham (London, 1977).

72. Letter CLXIV, *The Confessions and Letters of St. Augustine*, ed. Philip Schaff, A Select Library of Nicene and Post-Nicene fathers of the Christian Church, 1 (Buffalo, 1886), p. 521. For Epistola CLXIV.21 see also *Sancti Augustini, Hipponensis Episcopi*, Opera Omnia 40 (Paris, 1842), p. 318.
73. Northrop Frye, *The Secular Scripture: A Study of the Structure of Romance* (Cambridge, MA, 1976), pp. 99, 105.
74. See the Casket with scenes from the tale of the Prodigal Son, New York, Metropolitan Museum of Art, No. 41.100.159, French, 1325–50, reproduced in C. Jean Campbell, "Courting, Harlotry and the Art of Gothic Ivory Carving," *Gesta* 34.1 (1995), Fig. 4.
75. Except that here, Arthur's other hand is raised in a gesture of welcome instead of holding, as does Christ, a resurrection banner. See, for instance, the Harrowing of Hell in Sandler, *Gothic Manuscripts* I, Ills. 314, showing the Fitzwarin Psalter, Paris, MS Bibl. Nat. lat. 765, 1350–70, fol. 15r.

Untangling the Thread of Internal Progress in a Benedictine Community: An Abridgement of Augustine's *Confessiones* from Medieval Norwich

[1]Linda Olson

Here he narrates his Confessiones *as an example that others may do thus.*[2]

These informative words intrude upon Augustine's narrative in the midst of book II of his *Confessiones* in Cambridge, University Library, MS Kk.II.21 (fols. 102r[a]-115v[b]). In so doing, they act as a kind of explanatory, didactic gloss for readers of this particular copy of Augustine's autobiography. They occur at a point in the narrative where Augustine has himself interrupted the report of his wayward youth to question the audience and purpose of his text:

> To whom do I narrate these things? For not to you, my God, but with you I narrate these things to my kind, the human kind, however small a portion can fall upon these letters of mine. And for what [purpose do I do] this? Namely so that I and whoever reads these things may consider how one should cry out to you from a depth.[3]

The intrusion follows immediately upon this passage, indicating that the potentially and perhaps suggestively ambiguous "thus" refers first and foremost to the sinner's invocation of or confession to God. In this way, Augustine's narrative purpose is defined in MS Kk.II.21 as the presentation of exemplary confession for imitation by his readers, who might then narrate their own *confessiones*, with the obvious implication that those readers are to apply what they read in the *Confessiones* to themselves, examining their own spiritual natures, rising through hope and prayer from the depth of sin, and ultimately converting to ascetic Christianity like Augustine himself—that is, that they should follow the example of Augustine's spiritual progression as well as of his autobiographical devotion. The focus upon Augustine's *confessio* and *conversio* provided by this intrusion in MS Kk.II.21 serves as an excellent introduction to what is one of the most unique medieval English copies of the text extant today; indeed, it is indicative of how the medieval "editor" of these *Confessiones* intended to shape the interiorities of future readers through his carefully presented version of Augustine's self-writing. In addition, the strange ambiguity of the word "thus" in the intrusion—namely its ability to refer not only to the narration of the imitative *confessiones* of Augustine's readers, but also to the narration of Augustine's *Confessiones* themselves—allows the remark to be read as a claim that Augustine "narrates his *Confessiones* as an example that others may" also narrate his *Confessiones*, and thus as justification for the activities of MS Kk.II.21's intrusive "editor." For there can be little doubt that this active medieval reader of the *Confessiones* re-narrates Augustine's autobiography, and does so with a particular agenda in mind, revealing in the process some interesting readerly and editorial habits.

MS Kk.II.21 is an English volume produced in the first half of the fourteenth century and containing two inscriptions which identify it as the book of Robert de Donewico, a Benedictine monk and administrative official in the Cathedral Priory of Norwich during the same period; beside one of the inscriptions appears a characteristic Norwich library press-mark (N.lvij; N possibly over an erasure).[4] Both this press-mark and the usual practice of Benedictine monks at Norwich (as elsewhere) in bequeathing their private books to their communities suggest that the volume probably entered the monastic library upon Donewico's death, and we can assume that the manuscript was his personal possession until then.[5] Unfortunately, we do not know exactly when Donewico (or Donewich) entered the monastery at Norwich, or when he died, but he was already a trusted member of that community in 1329–30 when he was sent to London to buy "colours" for a new chapel.[6] Over the next several years, he was assigned other responsibilities appropriate to a capable, learned, and politically informed individual, including the arrangement of an essential loan for the monastery (1330) and participation *pro priore* in parliament in London (1333–34 and 1337–38). From 1331 until 1333 he was the community's hosteller, and thus responsible for the lodging and entertainment of guests. In 1333 he was appointed master of the cellar, the chief financial officer at Norwich, equivalent to the bursar or treasurer in other monastic houses. He held that position until November of 1341, when he recorded at the end of his accounts that he had greatly reduced the debt he inherited from his predecessor, that he had left more in the granary than was there when he came to office, and finally, that he had purchased land and entertained the king and queen. For a brief period in 1341 he acted as communar, the offical responsible for the fourteenth-century building program in the monastery's cloister, as well as for the distribution of funds for various other expenses. During the final years of his life, 1341 until 1344, he filled the office of chamberlain, providing clothing and other domestic necessities for his community, until, in 1343–44, he charged his office for medical treatment and then disappeared from the records.

These facts make it clear that Donewico was a monk linked always to the administration of his monastery, and thus never separated from the often contradictory concerns of both the cloister and the outside world. Though he must have been well educated, he probably did not attend university (or only for a very short period of time if he did), for he does not appear in the records as one of Norwich's many monk students, and very few university-trained monks held significant monastic offices at Norwich for long periods of time, particularly several of them consecutively.[7] As Joan Greatrex has argued, "in the majority of cases the longer a monk was absent at university the less likely he was to be found in the group of long-standing administrators on his return to the Norwich cloister."[8] Donewico was most probably, then, neither a great intellectual nor a deep spiritualist, and although he was entrusted with significant responsibilities, he is known for neither ill behaviour nor outstanding achievements in fulfilling them (excepting, of course, his own tribute to his accounting successes). He would seem, instead, to have lived a life of quiet but considerable accomplishment in both the cloister and the world. In a century when the *Confessiones* were read by some of the most powerful ecclesiastical and intellectual figures in England—men like Thomas Bradwardine and Richard FitzRalph, Thomas Buckingham and Robert Holcot, John de Grandisson and William Langland[9]—Robert de Donewico, who stands out more for being unexceptional, is not perhaps the type of person we might expect to find reading the *Confessiones.* And this is, of course, one of the main reasons why his copy of the *Confessiones* in MS Kk.II.21 is so particularly interesting.

However, the second main reason for a special interest in Donewico's *Confessiones*—their unique nature—is yet more compelling. For Augustine's autobiography as it appears in MS Kk.II.21 has been considerably abridged in the following ways: large passages and even entire books have been completely deleted; various short sections have been removed to form long condensed passages; significant brief passages have been included while the text around them has been deleted; and Augustine's language has been altered slightly in places in order to accommodate the omissions.[10] Donewico's *Confessiones* also present a unique pattern of unnumbered chapter-like divisions,[11] which are built right into the text (rather than appearing marginally, as is the case in most manuscripts of the *Confessiones*), and occasionally appear in combination with narrative rubrics—that is, rubrics explaining what is going on in the narrative as opposed to those more structurally oriented rubrics which mark the beginning and end of books. These rubrics are the product of the scribal hand which copied the main text,[12] though they are executed in red ink. Appearing, as they do, only at divisions marked by the same kind of colored capitals as those which signal the openings of books, rather than by the large paragraph marks which suffice for the other divisions, they emphasize how these capital-adorned and rubricated divisions are to be understood as more important—or at least more noteworthy—than the others.[13] Unfortunately, the narrative rubrics seem to be incomplete, for they, and the major divisions associated with them, curiously stop in book V and do not continue again until book IX, although the capitals and rubrics indicating book divisions continue through this section of the text.

As I intend to show in this article, the "editing" process of *abbreviatio* and *ordinatio* presented by MS Kk.II.21 produces a very different text of the *Confessiones*—one which does not appear to have existed outside of Norwich,[14] and one which reveals much about how the medieval "editor" (and of necessity those who encountered his version) read Augustine's autobiography. Although this "editor" may seem to the admirer of Augustine's *Confessiones* to present at best a mere skeleton of a complex literary structure, and at times to reveal himself as no great respecter of Augustine's rich and allusive style, there does appear to be a focused method to his madness. For his editing activities suggest a particular reading of the text designed to bring about certain specific effects in subsequent readers—effects hinted at in the intrusion which opens this paper. In fact, it is probable that Donewico's *Confessiones* were reshaped by a learned Norwich monk (though I suspect not Donewico himself) in an attempt to create a safe and uncomplicated, yet rich and sophisticated textual guide particularly for the use of young or newly converting and converted members of the Norwich community—those who were just beginning to fashion the monastic interiorities necessary for their learned devotional journeys of mind and soul toward their God.

Specifically, I believe that the "editor" of MS Kk.II.21 was attempting to create a version of the *Confessiones* designed to be read in the ways suggested by Augustine himself in his *Retractationes,* though necessarily with some biases of his own seasoning the text as well. Some form of Augustine's *retractatio* for the *Confessiones* appears as a prologue to virtually every medieval English copy of the autobiography, and Donewico's MS Kk.II.21 is no exception.[15] It contains an abbreviated version of the *retractatio* virtually identical to that which entered England through one textual tradition in the late eleventh century,[16] and it reads, in a literal translation, as follows:

> The books of my confessions regarding both [my] goods and evils praise God and into him excite the human intellect and affection. And thus they accomplish this in me and about me when they are read. From the first [book] all the way to the tenth they are written about me; the remaining three, about the holy scriptures. This work begins thus.[17]

While eliminating Augustine's reconsiderations of particular passages of his autobiography, this abbreviated *retractatio* retains in brief the most interesting and unique aspects of Augustine's strikingly personal comments on the *Confessiones,*[18] and the "editor" of MS Kk.II.21 appears to have taken them to heart. The most immediately obvious deletion in his version, for instance—namely the fact that books XI through XIII of the text are completely lacking—indicates that the "editor" has chosen to include only those books (I-X) which Augustine claims are written about himself. He thus implies not only that he pays close attention to Augustine's words in the *retractatio,* but also that he is attempting to present the *Confessiones* specifically as what we would call an autobiographical narrative. Also indicative of this trend is the removal of various passages of theological and philosophical speculation and polemic throughout the included books in favor of passages dealing with Augustine's personal experiences, spiritual development and relationship to God; the abstract questions and arguments of books VII and X in particular have frequently been deleted.[19] Finally, the occasional narrative rubrics in MS Kk.II.21, transcribed here with the major divisions where they appear indicated in relation to Verheijen's edition of the *Confessiones,* confirm this reading:

Book I:	**De infantia Augustini.** (6.4: *Quid* . . . , fol. 102r[b])
	De pueritia (7.45: *ecce* . . . , fol. 102v[a])
	Oratio Augustini. (10.13: *Vide* . . . , fol. 102v[b])
Book II:	**De furto. Augustini.** (4.1: *Furtum* . . . , fol. 103v[b])
Book III:	**De sompnio matris. Augustini.** (11.7: *somnium* . . . , fol. 105r[a])
Book IV:	**De amicitia et morte socij.** (4.1: *In* . . . , fol. 105v[a])
Book V:	**De aduentu fausti.** (3.2: *Iam* . . . , fol. 106v[a])
Book IX:	**De conuersatione matris et nutrice eiusdem.** (8.10: *non* . . . , fol. 112r[b])
Book X:	**De Gulositate.** (31.1: *Est* . . . , fol. 114r[b])
	De voluptate aurium. (33.1: *Voluptates* . . . , fol. 114v[a])
	De voluptate oculorum. (34.1: *Restat* . . . , fol. 114v[b])
	De Curiositate seculi. (35.53: *in* . . . , fol. 115r[a])
	De Adulatione. (36.13: *numquid* . . . , fol. 115r[b])

Two of the three narrative rubrics in book I of the *Confessiones* highlight stages of the young Augustine's development, namely "infancy" and "childhood," while others elsewhere in the text reveal a special interest in Augustine's personal activities, friends and sins. Thus these rubrics suggest that their inventor, who was presumably the same individual as the "editor," was attempting to emphasize Augustine's autobiographical narrative and align it with a couple of the "grid patterns" of medieval thought regarding the individual, his development and his Christian morality, namely the ages of man and the deadly sins.[20]

More complicated than the emphasis on Augustine's autobiographical narrative are the ways in which the "editor" of MS Kk.II.21 works to create a text which will readily achieve for himself, and perhaps for future readers, exactly what the abbreviated *retractatio* claims the *Confessiones* do for both their author and reader—"praise God and into him excite the human intellect and affection" (the use of the accusative, *in eum,* makes the rather odd sense of movement in the passage clear). This involves special attention to Augustine's devotional confession, his offerings of praise and admissions of sin; to his gradual conversion, the progression of his intellect and affection into God; and to the essential interiority of both as they are presented in the *Confessiones.*[21] Certainly a concern with praying to, praising and thanking God is central to the "editor's" mission, for he often selects for inclusion passages containing Augustine's most direct and explicit addresses and outbursts to God, like the opening devotions of book I,[22] the "Deus, deus meus" confession a few chapters later,[23] the powerful plea for acceptance at the beginning of book V—"Accept the sacrifice of my confessions from the hand of my tongue . . . "[24]—and many others. In one instance, this medieval "editor" even draws special attention with a narrative rubric to a prayer in which Augustine has used the first-person plural:

> Look mercifully at these [sins], Lord, and free us already calling upon you, [and] also free those who do not yet call upon you, so that they may call upon you and you might free them.[25]

Such a prayer could easily be appropriated by readers and used for their own devotional activities, especially with the rubric "Oratio Augustini" making the passage immediately accessible and lending it a certain amount of editorial and textual authority. Indeed, the ready potential for such devotional appropriation of Augustine's voice is suggested by the way in which the "editor" changes Augustine's third-person line in I.1—"For seeking they find him and finding they will praise him"—into the direct second-person address of prayer—"For seeking they will find you and finding they will praise you."[26]

In addition, the "editor" retains much of Augustine's discussion in book X of the usefulness of his devotional *Confessiones,* particularly including Augustine's assertions of how his is primarily an intimate confession to God,[27] yet one which Augustine hopes his readers will believe through charity,[28] so that his *Confessiones* will inspire in their audience similar tearful prayers of thanks, supplication and praise.[29] Finally, in book II he selects from the deleted text around them Augustine's questions about his *Confessions*—"To whom do I narrate these things?" "And for what [purpose do I do] this?"—as well as his subsequent description of how he wrote his text so that both he and his readers would consider "from what depth one should cry out" to God.[30] The "editor" then does something very unusual: he drives the point home by making the first of only two intrusions into Augustine's narrative to write the words cited earlier, the claim that Augustine "narrates his confessions as an example that others may do thus." As I mentioned above, the most obvious referent of the somewhat ambiguous "thus" is the sinner's invocation of or confession to God, which means that the "editor" of MS Kk.II.21 sees Augustine's narrative purpose as the presentation of personal confession for imitation by each of his readers in turn. The intrusion does not appear in red ink like the other narrative rubrics and is accompanied by no division, as though the "editor" inserted the words so naturally or automatically that he forgot to shift into rubrication mode and ink; as a result, his participatory comment has become part of the text itself, interpreting Augustine's words morally and personally, and encouraging the reader to engage in an Augustinian self-examination and the devout *confessio* which should follow.

From these few examples, then, we can see that Augustine's devotional *confessio* mode and its purpose to both communicate with God and motivate readers to engage in similar confessions were seen by the Norwich abbreviator as vital aspects of the text, worthy of inclusion and emphasis.[31] Also apparent in this abridged version of the *Confessiones* is a recognition that Augustine's *confessio* is first and foremost an internal process, consisting of what Augustine calls, in a passage retained by the abbreviator, "the words of the soul and the cry of thought," and thus, while "silent in noise, it cries out in affection."[32] Elsewhere in the text, passages explicitly describing Augustine's *confessio* as an internal activity are selected for inclusion. In book VI, for instance, the "editor" retains Augustine's brief acknowledgement that he considers God's "mercies" and confesses God's "praises" from his "innermost aspects," even though he eliminates the text all around—indeed, the entire context of—this sentence.[33] Again in book VII he selects Augustine's description of how the "silent contritions" of his "spirit" were the "great voices" by which he spoke in God's "ears," crying out for his "mercy."[34]

It is clear, then, that the "editor" of the *Confessiones* in MS Kk.II.21 made an effort to emphasize the essential interiority of Augustine's *confessio* mode, and thus presumably to let himself and future readers know that their *confessiones* should also originate and be offered within the heart.

And it is equally clear from his version of the text that he experienced a similar preoccupation with the interiority of Augustine's progressive conversion process—what Augustine calls in his *Retractationes* the movement of the "human intellect and affection" into God. Thus included while the text around it has been deleted is Augustine's description in book IV of how it is the "weak *soul*" which is "carried off and turned round, twisted and retwisted," so that the "light is beclouded for it and the truth is not distinguished."[35] Again in book VI the abbreviator retains, along with various other brief passages from chapter 16, Augustine's exclamation that it is his "*soul*" which is restless and insecure, desperately "turned and returned."[36] Even more revealing is the inclusion in book I of Augustine's statement of his spiritual wandering in youth: I was "far from your face, [God], in a dark affection. For one does not go from you or return to you with the feet or [through] the spaces of places."[37] The rich literary allusions to the parable of the prodigal son, the journey of Aeneas, the theme of exile central to the writings of Plotinus and the Old Testament which follow in the complete text are predictably deleted, as if the simple statement of the young Augustine's spiritual distance from his God and the essentially nonphysical, internal and specifically affective nature of the movement to and from that God is sufficient to the "editor's" needs. He doctors in similar ways chapter 10 of book VII in which Augustine, freshly inspired by reading the Platonic books, "enters into his innermost aspects," finds "eternal truth," fearfully discovers his own true nature in a "region of unlikeness" and hears the voice of his God "cry out from on high" and "from afar," for these essentials of the passage are retained, but everything else, everything extraneous to this basic message of internal revelation and turmoil, has been deleted.[38]

While we may not appreciate the "editor's" cursory treatment of some of Augustine's richest and most subtle passages, it is nonetheless clear that he presents Augustine's *confessio* mode and the journey of self-progression narrated by it as processes which take place on intellectual and emotional levels, and involve, on the part of the one confessing and progressing, a reflective turn towards one's own internal nature. Internal progression or *conversio* may in fact be the prime concern of the "editor" in abridging the text, for he appears to focus within the autobiographical narrative which is his priority upon the author's personal internal progress—upon how, as a retained passage notes, Augustine was first "confounded" and then "converted."[39] The encounter with Cicero's *Hortensius* in book III is particularly interesting in this regard, for the "editor" eliminates the descriptions of Cicero and his book, as well as Augustine's lengthy elaboration of philosophy, paring the passage down to Augustine's reading of the text, his subsequent internal change—"that book changed my affection, changed my prayers to you yourself, Lord, made my wishes and desires other" than they were, and thus "I began to rise up so that I might return to you"—and his lament over that book's lack of "Christ's name" which he had imbibed with his "mother's milk."[40] In this way, the exact nature of Augustine's internal conversion at this point and its limitations from a Christian perspective stand out. Further on in Augustine's development, in the abstract, philosophical explorations of book VII, the deletions are extensive and there is an attempt to select for inclusion only the most direct and memorable statements of Augustine's internal condition and progress, like those of chapter 10 and its "region of unlikeness" discussed above. Thus the lengthy first chapter of book VII is reduced to a few passages which clearly outline the current state of Augustine's inner nature. He is said to have passed from adolescence to youth, a physical and intellectual development which makes his lack of spiritual vision all the more wicked; he attempts to cleanse the "swarm of impurity from the sight of his mind," but it rushes back to "becloud" his inner vision; and he continues to think and understand in physical terms only, his "heart" seeking "images" like those his "eyes" perceive, because God has not yet "illuminated his darknesses."[41] It would seem that nothing else in the chapter—not the long summary of the correct doctrine Augustine already believed or the detailed description of his mistaken physical understanding of God and indeed himself (at 1.4–14, 18–31 and 33–52)—was deemed worthy of manuscript space by this active "editor;" and the pattern continues throughout book VII.

Similarly in book VIII, the book of the *Confessiones* which deals most explicitly with the concept of conversion, the abridging process appears to aim at a concise presentation of the key events and influences in Augustine's spiritual progress. Thus the "editor" follows in a condensed form the conversion of Victorinus,[42] shows some interest in the comments on the conversion of sinners which follow,[43] and clearly emphasizes the effect of Simplicianus's exemplary conversion story upon

Augustine by selecting from its deleted surroundings the statement of Augustine's intense desire to imitate Victorinus.[44] Similar attention is paid to Augustine's response to Ponticianus's inspirational narrative, for the medieval "editor" selects from chapter 7 the passages which describe how Augustine is forced by that story to "turn back" and honestly examine his "distorted and filthy, stained and ulcerous" inner "face;" how he assesses the weakness of his previous prayers to be given "chastity and continence, but not now;" how he is rebuked for his spiritual tardiness by his own "conscience;" and how, as Ponticianus speaks, he is "gnawed within and confounded by a powerful shame" until he turns to himself once again for further self-reflection.[45] Augustine's frustrated and motivating outburst to Alypius in chapter 8,[46] his movement into the Milanese garden soon afterwards,[47] and his gradual halting progress as he struggles with his own will in the chapters preceding the dramatic revelation there[48] are also selected as the narrative leads into Augustine's own conversion. Finally, the chapter (VIII.12) which relates that sudden inner transformation is condensed in a way which removes extraneous details and neatly lays emphasis upon the process of change Augustine undergoes.[49] More than any other section of the autobiography, then, book VIII of this abbreviated version reveals how the medieval "editor" focused intently upon Augustine's internal conversion from secular concerns to spiritual priorities—a conversion which not only takes place within the individual, but is also a conversion into more internal aspects of the self.

It is clear from these examples in book VIII and from passages selected elsewhere in the *Confessiones*—like those dealing with Cicero's *Hortensius* and the Platonic writings—that the "editor" of MS Kk.II.21 also pays considerable attention to Augustine's reflective and growthful encounters with narratives. Indeed, it would seem that he had a special interest in the role of narratives and the tellers or writers of those narratives in shaping the developing interiority of the individual listener or reader. Thus he specifically selects, for instance, along with Augustine's motivated response to Simplicianus's narrative, the autobiographer's brief explanation of how Simplicianus tells his story with the particular intention of inspiring in Augustine a desire to imitate Victorinus (cited above). That is, the "editor" (and not surprisingly) appears to acknowledge here that narratives are created and related in order to bring about certain results in those who encounter them, in this case, to encourage Augustine's conversion from secular rhetoric to ascetic Christianity. The "editor" has, of course, already demonstrated an interest in and understanding of this fact by noting in his intrusion in book II that Augustine narrates his *Confessiones* in order to encourage similar confessions in his readers and emphasizing in book III Augustine's response to Cicero's text. Furthermore, he continues to do so by including in his version not only Augustine's intense response to Ponticianus's story, but also his immediate conversion through reading Paul and the passages from the end of VIII.12 in which Augustine tells first Alypius, who follows him into conversion, and then Monnica of this transformation (quoted above). We can therefore reasonably assume in this "editor" a sophisticated level of self-awareness regarding the potential effects of his own carefully reshaped narrative upon future readers of the abridged *Confessiones,* and view his editorial activities, as I have already suggested, not simply as attempts to shorten a long work, but as deliberate efforts to influence his readers—certain readers, in fact—in certain ways.

Thinking about his abridgement in this way actually helps to clarify a few potentially confusing deletions in Ponticianus's conversion narrative (VIII.6). The first occurs when the "editor" includes the mention of Anthony the Egyptian monk and the monastery under Ambrose's care, but eliminates the text between the two, adding instead a simple *et cetera* after Anthony's name:

> When I had indicated to [Ponticianus] that I expended the greatest care on those writings [of Paul], a sermon arose, with he himself narrating, about Anthony the Egyptian monk, and so on. {And there was a monastery full of good brothers at Milan, outside the walls of the city under the nourisher Ambrose, and we did not know.[50]

The brief comment is the "editor's" second and last intrusion into Augustine's narrative, and it implies in its author and assumes in its reader an intimate familiarity with the conversion of Anthony, the father of monks, while it deletes Augustine's comments on Anthony's reputation among Christians, on the nearly contemporary nature of the miraculous events associated with him, and on the amazing ignorance of Augustine and Alypius with regard to Anthony's life. Thus eliminating what might be seen as repetitious and no longer of immediate relevance in the later Middle Ages, this version also neatly juxtaposes, though in a somewhat abrupt manner, two concrete examples of the Christian monastic life—the conversion of Anthony the hermit and the establishment of a monastic community by Ambrose. The "editor" then excludes from his version the whole of Ponticianus's report regarding the conversion of his two acquaintances, the aspect of Ponticianus's discourse which we might think of as the main point of his story. The narrative to which Augustine responds so powerfully is thus given a decidedly more monastic bias, a bias which would presumably have been entirely appropriate for influencing the spiritual development of readers in a Benedictine community like that at the Norwich Cathedral Priory. In fact, there could hardly be a better confirmation of Jean Leclercq's claim that medieval monks primarily sought in Augustine (as in the other Latin fathers) "all that could be helpful in leading the monastic life" they had chosen.[51]

I believe that the abridged *Confessiones* in MS Kk.II.21 should, then, be read as indicative not only of an active monastic reader's personal interests and preferences, but also of his attempts to influence future monastic readers in some rather specific ways, and this is the case particularly in those instances where he appears to be doing more than simply abridging or editing the text. For he frequently engages in a form of censorship, eliminating passages and ideas which might be potentially dangerous, misleading or even simply distracting in terms of reading the *Confessiones* as an inspiring and exemplary model for internal progress, especially in the Benedictine monastic life. Thus he cuts much of Augustine's report in book I of the pleasure he took in pagan literature and rhetorical exercises, including the implication that such literature instigates sins like adultery.[52] In book III he deletes the philosophical material in Augustine's encounter with the *Hortensius* (III.4, as cited above) and most of the Manichaean doctrine Augustine relates,[53] but includes Augustine's attempt to read the Bible almost in its entirety.[54] In book VI he eliminates a brief mention of Epicurus[55] and removes the reports of Alypius's fascination with the circus and gladiatorial games—indeed, he removes much of the material on Alypius himself and focuses instead on Augustine's relationship with him.[56] In book VII, although he retains most of Augustine's important discovery of Christian spiritual principles in the Platonic books, he deletes the description of idolatry and pagan ideals found in the same books,[57] and he also omits Augustine's report of the notably Plotinian light of truth he sees within himself in the following chapter.[58] In book VIII, he eliminates not only Augustine's lengthy discussion and refutation of the Manichaean dual approach to the human will,[59] but also the tempting allegory of Augustine's "old friends," while keeping the completely unobjectionable figure of Continence who urges Augustine on to chastity.[60] And finally, in VIII.12 (cited above) he omits the second mention of Anthony's conversion immediately before Augustine's own conversion experience, presumably not because it no longer interested him, but perhaps because he considered it unnecessary to repeat here, assuming (as he did in using *et cetera* in VIII.6) a shared reading culture, like a Benedictine monastery where the liturgy and other communal texts would introduce all members to exemplary *Vitae* like Anthony's. Maybe he even thought that it drew attention away from Augustine's conversion, rendering it less dramatic, and thus considered it distracting as well as repetitious in terms of his bare-bones technique of narrative presentation and his narrow focus upon Augustine's progress alone at this point. There can be no doubt that his version does present an uncluttered report of Augustine's dramatic conversion.[61]

These omissions, and various others found in the *Confessiones* of MS Kk.II.21,[62] strongly suggest that this medieval "editor" not only considered details extraneous to the main narrative thread of spiritual progression as distracting and expendable, but also regarded schools of thought which were opposed to Christianity with deep suspicion, and Augustine's expressions of doubt, difficulty, and temptation as potentially dangerous to either his own spirituality or that of his future readers. They also suggest that he took very seriously his own spiritual responsibility as an "editor" or "re-narrator" of Augustine's *Confessiones,* eliminating any passages which might lead his readers or himself astray, and ensuring that his version of the *Confessiones* would excite them internally in an appropriate manner and ultimately convert them all in the right direction. This is to say that the "editor" of Augustine's autobiography in MS Kk.II.21 appears to have designed his version of Augustine's text to be read as Augustine himself had intended, to "excite" into God "the human intellect and affection," and thus to serve as a textual guide or model for the self-reflective construction of a progressing inner self appropriate to the spiritual or ascetic Christian life—for the construction through *confessio* and *conversio* of what I would call progressive Augustinian interiority.[63] Yet he alters Augustine's exemplary autobiography, including only the books explicitly about Augustine, untangling the thread of spiritual progress, calling attention to passages of devotion, emphasizing the role of reading and narrative, prioritizing Augustinian interiority and eliminating potential dangers: in short, he plays up many of Augustine's own central concerns, eliminates his doubts, and does so with vigor and consistency, suggesting an intently focused mind and a carefully defined narrative mission.

Who, then, might this "editor" have been? And precisely why did he abridge the *Confessiones* in this way? Unfortunately, definitive answers to these questions are beyond the present state of our knowledge, but some reasonable conjecture is in order. For one, although we cannot know what has been lost (and this recognition must always inform our speculation), the fact that this version seems from a comparison with other extant English manuscripts of the *Confessiones* to have been known only at Norwich, combined with the monastic interests apparent in MS Kk.II.21, suggests that the abbreviator was probably one of the monks of the Norwich house, and thus Robert de Donewico springs immediately to mind. Certainly there are reasons to think that Donewico could have been the abbreviator of the *Confessiones* he owned. We might, for instance, consider the version in his manuscript relatively unsophisticated in theological and literary ways, and thus appropriate to a man who was more an administrator than a theologian, and no doubt educated, but probably not university trained, as I have already suggested. In addition, it is easy to see how a text like the abridged *Confessiones* would provide the kind of uncomplicated, prescriptive guide to the monastic life which a man busy with so many practical and political matters, and daily presented with the conflicts of the cloister and the world might find the most useful. Yet Donewico's career, dominated as it is by financial, administrative, and political officialdom, leaves little space and provides no clues to suggest that he would have had the duty or the time or even the inclination to abridge the *Confessiones*, and particularly to prepare such a text in such a way for his fellow monks—assuming, of course, that that is what is taking place in MS Kk.II.21—though certainly he could have made personal use of the abridged version. Finally, there is one major complication if we choose to see Donewico acting as the "editor" of MS Kk.II.21 and creating an abridged text either for his personal use or as a teaching aid for his community.

This is the presence of part of the abridged text found in MS Kk.II.21 in another, more scholastic-feeling copy of the *Confessiones* which also belonged to the Norwich priory: Cambridge, University Library, MS Ii.II.20.[64] We do not know whether this manuscript was made at Norwich or exactly when it entered the priory library, though its characteristic Norwich press-mark (G. or perhaps C.lxvj) indicates that it was there before the end of the fifteenth century, and perhaps long before then.[65] However, the *Confessiones* it contains (on fols. 79r[a]-121v[b]) were written in the late thirteenth or early fourteenth century, and the close relationship which exists between part of this copy and that in MS Kk.II.21 suggests that it, too, may have originated in the Norwich monastery, perhaps among Norwich monks newly returned from university.[66] In MS Ii.II.20, books V through X of the *Confessiones* present an abridged text almost identical to that in Donewico's manuscript, while the remaining books (I-IV and XI-XIII) represent a complete copy of the text, including a set of numbered chapter divisions and summaries which may also have been unique to Norwich.[67] Though the portion of the text which derives from each version appears in a different hand from the other,[68] the two hands are contemporary and the two scribes were clearly working closely enough that each had knowledge of the other's section of text.[69] Exactly why such a combined version of the *Confessiones* might have been created can only be a matter of speculation at present, though perhaps an urgent need to regain an important text from fragments left after the fire of 1272 which destroyed so many of Norwich's books was a factor.[70]

It would, of course, seem most obvious and reasonable to consider the portion of abridged text in MS Ii.II.20 a copy of the more complete abridged version in MS Kk.II.21, but this seems unlikely. For not only were the *Confessiones* in MS Ii.II.20 almost certainly written before Donewico's manuscript entered the Norwich library and probably before Donewico's volume was produced, but even if we were to assume that the abridged portion of the text was copied from Donewico's personal volume before it entered the priory library, the abridged text in MS Ii.II.20 presents some slight variations in the unnumbered textual divisions and some extensive additions to the narrative rubrics which are difficult to account for given MS Kk.II.21 as an exemplar. Certainly these new rubrics and divisions could have been the on-the-spot creation of the scribe (or the person supervising the scribe) who copied the abridged portion of MS Ii.II.20, but the narrative rubrics in MS Ii.II.20 are very much in keeping with the form of those in MS Kk.II.21, as with the emphasis upon Augustine's spiritual progress so predominant there, and those which overlap the rubrics in MS Kk.II.21 are identical to them. I therefore suspect that the relationship between the two manuscripts is somewhat more complicated. It may be the case that the abbreviated text in both MSS Kk.II.21 and Ii.II.20 derives from a third and earlier (perhaps late-thirteenth-century) copy of the text which was either abridged or contained indications of the intended abridgements, and which is now lost. This copy probably included a more or less full set of narrative rubrics, perhaps as marginal additions, which would make their appearance in subsequent copies somewhat more dependent upon scribal preference and thus explain the majority of the inconsistencies in the rubrics of MSS Kk.II.21 and Ii.II.20;[71] the situation might have been similar with the chapter divisions, which are all the more flexible because unnumbered.

If we accept the premise of a third, earlier, "complete" abridged version of the *Confessiones* at Norwich, the question of its reason for being and purpose in the community nonetheless remains, and, once again, the surviving manuscripts provide suggestive hints. For the abridged *Confessiones* as they stand in both MSS Kk.II.21 and Ii.II.20 seem eminently suited to teaching the spiritual life in a monastic environment: the frequent omissions of dangerous or confusing material would, for instance, make the text a "safe way" (to use Augustine's phrase: "uia tuta" at I.15.12) to teach novices and perhaps other children and youths entrusted to the monks for education; the rubrics outlining "infancy" and "childhood" would be especially relevant in a text designed for children or adolescents, while the more sophisticated narrative rubrics would be appropriate for guiding somewhat older or even adult novices carefully through a complex and spiritually beneficial text; and the relatively uncomplicated condensed form of the text might be appreciated by anyone new to the study of spiritual literature and Augustinian thought. I therefore propose that the original text behind the abbreviated version in MSS Kk.II.21 and Ii.II.20 may have been abridged, divided and rubricated by one of the monks responsible for instruction in the community's school for its junior monks.[72] Donewico's manuscript and the abridged part of MS Ii.II.20 could then have been made from this working "textbook." Although the records are almost silent on the monks responsible for instructing the Norwich novices, such an individual, depending on his precise dates, would be well educated and probably one of the many university-trained Norwich monks who, from the late thirteenth century on, returned from a short period at university in order to teach and preach to their brethren.[73] He would thus possess the intellectual sophistication required to abridge, divide, and rubricate a complex text like the *Confessiones* in this way, while his professional responsibilities as teacher and spiritual guide would conceivably necessitate his sometimes ruthless insensitivity to Augustine's literary project.

Yet the records are also deplorably silent on the specific training received in the cloister school at Norwich,[74] and it is difficult to know whether such a version of a patristic text would have been taught in a thirteenth- or fourteenth-century monastic school, and specifically in the Norwich school. Certainly, the speed and frequency with which the *Confessiones* were copied in Benedictine houses during the late eleventh and early twelfth centuries (often in the first phases of manuscript production along with the Bibles, liturgical texts and patristic commentaries)[75] indicates that those responsible for building or rebuilding Benedictine libraries at that time thought the text a necessity for their communities and perhaps even considered it a "precious model" for initiating new converts "into the monastic and contemplative life," as Pierre Courcelle claimed over thirty years ago.[76] It was, of course, such essential texts which were being replaced in late-thirteenth-century Norwich after the devastating fire of 1272.[77] In addition, Jean Leclercq's claim that the rich and allusive style of medieval monastic writing derives ultimately from Augustine's *Confessiones*,[78] as well as the intriguing links between Augustine's self-reflective reading experiences in the *Confessiones* and the meditative *lectio divina* which Leclercq places at the heart of the monastic life,[79] suggest that the *Confessiones* may well have found a place in the monks's own schools. In a simplified and directed version like that of MS Kk.II.21, which nonetheless retains long chunks of Augustine's admirable prose, the *Confessiones* could have been used as an influential model for internal conversion to and progress within the monastic life of devotion, as indeed for manifesting that conversion and progress in external behaviour, at the same time as they provided fine passages richly interwoven with quotations from the Bible with which to teach the "monastic style," and excellent readerly episodes through which to demonstrate the benefits of meditative and self-reflective reading—the benefits of reading this very text in an active ethical way as an personal exercise in self-knowledge and self-improvement.[80]

This is to say that the *Confessiones* may well have been for the Norwich Benedictines what Brian Stock might call a kind of "textual community" text: a text which acted as an "ascetic model" for shaping the "moral conduct" of the community's members; a text which served as a step or steps "by which the individual climbed towards a perfection" found in relation to God; a text which was mastered by a learned and influential interpreter—in this case, the "editor" who abridged, divided and rubricated the text—who then "utilized it for reforming [the] group's thought and action."[81] Evidence of the communal use of the *Confessiones* in medieval England is found, for one, in the existence of numerous copies of the *Confessiones* (and medieval catalogue listings for several others) which originally belonged to communities rather than to individuals.[82] More specifically, however, evidence is found within the folios of some of these manuscripts. The earliest, Cambridge, Trinity College, MS B.3.25, was produced at Canterbury Cathedral in the second half (probably the last quarter) of the eleventh century, and remained in the community library throughout the Middle Ages.[83] This copy of the *Confessiones* contains, for one, marginal annotations in the style of and very possibly in the hand of Lanfranc of Bec.[84] In the form of an "**a**" for *attende* and an "**N**" for *Nota*, these tiny guides to the text highlight passages of devotion, spiritual progress, contemplation and the communal life, and give every indication of being designed, like the corrections which appear in the same hand, for future readers as much as (if not more than) for the annotator himself. Given that the manuscript also contains stress accents for public reading,[85] it can be assumed that the text was used for the benefit of the community as a whole, though it is difficult to know where and in what context it may have been read aloud to the monks of Christ Church.

A clue is provided, perhaps, by a couple of slightly later copies of the *Confessiones*, for both Cambridge, Corpus Christi College, MS 253, most probably from St Augustine's Abbey, Canterbury, and London, British Library, MS Royal 5.B.xvi, from Rochester Cathedral, reveal some intriguing associations with the precentors and formal musical devotions of these Benedictine communities.[86] One wonders, then, if the *Confessiones* were put to any kind of liturgical use in these English Benedictine communities, as they were, for instance, in an Office of Augustine celebrated particularly among houses of canons on the continent.[87] While such liturgical use would correspond rather nicely with the extensive devotional use of the *Confessiones* in medieval England indicated by the *marginalia* annotating and literature engaging the text, as indeed by the abridgement in MS Kk.II.21,[88] monastic precentors were also associated with the book collections and learned activities of their monastic communities, and their personal connection with copies of the *Confessiones* may thus stand as further evidence of the more general importance of the text in Benedictine collections and its didactic use in those houses.[89] Another possible communal use is suggested by an intriguing marginal note in Cambridge, Pembroke College, MS 135, dateable to the last quarter of the thirteenth century (the very period in which I have suggested the abridged Norwich version of the *Confessiones* was first created).[90] This copy of Augustine's autobiography, like that associated with Lanfranc, contains marginal annotations contemporary with the main text of the *Confessiones*, and these annotations not only emphasize matters like confession, spiritual progress, and the communal life,[91] but at one point the scribe of the marginal apparatus even indicates that the *Confessiones* are to be read "at the table,"[92] presumably in a refectory during meals as were other saints's lives.[93] Although we unfortunately do not know where this manuscript was made and originally read,[94] it was probably the product of a house of monks or friars, and it provides concrete evidence of the intention to use the text communally, with all members digesting its contents along with their daily bread, and ideally applying the spiritual nutrition thus obtained to the growth and maintenance of their own progressive Christian interiorities, as surely as the food eaten would be used for the growth and maintenance of their physical bodies.

It is clear, then, that medieval English religious communities did use the *Confessiones* in communal ways, with the implication that this autobiography contained something thought to be useful for shaping the spiritual nature and "moral conduct" of the community, as well as of each of its members. And it is equally clear that the *Confessiones*, with their narrative of the personal progress from sinner to saint of the learned and authoritative Augustine, could very well have provided an appropriate textual pattern of steps "by which the individual climbed towards a perfection" found in relation to God. In addition, the abridged *Confessiones* of MS Kk.II.21 (even more effectively than the annotated copies I have just discussed) would have served as both the text itself and the vital interpretation of that text for shaping the minds and souls of new converts to the monastic life, and for guiding the continual construction of progressive interiority within more established members of the community. It would seem, then, that in the abridged *Confessiones* of MS Kk.II.21 we may have some rather convincing manuscript evidence of a monastic community using a text in the ways which Stock claims a medieval "textual community" should have. Yet instead of "reforming [the] group's thought and action" in any new or radical way, the Norwich abridgement appears to work towards bringing novices to the Benedictine life as they always had been, through a personal intellectual and emotional call to the ascetic life of the spirit, a call inspired in the fourteenth century, as in the twelfth (though with some new twists), by Augustine's exemplary *confessio* and *conversio*. It is easy to imagine how such a prescriptive yet learned, traditional yet appealing textual call to the monastic ideal would have been welcomed in a period when Benedictines may have felt their intellectual and spiritual ascendency threatened by the success of the friars and the scholastic thought associated with them, and especially in a house which was reported at this very time as lacking some of its original spiritual vigor.[95] Indeed, by using inventive forms of *ordinatio* which are often connected with the friars and university thinking, the abridgement of the *Confessiones* in MS Kk.II.21 presents Augustine's text in a scholastically attractive and intellectually fashionable way, while emphasizing its traditional monastic spirituality and eliminating ideas which might have been considered theologically or philosophically dangerous.[96]

There can, in any case, be no doubt that the *Confessiones* were in special demand in the Norwich monastery, for three copies of the *Confessiones* survive from medieval Norwich (the third being Cambridge, Corpus Christi College, MS 34, a complete version of the text most probably produced in the second half of the thirteenth century)[97]—the largest number to survive from any English house—and the community probably owned at least four (presuming a lost exemplar for MSS Kk.II.21 and Ii.II.20)—the largest number for which any English house provides evidence. Similarly, there can be no doubt that the level of readerly participation in the text of the *Confessiones* at Norwich is striking, for no other medieval English religious community appears to have edited and generally "fiddled with" Augustine's autobiography so extensively and variously as the Norwich monks who reorganized, rubricated, abridged, capitulated, and summarized the text. Indeed, given the strange combined version of MS Ii.II.20, made at a time when a complete version of the *Confessiones* may already have been available in the Norwich library,[98] it would seem that the Norwich monks, faced with extensive manuscript losses due to the fire, may have been so anxious to obtain a carefully edited and pre-interpreted version of this text that they would rather have blended two versions with entirely different forms of *ordinatio* than settle for a complete but unedited copy.[99] The implication is that a version of the text appropriate for those who were just learning to read as spiritual men and were not familiar with the *Confessiones* or in fact with the concepts it narrates—for those, that is, who should be carefully instructed and not be led astray in their reading—was desperately needed, and thus that the text was used both frequently and regularly in the community, most probably as the spiritual teaching aid which the version in MS Kk.II.21 appears so obviously to be.[100]

How, then, did the abridged *Confessiones* come to be in the only extant manuscript owned by the monastic official Robert de Donewico? As I have already noted, Donewico's administrative and political career provides no indication of his having been the learned *magister* of novices and monks who appears to have professionally abridged the text for his community, though Donewico's involvement should not be ruled out as a complete impossibility. I would propose instead, however, that he may have been among the novices who were introduced to the abridged *Confessiones* as a kind of practical and ethical textbook in the cloister school at Norwich. He could well have been educated there in the late thirteenth or early fourteenth century and he could possibly have known Augustine's autobiography only in this abridged form—an intriguing thought. Perhaps his copy of the text which survives in MS Kk.II.21 was his student's copy (certainly it is not a lavish volume, although it is hardly shabby either), and (though there is no specific evidence to suggest an earlier owner) it could even have been given to him or compiled for him by one of his teachers, since its contents—an *Expositio super Regulam Beati Benedicti* by Bernard Cassinensis, the *Liber Eruditionis Religiosorum* by Humbert de Romanis, and the *De Claustro Animae* by Hugh de Fouilloy, as well as the abridged *Confessiones*[101] —would be almost as appropriate for an educational volume owned or devised by a learned monastic teacher, which Donewico does not appear to have been, as for a book of personal guidance on the devotional life of internal progression.

On the other hand (and this seems to me the more likely scenario), he might have had the copy made from the Norwich school's text later in his life when, burdened with responsibilities which could easily have pulled his mind and soul away from monastic ideals, he might have felt a personal desire to renew the spiritual lessons he had learned as a novice and thus a need for texts on the inner life, like Augustine's *Confessiones* and Hugh's *De Claustro Animae*, and particularly on the Benedictine life, like Bernard's *Expositio* on Benedict's Rule. Certainly the only other extant manuscript which has been identified as containing the same scribal hand as Donewico's manuscript, Cambridge, University Library, MS Ii.III.10, can be dated from its contents to the 1330s or later, when Donewico was already undertaking administrative and political tasks for his community.[102] In addition, the way in which the narrative rubrics for the abridged *Confessiones* in MS Kk.II.21 appear (in comparison with those in MS Ii.II.20) to have been themselves edited and abridged, even removed from a large section of the text (books V-IX), suggests an intended reader already familiar with the *Confessiones*, though one who wished to attend carefully, as the mature Augustine had when he wrote book X of his autobiography, to the daily temptations of the world, like "gluttony," "flattery," "curiosity" and the desires of "ears" and "eyes" highlighted by the rubrication of MS Kk.II.21 (quoted above). In any case, although we might lament the loss of the "editor's" own copy of the *Confessiones* and the suggestive *ordinatio* and *marginalia* for fashioning his re-narration which it may well have contained, Robert de Donewico is precisely the kind of educated and dedicated monk for whom the Norwich *Confessiones* must have been abridged, and in whom their "editor" must have hoped to "excite" both "intellect and affection" so that the construction of a progressive Augustinian interiority might begin and continue without complication in a busy monastic order and hectic political world.

University of Victoria

Notes

1. I would like to thank Kathryn Kerby-Fulton and Maidie Hilmo for reading and providing comments on drafts of this paper, and Mark Vessey for inviting me to present an earlier version to the twenty-seventh annual medieval workshop at the University of British Columbia: "History, Apocalypse and the Secular Imagination: An Interdisciplinary Symposium on Augustine's *City of God*," September 18–20, 1997. I am also most grateful to the Syndics of Cambridge University Library for granting me permission to quote extensively from Cambridge, University Library, MS Kk.II.21, and to the Social Sciences and Humanities Research Council of Canada for the funding which enabled my research.
2. Cambridge, University Library, MS Kk.II.21, fol. 103v[b]: "hic narrat confessiones suas supra exemplum. vt alii ita agant."
3. *Confessiones* II.3.6–10: "Cui narro haec? Neque enim tibi, deus meus, sed apud te narro haec generi meo, generi humano, quantulacumque ex particula incidere potest in istas meas litteras. Et ut quid hoc? Vt uidelicet ego et quisquis haec legit cogitemus, de quam profundo clamandum sit ad te." All citations from the *Confessiones* are either from the edition by Lucas Verheijen, ed., *Sancti Augustini: Confessionum Libri XIII*, Corpus Christianorum: Series Latina, vol. 27 (Turnhout, 1981), as this quotation and all italicized references to the text are, or (when specifically indicated) from the version in Cambridge, University Library, MS Kk.II.21. In both instances, quotations are accompanied by book, chapter and line numbers drawn from Verheijen's edition, and, if relevant, by the manuscript's folio numbers along with **r** or **v** for *recto* or *verso* and a superscript [a] or [b] indicating column.
4. On the front fly-leaf is the inscription "Liber fratris Roberti de Donewico" and on fol. 3r is the inscription "Roberti de donewic'.N.lvij;" see also N. R. Ker, "Medieval Manuscripts from Norwich Cathedral Priory," in *Books, Collectors and Libraries: Studies in the Medieval Heritage*, ed. Andrew G. Watson (London and Ronceverte, 1985), p. 260, and C. Hardwick, *A Catalogue of the Manuscripts Preserved in the Library of the University of Cambridge*, vol. 3 (Cambridge, 1858), pp. 619–20, but Hardwick's fifteenth-century date for the manuscript is incorrect. In all transcriptions from MS Kk.II.21, the following conventions have been observed: abbreviations (with the exception of Donewico's name) have been silently expanded; corrections made to the text by either the main scribe or later readers are not individually noted, but the text is corrected accordingly if warranted by sense; the use of **c** and **t** has been adjusted to conform with classical spelling, but all other aspects of the medieval spelling have been retained from the manuscript; word division has been retained from the manuscript, as has the use of upper and lower case letters; a full stop (**.**) indicates the same mark in the manuscript; a semi-colon (**;**) indicates a *punctus*

elevatus in the manuscript; a question mark (?) represents the same mark in the manuscript; a forward slash (/) represents a similar vertical stroke in the manuscript; a curved bracket or brace ({) represents a paragraph mark or *capitulum*, indicating a minor division of the text; an upper case letter in bold font (**A**) represents a large colored capital, indicating a major division of the text; and square brackets ([and]) have been reserved for my own emendations.

5. See Ker, "Medieval Manuscripts from Norwich," p. 249, who notes how the book collection at Norwich (as at Christ Church, Canterbury) grew considerably through the gifts of monks who died in the late thirteenth and the first half of the fourteenth century. Ker also discusses there how books donated to the priory in this way "were marked with the donor's name in the genitive case preceded by a press-mark consisting of a capital letter and a Roman number," but only consistently from 1315 until 1325. "After about 1325 the press-mark is the only regular feature: the inscription of ownership varies in form and is often absent" (p. 249). Although the presence of both in MS Kk.II.21 would therefore suggest that the volume was in the Norwich library by c.1325 at the latest, there are plenty of volumes which contain both name and press-mark but which did not enter the library until after 1325 (pp. 252–53 and 258–61), and the name in any case precedes (rather than follows) the press-mark in MS Kk.II.21; in addition, the name and press-mark "are entered independently, in different ink and by a different hand," as with many of the manuscripts acquired after c.1325 (p. 253). Ker places the volume among the books acquired after c.1325 (p. 260), and working from the inscription (and no doubt from Donewico's dates), determines that MS Kk.II.21 was acquired by the Norwich library in the mid-fourteenth century (p. 253); he also notes that this "seems to be the last appearance of the old form of inscription in which the words 'liber' and 'fratris' are omitted" (p. 260). They are of course present in the second inscription of MS Kk.II.21. For volumes donated to their monastic communities by other medieval Benedictines, see the List of Donors in Ker, *Medieval Libraries of Great Britain: A List of Surviving Books*, 2nd ed. (London, 1964), pp. 225–321.
6. I am most grateful to Joan Greatrex for her generous assistance with Robert de Donewico, and for sending me the entry for Donewico for her *Biographical Register of the English Cathedral Priories of the Province of Canterbury c.1066–1540* (Oxford, 1997) prior to its publication. The information presented here on Donewico's life and career has been drawn from both that Register and Greatrex's correspondence.
7. For lists of Norwich's monk students, see appendices I-III in Greatrex, "Monk Students from Norwich Cathedral Priory at Oxford and Cambridge, c. 1300 to 1530," *English Historical Review* 106 (1991), pp. 579–83. On pp. 568–70, Greatrex discusses the monastic career of university-trained Norwich monks, stating that "under one-third of the university group can be identified as office-holders within the priory for periods of more than two years; and only half of this third, fifteen in all, are known to have been appointed to internal administrative offices for more than five years. Eleven of these had spent only a short period at university" (p. 569). However, the possibility of Donewico having been trained at a university, at least for a short time, should not be ruled out.
8. "Monk Students from Norwich," p. 570.
9. Both Thomas Bradwardine in his *De Causa Dei* and Richard FitzRalph in his *Summa Domini Armacani in Questionibus Armenorum* make use of the language, style and content of the *Confessiones* in presenting their own conversions: see I.35 of the early

printed edition of Bradwardine's *De Causa Dei*, ed. Henry Savil, *Thomae Bradwardini Archiepiscopi Olim Cantuariensis, De Causa Dei, Contra Pelagium, et de Virtute Causarum, ad suos Mertonenses, Libri Tres* (London, 1618), and XIX.35 of the early printed edition of FitzRalph's *Summa Domini Armacani*, ed. John Sudor, *Ricardi Fitzralph Summa Domini Armacani in Questionibus Armenorum Nouiter Impressa et Correcta a Magistro Nostro Johanne Sudoris. Cum Aliquis Sermonibus Eiusdem de Christi Dominio* (Paris, 1512). Thomas Buckingham, Robert Holcot and John de Grandisson each owned a copy of the *Confessiones*—Oxford, Merton College MS 1, Cambridge, University Library, MS Kk.II.5 and London, Lambeth Palace, MS 203 respectively. Buckingham has possibly and Grandisson has certainly left personal responses to the autobiography in the margins of their manuscripts: see especially my study of Grandisson's *marginalia* in "Reading Augustine's *Confessiones* in Fourteenth-Century England: John de Grandisson's Fashioning of Text and Self," *Traditio* 52 (1997), 201–57. William Langland misquotes the *Confessiones*, presumably deliberately, at a moment of conversion both in his poetic enterprise and in his narrator's progression: see George Kane, ed., *Piers Plowman: The A Version: Will's Visions of Piers Plowman and Do-Well*, rev. ed. (London and Berkeley, 1988), XI:302–13 (where the A Text breaks off); Kane, and E. Talbot Donaldson, eds, *Piers Plowman: The B Version: Will's Visions of Piers Plowman, Do-Well, Do-Better and Do-Best*, rev. ed. (London and Berkeley, 1988), X:458–71; and Derek Pearsall, ed., *Piers Plowman by William Langland: An Edition of the C-text* (Berkeley and Los Angeles, 1979), XI:288–98.

10. There is one other English copy of the *Confessiones* (Oxford, St John's College, MS 206, also produced in the first half of the fourteenth century) which I would call an abridgement of the text, though one very different from the version in MS Kk.II.21. It attempts to present Augustine's narrative as a whole, while removing many passages, moving others about in the text (something which does not occur in MS Kk.II.21) and including a unique system of division. St John's MS 206 is the only extant fourteenth-century English copy of the *Confessiones* which has not yet been associated with a particular fourteenth-century community or individual. On MS 206 and other extant English manuscripts of the *Confessiones*, including MS Kk.II.21 and those listed in the preceding note, see the entries in appendix A of Olson, "The Textual Construction of Monastic Interiority: Reading Augustine's *Confessiones* in England c. 1066–c. 1200," (DPhil diss., University of York, 1998); medieval English catalogue entries for the *Confessiones* appear in appendix B. MS Kk.II.21, along with other manuscripts associated with fourteenth-century individuals, is also listed in appendix B of "Grandisson's Fashioning of Text and Self." I am most grateful to my partner, Bob Olson, and my daughter, Linda D. Olson, for their generous help with the initial collation of the abridged *Confessiones* in both MS Kk.II.21 and MS 206.
11. These divisions are unique in that they differ from those found in most English manuscripts of the *Confessiones*, from those linked with Robert Kilwardby's work in the thirteenth century, and from those in modern editions of the text (all of which are somewhat similar). On the divisions in the English manuscripts, see the brief discussion in Olson, "Grandisson's Fashioning of Text and Self," pp. 210–11. On the Dominican friar Robert Kilwardby and his forms of *ordinatio* for the fathers, see especially Daniel A. Callus, "The 'Tabulae super Originalia Patrum' of Robert Kilwardby O.P.," in *Studia Mediaevalia in Honorem Admodum Reverendi Patris Raymundi Josephi Martin* (Bruges, 1948), pp. 243–70, and "New Manuscripts of Kilwardby's *Tabulae Super Originalia Patrum*," *Dominican Studies* 2 (1949), 38–45; Kilwardby's

chapter divisions for the *Confessiones* can be determined from the copy of his summaries in Paris, Bibliothèque Nationale, MS lat. 2117, dating to the last quarter of the thirteenth century (I would like to thank Patricia Stirnemann for consulting this manuscript for me and kindly providing the revised date). Only one other English manuscript of the *Confessiones* sports unnumbered chapter-like divisions: Oxford, St John's College, MS 206, which also contains the only other extant medieval English abridgement of the text (see the preceding note).

12. Although the rubricating hand of MS Kk.II.21 makes an effort at a slightly more formal presentation than the text hand, the perpendicular ductus and the letter forms of both are the same, with the letters "r" and "a" particularly exemplary and consistent throughout both text and rubrication.
13. Every capital-adorned division in the text of the *Confessiones* in MS Kk.II.21 is accompanied by rubrication, either structural or narrative.
14. Certainly I know of no other English manuscripts containing this abridged version of the *Confessiones.* I have not, however, consulted the many continental medieval copies of the text, and given Norwich's connections with the continent in the fourteenth century, it is not impossible (though I have not explored the possibility here) that continental influences are at work in the abridgement found in Donewico's *Confessiones.*
15. The only two extant English manuscripts which do not contain a *retractatio* are Durham Cathedral, MS B.II.12, a fourteenth- century copy of the *Confessiones,* and the abridged version of the text in St John's MS 206, mentioned in previous notes.
16. As Teresa Webber, "The Diffusion of Augustine's *Confessions* in England during the Eleventh and Twelfth Centuries," in *The Cloister and the World: Essays Presented to B. F. Harvey,* ed. W. J. Blair and B. J. Golding (Oxford, 1996), pp. 29–45, has shown, the *Confessiones* appear to have been disseminated in late-eleventh- and twelfth-century England from only two traditions of the text: see also the Introduction of Olson, "Textual Construction of Monastic Interiority," and the information on the textual traditions of individual manuscripts provided in appendix A of that dissertation. One of the two textual traditions derives ultimately from Paris, Bibliothèque Nationale, MS lat. 1913A, a ninth-century continental volume, to the front end-leaf of which was added, in a mid-eleventh-century hand, an abbreviated text of Augustine's *retractatio* for the *Confessiones*; this abbreviated text appears in many of MS lat. 1913A's derivatives, and is the version found in MS Kk.II.21. I would like to thank Teresa Webber for kindly providing me with a copy of her article prior to its publication, and for her generous help with so many of the English manuscripts of the *Confessiones.*
17. MS Kk.II.21, fol. 102r[a]: "Confessionum mearum libri et de bonis et de malis deum laudant atque in eum excitant humanum intellectum et effectum./Itaque hoc agunt cum leguntur in me et de me a primo usque ad. decimum. de me scripti sunt. Reliqui tres de scripturis sanctis. Hoc opus sic incipit." Compare the complete *retractatio* found in Almut Mutzenbecher, ed., *Sancti Augustini: Retractationum Libri II,* Corpus Christianorum: Series Latina, vol. 57 (Turnhout, 1984), II.6.2–20. The abbreviated *retractatio* is also transcribed from Paris MS lat. 1913A in Martin Skutella, ed., *S.Aureli Augustini Confessionum Libri XIII,* corrected by H. Juergens and W. Schaub (Stuttgart, 1969), pp. xi-xii, and in chapter 1 of Olson, "Textual Construction of Monastic Interiority," where it and the complete *retractatio* are discussed further.

18. As Kenneth Steinhauser, "The Literary Unity of the *Confessions*," in *Augustine: From Rhetor to Theologian*, ed. Joanne McWilliam, with Timothy Barnes, Michael Fahey and Peter Slater (Waterloo, Ontario, 1992), p. 19, has noted about Augustine's *retractatio* for the *Confessiones*, "nowhere else in his *Retractationes* does Augustine mention reading one of his own books for personal inspiration."
19. Book VII, one of the longest of the early books of the *Confessiones*, has been reduced to less than three and a half columns in MS Kk.II.21 (fols. 109r[b]-110r[a]) through the removal of long passages of speculation (particularly of an erroneous sort) on the nature of God and Christ (as, for example, at VII.1.4–14: *Non . . . potest*; 1.18–31: *ut . . . arbitrabar*, 1.33–52: *nec . . . ita*; and 4.1–8: *Sic . . . incorruptibilis*, all of which are deleted, along with the whole of VII.18, and all but one sentence [at 19.33–35: *Improbatio . . . infirmos*] of VII.19); of elaboration on Manichaean doctrine (like the whole of VII.2); of exploration into the nature of sin (the whole of VII.5, for instance, and all but two sentences [at 7.2–4: *me . . . tuam*, and 11–13: *Et . . . mei*] of VII.7); of discussion on astrologers (like all but two sentences [at 6.1–2: *Iam . . . reieceram*, and 80–82: *Tu . . . audire*] of VII.6); of explanation regarding creation and its creator (like the whole of VII.11 and 15, and large chunks of VII.12 [12.1–13: *Et . . . bona sunt*] and 13 [13.6–23: *Et . . . pendebam*); of revelation about what prevented Augustine from a correct knowledge of God (the whole of VII.18, for example); and of acknowledgement regarding the idolatry and pride instilled along with truth through the Platonic writings (as at VII.9.43–66: *Qui . . . creatori*, and 20.11– 27: *Iam . . . didicisset*). The deletions in book X are too extensive to list here, but they generally keep to the same pattern as those of VII, though in book X (fols. 113r[b]-115v[b]) the editor seems to be choosing occasional sections for inclusion rather than for deletion, and, in the process, leaving out numerous whole chapters and lengthy passages.
20. John Burrow, "Autobiographical Poetry in the Middle Ages: The Case of Thomas Hoccleve," Sir Israel Gollancz Memorial Lecture, *Proceedings of the British Academy* 68 (1982), 396, discusses the scheme of the seven deadly sins in the fourteenth and fifteenth centuries as "the moral grid-system most commonly used by men of the period whenever they attempted to map their inner lives," and emphasizes how that was the way in which medieval "people thought about themselves."
21. For a detailed exploration of these matters in terms of the eleventh and twelfth-century English reception of the *Confessiones*, see Olson, "Textual Construction of Monastic Interiority."
22. The "editor" of MS Kk.II.21 selects carefully from these opening chapters, including many passages from chapters 1–5. For the sake of comparison with the complete text, his version of I.1 reads: "**M**agnus es domine et Laudabilis valde magna uirtus tua. et sapientiae. tuae. non est numerus. Et laudare te uult homo aliqua portio creature tue et homo circumferens mortalitatem suam. testimonium peccati sui. quia superbis resistis. Tu excitas ut laudare te delectet quia fecisti nos ad te. et inquietum est cor nostrum donec requiescat in te. Da mihi domine scire et intellegere vtrum sit prius inuocare. an laudare te. et scire te prius sit. an inuocare te. Querentes enim inuenient te; et inuenientes Laudabunt te. Queram te domine inuocans te; et inuocabo te credens in te" (fol. 102r[a]).
23. See I.9.1–7 in Kk.II.21, where Augustine confesses the evils of an education which taught him to succeed through deceit and punished him with beatings if he did not attend to it: "{Deus meus quas ibi miserias expertus sum et Ludificationes quando

quidem recte mihi uiuere puero id proponebatur obtemperare monentibus vt in hoc seculo florerem et excellerem linguosis artibus ad honorem hominum; et falsas diuitias famulantibus. Inde in scholam datus sum vt discerem litteras. in quibus quid vtilitatis esset ignorabam miser. et tamen si segnis in discendo essem; uapulabam" (fol. 102v[a-b]).

24. Kk.II.21, V.1.1–3: "Accipe sacrificium confessionum mearum de manu lingue mee quam formasti et excitasti vt confiteatur nomini tuo et sana omnia ossa mea et dicant. domine Quis similis tibi?" (fol. 106v[a]).
25. I.10.13–15, reading in MS Kk.II.21: "Vide domine ista misericorditer. et libera nos iam inuocantes te. Libera etiam eos qui non dum te inuocant. vt inuocent te et liberes eos" (fol. 102v[b], but with a second "et liberes" mistakenly written by the scribe beside the first deleted).
26. Augustine's line as it appears in Verheijen's Corpus Christianorum edition reads "Quaerentes enim inueniunt eum et inuenientes laudabunt eum" (I.1.13–14), while the same line in MS Kk.II.21 (as cited in a previous note) reads "Querentes enim inuenient te; et inuenientes laudabunt te."
27. The "editor" retains, for instance, all of X.2 (with the exception of a couple of lines at 2.4–6: *tu . . . eligam te*), the chapter in which Augustine deals most explicitly with his personal and internal *confessio* to God (fol. 113v[a]).
28. The passages retained from X.3 focus upon this idea: 3.1–7: *Quid . . . est*; 10–14: *Sed . . . aperit*; and 34–35: *Dicit . . . mihi* (fol. 113v[a]).
29. The version of X.4 presented by the abbreviator highlights these concerns beautifully. From the first paragraph in Verheijen (4.1–19), he retains the following text on the fruit of the *Confessiones* as the prayer, both of thanks and sorrow, of Augustine's readers: "Sed quo fructu id uolunt? An congratulati mihi cupiunt et orare pro me cum audierint quantum recorder pondere meo. Non. enim. paruus est fructus ut a multis tibi gratie agantur de nobis. et a multis rogeris pro nobis. Amet in me fraternus animus quod amandum doces. et doleat in me; quod dolendum doces. Animus ille hoc faciat fraternus; non extraneus. Quia siue approbet me improbet me; diligit me. respirent in bonis meis . . . " through to the end of the paragraph at 4.19: . . . *mea* (fol. 113v[a-b]). From the second paragraph he selects passages dealing with how Augustine's *Confessiones* address his fellow Christians in particular (fol. 113v[b]).
30. The passage (II.3.6–10, cited from Verheijen's edition of the *Confessiones* in the opening paragraph of this paper) reads in MS Kk.II.21 as follows: "Cui narro hec. Et ut quid hoc? ut uidelicet ego et quisquis hec legit cogitemus de quo profundo clamandum sit ad te" (fol. 103v[b]).
31. The abridged *Confessiones* in MS Kk.II.21 could certainly be cited as confirmation of Jean Leclercq's claim that monastic readers "separated the essence of the Augustinian confession from all the philosophical developments which, in the *Confessions*, envelop it as with a matrix, very valuable in itself but alien to Augustine's life of prayer:" *The Love of Learning and the Desire for God: A Study of Monastic Culture*, trans. Catharine Misrahi (New York, 1961), p. 124.
32. See X.2.7–9 and 13–14, which read in MS Kk.II.21: "et quo fructu tibi confitear dixi. neque id ago uerbis carnis et uocibus; sed uerbis anime et clamore cogitationis quem nouit auris tua . . . Confessio itaque mea deus meus in conspectu tuo tibi tacite fit a non tacite. Tacet enim strepitu; clamat affectu" (fol. 113v[a]).

33. VI.7.42–43, reading in MS Kk.II.21: "Taceat laudes tuas; qui miserationes tuas non considerat que tibi de medullis meis confitentur" (fol. 108v[b]). The only other portion of VI.7 retained by the abbreviator is the opening passage about Augustine's friends, Nebridius and especially Alypius (7.1–8: *Congemescebamus . . . eminebat,* fol. 108v[a-b]).
34. VII.7.11–13, which read in MS Kk.II.21: "et ibi erant aures tue nesciente me et cum in silentio fortiter quererem magne voces erant ad misericordiam tuam. tacite contritiones animi mei" (fol. 109v[a]). As with the last example, only one other portion of this chapter is retained, that in which Augustine makes a statement of his unwavering faith (7.2–4: *me . . . tuam,* fol. 109v[a]).
35. IV.14.38–41, reading in MS Kk.II.21: "Ecce vbi latet infirma anima non dum herens soliditati ueritatis. Sicut aure linguarum flauerint a pectoribus opinantium; ita fertur et uertitur. torquetur ac retorquetur. et obnubilatur ei lumen et non cernitur veritas" (fol. 106r[a-b]). Italicizing in the translation here and in the next example is my own. Three other brief passages are retained from IV.14 (14.10–12: *ex . . . creditur,* 18–20: *Non . . . amari;* and 26–27: *Ergone . . . sim homo*), but they are neither close nor particularly related to the one cited here (fol. 106r[a]).
36. MS Kk.II.21, VI.16.21–24: "{Ve anime audaci que sperauit si a te recessisset se aliquid melius habituram uersa et reuersa in tergum et in latera et in uentrem. et dura sunt omnia. et tu solus requies" (fol. 109r[b]). The other passages retained from VI.16 report Augustine's struggles with carnal pleasures (16.3–7: *Nec . . . malorum;* 10–13: *Et . . . pertinere,* 16–17: *Nec . . . conferebam,* fol. 109r[b]).
37. I.18.10–12, which reads in MS Kk.II.21: "{Vultum tuum domine requiram. Nam isti longe a uultu tuo in affectu tenebroso. Non enim pedibus aut spatiis locorum itur abste; aut reditur ad te" (fol. 103r[b]). The "editor" also selects from I.18 two passages dealing with the way in which grammarians attend to the eloquence of their language, while ignoring the moral value of its content, commending beautifully expressed falsehoods and vices, while condemning awkwardly expressed truths and virtues (18.1–6: *Quid . . . gloriabantur,* and 18–24: *Vide . . . homo,* fol. 103r[b]).
38. VII.10 in MS Kk.II.21 reads as follows: "Et inde ammonitus redire ad memet ipsum intraui in intima mea duce te. et potui. quoniam factus es adiutor meus. {O eterna veritas. et uera caritas et cara eternitas. tu es deus meus. tibi suspiro die at nocte. Et contremui amore. et horrore. et inueni longe me esse a te in regione dissimilitudinis tamquam audirem vocem tuam de excelso. Cibus sum grandium; cresce et manducabis me. nec tu me in te muta[bis] sicut cibum carnis tue; sed tu mutaberis in me. Et clamasti de longinquo. ego sum qui sum. et audiui sicut auditur in corde et non erat prorsus unde dubitarem. faciliusque dubitarem uiuere me quam non esse ueritatem que per ea que facta sunt intellecta conspicitur;" (fol. 109v[b]). I have added "bis" to the end of "muta" on the assumption that it was omitted erroneously; and I have also removed the letters "un" from the final word "conspiciuntur" to form the more correct "conspicitur."
39. See VI.4.11–14 in MS Kk.II.21, with the surrounding text deleted: "{Itaque confundebar et conuertebar. et gaudebam deus meus quod ecclesia unica corpus unici tui in qua mihi nomen Christi infanti est inditum; non saperet infantiles nugas" (fol. 108r[b]).
40. As it appears in MS Kk.II.21, III.4 reads as follows: "Inter hos ego inbecilla etate discebam libros eloquentie in qua eminere cupiebam fine dampnabili et uentoso per gaudia uanitatis humane. Et vsitato iam discendi ordine perueneram in librum

quondam cuiusdam cicheronis qui uocatur hortensius. Ille vero liber mutauit affectum meum. et ad te ipsum domine mutauit preces meas. et uota ac desideria mea fecit alia. viluit mihi repente omnis vana spes et surgere iam ceperam; vt ad te redirem. Non ergo ad acuendam linguam referebam illum cum agerem annum etatis unde vicesimum iam defuncto patre ante biennium. {Quomodo ardebam deus meus reuolare a terrenis ad te; et nesciebam quid ageres mecum. apud te enim est sapientia. Et hoc solum me in tanta flagrantia re[f]rangebat quod nomen christi non erat ibi quoniam hoc nomen saluatoris mei filii tui in ipso adhuc lacte matris tenerum cor meum pie biberat et alte retinebat. et quicquid sine hoc nomine fuisset quamuis litteratum et expolitum et venditum. non me totum rapiebat'' (fol. 104v[a]). I have changed the mistaken ''g'' in ''regrangebat'' to an ''f'' to read ''refrangebat.'' The passage, which contains minor textual adjustments to accommodate the many deletions, presents a particularly fine example of the way in which the ''editor'' of MS Kk.II.21 works.

41. From a chapter of fifty-three lines (in Verheijen's edition of the *Confessiones*) and much theological explanation, the ''editor'' of MS Kk.II.21 has retained only the following: ''Iam mortua erat adolescentia mea mala et nefanda; et ibam in iuuentutem. Quanto etate maior; tanto uanitate turpior; qui cogitare aliud substantie nisi tale non poteram quale per hos oculos uideri solet. Clamabat uiolenter cor meum aduersus omnia fantasmata mea. et donabar abigere circumuolantem turbam immunditie ab acie mentis mee. et uix dimota in ictu oculi; ecce conglobata rursus aderat et irruebat in aspectum meum; et obnubilabat eum. per quales. enim. formas ire solent oculi mei; per tales ymagines ibat cor meum. Sed nondum illuminaueras tenebras meas'' (fol. 109r[b]). There could hardly be more convincing evidence of his focus upon Augustine's personal internal progression.

42. The ''editor'' has removed numerous passages, both long and short, from VIII.2, with the remaining text consisting of the following sections: 2.1–8: *Perrexi . . . mundi*; 9–10: *Deinde . . . humilitatem*; 11–13: *Victorinum . . . silebo*; 14–15: *quemadmodum . . . peritissimus*; 17: *qui . . . magisterii*; 18–19: *statuam . . . acceperat*; 25–27: *non . . . opprobrium*; 30–36: *Legebat . . . christianos*; 38–39: *Amicos . . . daemonicolas*; 41–43: *Sed . . . confiteri*; 47–49: *ait . . . fieri*; 49–52: *Vbi . . . ecclesia*; and 70–72: *Pronuntiauit . . . erant* (fol. 110r[b]-v[a]).

43. The ''editor'' selects for inclusion several passages from VIII.3–4 which explore the conversion of sinners, especially those who are influential and thus inspirational to others, and also shows an interest in Augustine's examples of joy following hardship: 3.1–2: *Deus . . . animae*; 2–3: *quam . . . affuisset*; 3–5: *Etenim . . . paenitentia*; 18–26: *Triumphat . . . ambularet*; 29–34: *Edendi . . . dilatam*; 37–38: *ubique . . . praeceditur*; 4.6–8: *Quando . . . alterutro*; 11–13: *Absit . . . elegisti*; 14–15: *et contemptibilia . . . euacuares*; and 20–23: *Plus . . . auctoritatis* (fol. 110v[a]).

44. VIII.5.1–2: ''{Vbi mihi homo tuus simplicianus de victorino ista narrauit; exarsi ad imitandum. Ad hoc. enim et ille narrauit'' (fol. 110v[a]). The rest of the passages selected from VIII.5 reveal, once again, an interest in Augustine's internal state, particularly in the way in which he is held back from further progress by custom and a struggle of the will: 5.8–17: *Cui . . . roboratam*; 24–26: *ex . . . perueneram*; 33: *Ita . . . premebar*; 41– 43: *sed . . . Christus*; and 45–47: *nisi . . . ibat* (fols. 110v[a-b]).

45. The text of VIII.7 in MS Kk.II.21 has been abridged to read: ''Tu domine inter verba eius retorquebas me ad me ipsum. auferens me a dorso meo vbi me posueram dum nollem me attendere et constituebas me ante faciem meam ut uiderem quam turpis

essem. quam distortus et sordidus maculosus et vlcerosus. et uidebam et horrebam; et quo a me fugerem non erat. {Et ego adolescens miser ualde miser. in exordio ipsius adolescentie petieram a te castitatem et dixeram. Da mihi castitatem et continentiam; sed noli modo. Timebam. enim. ne me cito exaudires et cito sanares a morbo concupiscentie quem malebam expleri quam extingui et ieram per uias prauas superstitione sacrilega. Et venerat quo nudarer mihi et increparet me conscientia mea. Vbi est lingua. Nempe tu dicebas propter incertum uerum nolle te abicere sarcinam uanitatis. Ecce iam certum est; et illa te adhuc premit. Ita rodebar intus. et confundebar pudore vehementi cum pontianus talia loqueretur. Terminato autem sermone et causa quam uenerat; abiit ille et ego ad me" (fols. $110v^{b}$-$111r^{a}$). The odd spelling ("pontianus") of the name Ponticianus seems to have been fairly common in the Middle Ages, appearing in other medieval English manuscripts of the *Confessiones*, so I have retained it here.

46. VIII.8.1–7, which read in MS Kk.II.21: "{Tum in illa grandi rixa tam uultu quam mente turbatus inuado alipium. exclamo. Quid patimur? Quid est hoc? Quid audisti? Surgunt indocti et celum rapiunt et nos cum doctrinis nostris sine corde ecce ubi uoluptamur in carne et sanguine? An quia precesserunt pudet sequi. et non pudet nec saltem sequi?" (fol. $111r^{a}$).
47. Selecting in MS Kk.II.21 the following passages from the remainder of VIII.8: 11–12: *Hortulus . . . domo*; 13: *Illuc . . . impediret*; 17: *Abscessi . . . hortum*; 18–19: *non . . . aderat*; 19–23: *Sedimus . . . laudibus*; 25–26: *Nam . . . ire*, and 40–42: *facilius . . . anima* (fol. $111r^{a}$).
48. Several passages dealing with Augustine's struggle of the will (also emphasized in the abridgement of VIII.5, as noted above) are selected from VIII.9–10 for inclusion in MS Kk.II.21: 9.4–5: *Vnde . . . statim*; 6–9: *Imperat . . . tamen*; 9–18: *Imperat . . . praegrauatus*; and 10.13–18: *Ego . . . meae* (fol. $111r^{a-b}$).
49. The version of VIII.12 in Kk.II.21 (to which I will return below) reads as follows: "Vbi in conspectu cordis mei oborta est procella ingens ferens ingentem ymbrem lacrimarum et ut totum effunderem cum uocibus suis. surrexi ab alipio. et secessi remotius ne esset mihi honerosa eius presentia. mansit ergo ille ubi sedebamus nimium stupens. {Sub quadam fici arbore straui me nescio quo modo et dimisi habenas lacrimas et proruperunt flumina oculorum meorum acceptabile sacrificium tuum. non quid[em] hiis verbis; sed in hac sententia multa dixi tibi. vsquequo domine irasceris. Iactabam uoces miserabiles. Quamdiu; quamdiu. Cras et cras. Quare non modo? Quare in hac hora finis turpitudinis mee; dicebam hec. et flebam amarissima contritione cordis mei. Et ecce audio uocem de uicina domo cum cantu dicentis et crebro repetentis quasi pueri an puelle nescio. Tolle lege. Tolle lege. statimque mutato uultu intentissimus cogitare cepi vtrum nam solerent pueri in aliquo genere ludendi cantare tale aliquid; nec occurrebat omnino audisse me uspiam. Represso que impetu lacrimarum; surrexi nihil aliud interpretans diuinitus mihi iuberi; nisi vt aperirem codicem et legerem quod primum inuenissem. Itaque concitus redii in illum locum ubi sedebat alipius. Ibi. enim. posueram codicem apostoli; cum inde surrexeram. Arripui et legi in silentio. capitulum quo primum coniecti sunt oculi mei. Non in comessationibus et ebrietatibus non in cubilibus. et inpudicitiis. non in contentionibus. et emulatione; sed induite dominum iesum christum. et carnis prouidentiam non feceritis in concupiscentiis. nec ultra uolui legere. nec opus erat. Statim omnes dubitationis tenebre diffugerunt. Tum interiecto digito aut nescio quo alio signo; codicem clausi et tranquillo iam uultu indicaui alipio. At ille quid in se

ageretur quod ego nesciebam sic indicauit. petit uidere quid legissem. ostendi et attendi etiam ultra quam ego legeram. et ignorabam quid sequeretur. Sequebatur vero infirmum in fide recipite. quod ille ad se retulit. mihi que apperuit. et tali admonitione firmatus est. Inde ad matrem ingredimur indicamur. gaudet. Narramus quemadmodum gestum sit. exultat et triumphat et benedicebam tibi qui potens es vltra quam petimus et intelligimus facere. {Conuertisti me ad te ut nec vxorem quererem. nec aliquam spem huius seculi stans in ea regula fidei in qua me ante tot annos ei reuelaueras. et conuertisti luctum eius in gaudium. multo vberius quam uoluerat. et multo carius atque castius quam de nepotibus carnis mee requirebat'' (fol. 111r[b]-v[a]). I have added *em* to the end of *quid* to make the word *quidem* on the assumption that the scribe simply forgot to add an abbreviation mark, but in all other cases I have left the text as it reads in the manuscript, since the variations are not grammatically incorrect.

50. The passage comes after the introduction of Ponticianus, the report of how he delights in finding Paul's Epistles lying on Augustine's table and the explanation of his devout Christianity (VIII.6.23–32: *uenit . . . orationibus*, fol. 110v[b]), when MS Kk.II.21 reduces the next fourteen lines in Verheijen to the following: ''Cui cum ego indicassem illis me scripturis curam maximam impendere; ortus est sermo ipso narrante de Antonio egyptio monacho et cetera. {Et erat monasterium mediolani plenum bonis fratribus extra urbis menia sub Ambrosio nutritore; et non noueramus'' (fol. 110v[b]). The remainder of the chapter is then deleted.

51. *Love of Learning*, p. 124.

52. In I.10, for instance, the passage in which Augustine describes his fascination with stage plays has been deleted (10.7–13: *et . . . peruenire*), and the same is the case with almost the whole of I.16, where Augustine writes at length about pagan literature and its encouragement to sin (only the final lines of the chapter, from 16.31: *non accuso . . .*, are partially retained at fol. 103r[b]), as with the whole of I.17, where Augustine speaks of the rhetorical exercises of his childhood.

53. From III.6, 7 and 10, in which Augustine describes the Manichaean faith and the way in which he was deceived by it, the ''editor'' of MS Kk.II.21 selects for inclusion only those passages which present Augustine's spiritual regression into heresy, and carefully eliminates any descripion of the Manichaeans which is not necessary to this mission. The text he retains reads as follows: [III.6.1–9, 22–24 and 53–62] ''Itaque incidi in homines superbe delirantes carnales nimis et loquaces in quorum ore laquei diaboli et uiscum confectum commixtione sillabarum nominis tui et domini iesu christi et peracliti consolatoris spiritus sancti. hec nomina non recedebant de ore eorum. sed tenui sono et strepitu lingue. et dicebant veritas veritas et nusquam erat in eis sed falso loquebantur non de te tantum qui vere veritas es; sed etiam de istis elementis huius mundi creatura tua. et tamen quia te putabam manducabam non auide quidem quia nec sapiebas in ore meo sicuti es. neque. enim tu eras illa figmenta inania {Ve ue quibus gradibus seductus sum in profunda inferi quippe laborans et estuans inopia veri cum te non secundum intellectum mentis; sed secundum sensum carnis querem. Tu autem eras interior intimo meo et superior summo meo. offendi illam mulierem audacem inopem prudentia enigma salomonis sedentem super sellam in foribus et dicentem. Panes occultos libenter edite et aquam dulcem furtiuam bibite. que me seduxit. quia inuenit foris habitantem in oculo carnis me. [III.7.57–60] Et reprehendebam cecus pios patres non solum sicut deus

iuberet atque inspiraret vtentes presentibus. uerum quoque sicut deus reuelaret futura prenuntiantes . . . [III.10.1–2 and 10–11] hec ego nesciens irridebam sanctos seruos et prophetas tuos. {Et credidi miser magis esse misericordiam prestandam fructibus terre; quam hominibus propter quos nascerentur'' (fol. 104v[a-b]).

54. III.5 (fol. 104v[a]), from which only the last phrase regarding Augustine's pride (5.10: *et . . . uidebar*) is deleted in MS Kk.II.21.
55. VI.16.7–10: *Epicurum . . . noluit.*
56. After including Augustine's introduction to Alypius and his friendship with him, the ''editor'' deletes the whole of VI.7 on the circus games (with the exception of Augustine's assertion of internal confession at 7.42–43, cited above), all of VI.8 describing the way in which the gladiatorial games corrupted Alypius, the whole of VI.9 in which Alypius is arrested as a thief, and much of VI.10 regarding Alypius' integrity as an assessor, while retaining the opening lines of that chapter on the strong bond between the two men (10.1–3: *Hunc . . . desereret*), as well as the line in which Augustine notes how Alypius is also searching for an appropriate mode of living (10.27–28: *mecumque . . . modus*); the ''editor'' also retains the following introduction to Nebridius (10.29–37, fol. 108v[b]).
57. A long passage at the end of VII.9 (9.43–66: *Qui . . . creatori*) which describes how the learned who are proud become fools and how Augustine encountered idolatry in the Platonic writings but ignored it is deleted from MS Kk.II.21.
58. See (cited above) the text retained from VII.10 in MS Kk.II.21. The Plotinian image of internal light as truth is also deleted from Augustine's conversion in VIII.12: see the text (cited above) retained from that chapter.
59. As noted above, only one brief passage is retained from VIII.10 in MS Kk.II.21, and it concerns Augustine's conclusion that it is entirely his own responsibility (rather than the work of two opposed natures) when he weakly wills contrary things: ''Ego cum deliberabam ut iam seruirem domino deo meo; ego eram qui uolebam; ego qui nolebam. Ego eram. nec plene uolebam. nec plene nolebam. Ideo mecum contendebam. et dissipabar a me ipso. et ipsa dissipatio me inuito quidem fiebat. nec tamen ostendebat naturam mentis aliene; sed pene mee'' (10.13–18, fol. 111r[b]).
60. After selecting from the opening lines of VIII.11 passages which highlight the precise nature of Augustine's spiritual condition and hesitation at this point in the narrative (11.1–3: *Sic . . . exiguo tenebar,* 7–8: *Dicebam . . . Ecce modo fiat;* 8–9: *et . . . non faciebam;* and 13–14: *haesitans . . . insolitum*), the entire report of Augustine's *antiquae amicae* is deleted, and the encounter with Continence (11.31–44) is retained in an edited form: ''{Aperiebatur ab ea parte quo intenderam faciem casta dignitas continentie serena. et extendens ad me suscipiendum et amplectendum pias manus plenas gregibus bonorum exemplorum. Ibi tot pueri et puelle. ibi inuentus multa et graues indue et uirgines anus. et in omnibus ipsa continentia nequaquam sterilis. sed fecunda mater filiorum gaudiorum de marito te domine. Et irridebant me irrisione oratoria quasi diceret. Tu non poteris. quod isti. quod iste? An uero isti uel iste in se ipsis possunt an non in domino deo suo? Quid in te stas et non stas? proice te in eum. noli metuere; non se subtrahet vt cadas. proice te securus excipiet et sanabit te. et erubescebam nimis'' (fol. 111r[b]).
61. Here, as in other places in his abridged text, the ''editor'' of MS Kk.II.21 reveals a tendency to restrict himself to what he appears to have seen as the main narrative thread—namely, the spiritual autobiography—of the *Confessiones,* and an awareness

of digression from this central progression. The chapter summaries for the *Confessiones* written by the thirteenth-century Dominican Robert Kilwardby reveal a similar preoccupation with narrative progression, for he frequently notes how Augustine returns to a particular "confession" (*confessio*) or to his "plan" or "intention" (*propositum*) after digressions. My knowledge of Kilwardby's *capitula* for the *Confessiones* is based upon their appearance in Paris, Bibliothèque Nationale, MS lat. 2117, from which I am currently preparing an edition of these fascinating summaries. See also Callus, "'Tabulae super Originalia Patrum'," and "New Manuscripts of Kilwardby's *Tabulae.*"

62. Like the subtle linguistic changes seen at III.6.53, where the "editor" substitutes *seductus* ("seduced") for *deductus* ("led down") when Augustine talks of the effect of Manichaean falsehoods upon him, and at VII.1.16, where he substitutes *donabar* ("I was given") for *conabar* ("I attempted") in Augustine's description of how he tried to cleanse the unclean phantasms from his inner eye. Verheijen lists neither of these substitutions as manuscript variants (see pp. 32 and 92 of his edition), though certainly they could represent errors in the English traditions of the text or on the part of MS Kk.II.21's scribe. Both of the relevant passages are cited in the notes above.

63. On the concept of progressive Augustinian interiority, particularly in relation to the predominantly monastic English readers of the *Confessiones* in the eleventh and twelfth centuries, see Olson, "Textual Construction of Monastic Interiority." Good modern studies of Augustine's role in the cultural construction of interiority are Charles Taylor, *Sources of the Self: the Making of Modern Identity* (Cambridge, Mass., 1989), pp. 127–42; and Denys Turner, *The Darkness of God: Negativity in Christian Mysticism* (Cambridge, 1995), pp. 50–101.

64. See Hardwick, *Catalogue of Manuscripts in the Library of the University of Cambridge*, pp. 394–95, for the contents of this manuscript, including commentaries on Fulgentius and Ovid's *Metamorphoses*; however, the dating in this catalogue of the hands in MS Ii.II.20 to the fifteenth century is mistaken (see Ker, "Medieval Manuscripts from Norwich," p. 262, and *Medieval Libraries of Great Britain*, p. 136, for the correct dates).

65. See Ker, "Medieval Manuscripts from Norwich," pp. 252–54 and 262; on p. 250 Ker notes how the letter and number of the press-mark provide some as of yet uncertain "indication of the date at which the book was acquired" by the Norwich library, and if Ker's examples give a fair picture of the pattern, MS Ii.II.20 may have entered the library in the late thirteenth century (assuming a C press-mark) or the early fourteenth century (assuming a G). The presence in MS Ii.II.20 of notes in the hand of Robert Talbot, prebendary of Norwich from 1547 through 1558, confirms the assignment to Norwich and the manuscript's presence there by the sixteenth century (see Ker, pp. 246, 255 and 262).

66. Although it is possible that MS Ii.II.20 originated in a university environment, there is to my knowledge no evidence of either the abridged version found both in it and in MS Kk.II.21 or the chapter summaries and divisions which it contains having circulated at Oxford or Cambridge. However, the techniques for organizing texts which are applied to the *Confessiones* in MS Ii.II.20 would no doubt be familiar to individuals trained at a thirteenth-century English university.

67. The numbered divisions in books I-V and XI-XIII of MS Ii.II.20 do not resemble those in MS Kk.II.21, in the majority of the English manuscripts of the *Confessiones*,

or in the work associated with Robert Kilwardby in the thirteenth century, although Eton College MS 47, a fifteenth-century volume which was copied by and belonged to Master John Malberthorpe, has chapter divisions which are at times and especially in the first four books of the text similar to those in MS Ii.II.20. In addition, I have not discovered in the medieval English manuscripts any chapter summaries for the *Confessiones* which resemble the partial set of summaries in MS Ii.II.20. On both MS Ii.II.20 and Malberthorpe's *Confessiones*, see the entries in appendix A of Olson, "Textual Construction of Monastic Interiority."

68. Not only is the overall appearance of the two hands very different, with the scribe who writes the middle, abridged section of the text (Scribe B) producing a spikier, less-rounded script than the scribe of the beginning and final sections of the text (Scribe A), but the letter forms also differ: the stem of "r," for instance, boasts a foot which generally curves up and to the right in the work of Scribe B, but usually ends abruptly in Scribe A's section; the letter "g" provides another useful example, for Scribe A gives it a large rounded tail in most instances, while Scribe B produces a smaller, flatter tail. In addition, Scribe A uses wider columns than Scribe B.

69. The physical layout of both hands in the manuscript suggests that neither hand preceded the other by a significant period of time: if we try to assume, for instance, that books I-IV and XI-XIII of the complete text were written earlier and the abridged portion was later added to replace a lost part of the text, then the fact that Scribe A begins book XI immediately after the close of Scribe B's book X in the middle of not only a quire and folio, but also a column (fol. 102v[b]) presents a problem; if, on the other hand, we assume that the abridged portion was the sole survivor of an older manuscript and the complete version was added to finish the text on either end, then the fact that Scribe B begins the abridged version (fol. 93r[a]) with a long correction, adding a large chunk of missing text to the end of book IV of the complete version, presents a problem. The logical solution is that the two parts of the *Confessiones* in MS Ii.II.20 were produced very near in time, almost certainly in narrative order, and with the scribe of each having knowledge of the other part of the text—that is, that the text in MS Ii.II.20, despite its haphazard appearance, was the product of a single project.

70. On this fire, see Ker, "Medieval Manuscripts from Norwich," pp. 248–49. I hope to explore the intriguing version of the *Confessiones* in MS Ii.II.20 further in a future study of medieval chapter divisions and summaries for the *Confessiones.*

71. This scenario could explain the fact that the extensive narrative rubrics in MS Ii.II.20 tend to be somewhat more intellectually sophisticated than those in MS Kk.II.21. Perhaps the running commentary on the *Confessiones* provided by these rubrics was played up slightly in MS Ii.II.20 to match the informative chapter summaries elsewhere in the text, or was watered down slightly in Donewico's copy of the text for the personal use of one who had already studied the text; indeed, a combination of both may well lie behind the two related sets of rubrics extant today. The sophisticated nature of the rubrics, as indeed of the chapter summaries, in MS Ii.II.20 is one of the aspects of this manuscript which gives it a scholastic feel.

72. On this school, see Norman P. Tanner, *The Church in Late Medieval Norwich 1370–1532* (Toronto, 1984), pp. 33–34; Tanner also notes (pp. 32–33) that a Song School and Almery School, where prospective priests might be educated, were attached to the Cathedral Priory.

73. See Greatrex, "Monk Students from Norwich," p. 562, who notes that although "there are few references to the novices, none to novice masters and only one to a lector" at Norwich, "it is likely that some of the university monks, on their return to the community, assumed the task of lecturing to their brethren, as was the practice at Canterbury from 1314 on, and they may have provided basic instruction in grammar, and perhaps also in logic and philosophy;" see also p. 563 on the fact that a long period at university was not considered necessary to instruct the brethren at Norwich, p. 574 on the lack of records concerning the instructor or lector of the Norwich community, and pp. 557 and 579–83 on the many Norwich monks who attended university between 1290 and 1500.
74. See Greatrex, "Monk Students from Norwich," p. 557, who notes how "nothing is known of the religious formation or of the preliminary training which the monks must have received within the cloister school at Norwich." William J. Courtenay, *Schools and Scholars in Fourteenth-Century England* (Princeton, 1987), p. 107, has suggested that the Norwich "cathedral priory gave instruction in grammar, philosophy, and theology both to monks and to future diocesan clergy," but as Greatrex, "Monk Students from Norwich," p. 576 n. 3, points out, Courtenay "fails to provide any reference" to substantiate this claim. See also Tanner, *Church in Late Medieval Norwich*, pp. 32–35.
75. On the rapid dissemination of the *Confessiones* in late-eleventh- and twelfth-century England, see Webber, "Diffusion of Augustine's *Confessions* in England," and the Introduction to Olson, "Textual Construction of Monastic Interiority."
76. *Les Confessions de Saint Augustin dans la Tradition Littéraire: Antécédents et Postérité* (Paris, 1963), p. 305, where Courcelle's discussion of the twelfth-century use of the *Confessiones* concludes with the assertion that "les *Confessions* fournissent surtout un modèle précieux en vue de l'initier à la vie monastique et contemplative."
77. Ker, "Medieval Manuscripts from Norwich," pp. 248–49, discusses the effect of this fire on the Norwich collection, which is made up largely of late-thirteenth- and fourteenth-century volumes, instead of containing the large proportion of twelfth-century manuscripts found in most monastic English houses.
78. *Love of Learning*, p. 123: "Augustine's influence was paramount in the formation of the 'monastic style.' In his sermons and particularly in his *Confessions*, he had produced a model of artistic prose in which all the procedures used in ancient rhythmical prose were put to the service of his Christian enthusiasm."
79. On the relationship between Augustine's reading experiences in the *Confessiones* and the monastic practice of *lectio divina* as described by Leclercq (*Love of Learning*, pp. 18–20 and 89–90), see especially Olson, "The Textual Self: Autobiographical Self-Expression in Augustine's *Confessiones*," MA thesis, University of Victoria, 1993.
80. This is in keeping with Brian Stock's argument in *Augustine the Reader: Meditation, Self-Knowledge, and the Ethics of Interpretation* (Cambridge, Mass., and London, 1996), especially pp. 1–121, that Augustine presents himself in the *Confessiones* as reading in progressively ethical ways and ascending spiritually and mentally through the course of his life as a consequence, and that this theory of ethical reading was highly influential for Augustine's readers. See also Douglas Gray, "Saint Augustine and Medieval Literature: Part I," in *Saint Augustine and His Influence in the Middle Ages*, Sewanee Mediaeval Studies 3, edited by Edward B. King and Jacqueline T. Schaefer (Sewanee, Tennessee, 1988), p. 29, who notes how "the *Confessions* encouraged religious writings of self-exploration; it encouraged the development of the old idea

of 'nosce te ipsum' in moral and mystical writing." I discuss Augustine's progress through reading in "Textual Self" and "Textual Construction of Monastic Interiority," the latter of which presents various eleventh- and twelfth-century English examples of Augustine's *Confessiones* being read in the ways suggested here.

81. The quotations are from *The Implications of Literacy: Written Language and Models of Interpretation in the Eleventh and Twelfth Centuries* (Princeton, 1983), p. 90, where Stock describes his understanding of "textual communities."
82. See the entries on the extant English manuscripts of the *Confessiones* in appendix A and those on manuscripts listed in medieval catalogues in appendix B of Olson, "Textual Construction of Monastic Interiority."
83. On MS B.3.25, see M. R. James, *The Western Manuscripts in the Library of Trinity College, Cambridge: A Descriptive Catalogue*, vol. I (Cambridge, 1900), p. 123; and the entries in appendices A and B of Olson, "Textual Construction of Monastic Interiority."
84. On Lanfranc and the annotations in MS B.3.25, see chapters Two and Six in Olson, "Textual Construction of Monastic Interiority;" and on the many other manuscripts containing annotations in the Lanfrancian style, see R. W. Southern, *Saint Anselm: A Portrait in a Landscape* (Cambridge, 1990), pp. 35–38; Z. N. Brooke, *The English Church and the Papacy from the Conquest to the Reign of John* (Cambridge, 1952), pp. 231–35; and Webber, "Diffusion," p. 43. As Brooke, pp. 68–71, demonstrates, and Southern, p. 36, explains, "some of the annotation . . . certainly goes back to Lanfranc himself."
85. See Webber, "Diffusion," p. 43, n. 74, where she notes their presence throughout the manuscript, but especially in book I of the *Confessiones.*
86. Corpus Christi College, MS 253 and British Library, MS Royal 5.B.xvi are both late-eleventh- or early-twelfth-century volumes in the textual tradition of Boulogne-sur-Mer, Bibliothèque Municipale MS 46, the same tradition as that of Trinity College, MS B.3.25 (as opposed to Paris MS lat. 1913A, from which the abbreviated *retractatio* of MS Kk.II.21 is derived); MS 253 is in fact a copy of MS B.3.25, and contains some of the Lanfrancian *marginalia.* MS 253 also contains the new-style sequence *Interni festi gaudia,* and thus might have been associated with a precentor or other individual responsible for the musical devotions of St Augustine's Abbey; while MS Royal 5.B.xvi certainly belonged to Peter the Precentor of Rochester. On these two manuscripts see chapters Two, Three and Six and the entries in appendices A and B of Olson, "Textual Construction of Monastic Interiority;" and see also James, *A Descriptive Catalogue of the Manuscripts in the Library of Corpus Christi College, Cambridge,* vol. 2 (Cambridge, 1912), pp. 4–5, and G. F. Warner and J. P. Gilson, *British Museum: Catalogue of Western Manuscripts in the Old Royal and King's Collections,* vol. 1 (London, 1921), p. 105.
87. See especially Étienne Gilson, "Sur l'Office de Saint Augustin," *Mediaeval Studies* 13 (1951), 233–34, and the discussion of possible liturgical associations for the *Confessiones* in eleventh- and twelfth-century England in chapter 3 of Olson, "Textual Construction of Monastic Interiority." This Office, found in various medieval manuscripts, uses Augustine's discovery of himself in a *regio dissimilitudinis* from VII.10 of the *Confessiones.*
88. The personal devotional use of the *Confessiones* and the literary adoption of Augustine's *confessio* mode are extremely common among the eleventh- and twelfth-century English readers of the *Confessiones* whom I have studied in detail in "Textual Construction of Monastic Interiority."

89. On the role of monastic precentors, see my discussion of Peter the Precentor of Rochester and MS 253 in chapter 3 of "Textual Construction of Monastic Interiority," as well as the many references cited there, especially David Knowles, *The Monastic Order in England: A History of its Development from the Times of St Dunstan to the Fourth Lateran Council (943–1216)* (Cambridge, 1940), pp. 428–29.
90. On Pembroke College, MS 135, see the entries in appendices A and B of Olson, "Textual Construction of Monastic Interiority," and appendix B of Olson, "Grandisson's Fashioning of Text and Self," as well as James, *A Descriptive Catalogue of the Manuscripts in the Library of Pembroke College* (Cambridge, 1905), pp. 134–35. I would like to thank Malcolm Parkes for his kind assistance with dating the scribal and annotating hands in MS 135, and for his fascinating and informative comments on other manuscripts of the *Confessiones*.
91. It is worth noting that both Trinity College, MS B.3.25 and Pembroke College, MS 135 contain an annotation in book X beside Augustine's expression of his fears on account of his "sins and miseries," his desire to "flee into solitude" and God's prohibition of this lifestyle for him (43.28–30: "Conterritus peccatis meis et mole miseriae meae agitaueram corde meditatusque fueram fugam in solitudinem, sed prohibuisti me"): Lanfranc leaves his characteristic **.a.** beside the passage (fol. 63r), while the annotator of Pembroke MS 135 makes the judgement that the "common life is to be preferred to the solitary" ("vitam communem preferendam esse solitarie:" fol. 194v[a]).
92. The note (which is somewhat rougher than many of the notes comprising the marginal apparatus in MS 135, but still very similar in its letter forms to and probably the product of the scribal hand which writes both the apparatus and the text of the *Confessiones*) reads as follows: "'A' Potes in lectione mense ab hac figura transire usque ad locum ubi subsequens figura subscribitur. 8" (it appears on fol. 189r[b] beside X.8.4–6, with a corresponding 'A' at *Ibi* . . . in line 4, and a corresponding 8 at X.17.1, fol. 190v[b]). The note thus allows the reader to eliminate a large chunk of Augustine's complicated discussion of memory and forgetfulness, a practical move for reading the text aloud to a large and somewhat varied audience, and one with some interesting implications of its own.
93. Frances Beer, *Women and the Mystical Experience in the Middle Ages* (Woodbridge, 1992), p. 22, notes how the works of the fathers were also read aloud at mealtimes in Benedictine houses.
94. We do know, however, that it might well have been associated with a Master John de Tynmouth and Cambridge's Pembroke Hall in the fourteenth century: on Tynmouth's connection with Pembroke MS 135, see the entries in appendices B of Olson, "Textual Construction of Monastic Interiority" and "Grandisson's Fashioning of Text and Self." I would like to thank Jayne Ringrose for her generous assistance with Tynmouth and MS 135.
95. See Tanner, *Church in Late Medieval Norwich*, pp. 51–52, on the lack of spiritual vigor found among the monks of Norwich in the 1309 visitation of Bishop Salmon.
96. On the friars, the universities and *ordinatio*, see especially the study by M. B. Parkes, "The Influence of the Concepts of *Ordinatio* and *Compilatio* on the Development of the Book," in *Scribes, Scripts and Readers: Studies in the Communication, Presentation and Dissemination of Medieval Texts* (London, 1991), pp. 35–69; and see also Callus, "The Contribution to the Study of the Fathers Made by the Thirteenth-Century Oxford Schools," *Journal of Ecclesiastical History* 5 (1954), 139–48; and Richard H.

and Mary A. Rouse, "Statim inuenire: Schools, Preachers, and New Attitudes to the Page," in *Renaissance and Renewal in the Twelfth Century*, edited by Robert L. Benson and Giles Constable (Oxford, 1982), pp. 201–25, and "The Development of Research Tools in the Thirteenth Century," in *Authentic Witnesses: Approaches to Medieval Texts and Manuscripts* (Notre Dame, Indiana, 1991), pp. 221–55. Since Courtenay, *Schools and Scholars*, p. 79, has speculated that instruction in philosophy and theology at Norwich was probably in the hands of the Franciscans in the latter half of the thirteenth century, whereas such Benedictine houses would have become academically self-sufficient by the early years of the fourteenth century, the friars may have in fact had a rather direct influence upon the methods of *ordinatio* found in MSS Kk.II.21 and Ii.II.20. However, if a Franciscan friar was in any way responsible for the abridged version of the *Confessiones* studied here, he worked with some notably monastic biases.

97. On Cambridge, Corpus Christi College, MS 34 (in which the *Confessiones* appear on pp. 464[a]-546[b]), see the entry in appendix A of Olson, "Textual Construction of Monastic Interiority;" and James, *Catalogue of Manuscripts in Corpus Christi College*, vol. 1, pp. 66–69.

98. Assuming that Corpus Christi College, MS 34 was at Norwich soon after its production, which is by no means certain since it can only be placed at Norwich without doubt in the late fifteenth and mid sixteenth centuries: see Ker, "Medieval Manuscripts from Norwich," pp. 246, 252, 254 and 264 on the press-mark and Robert Talbot's hand in MS 34.

99. The *Confessiones* in MS 34 are remarkably free of *ordinatio*, for they contain no chapter divisions, and are missing all of the capitals and some of the rubrics which should open their separate books.

100. The copies of the *Confessiones* in both MSS Ii.II.20 and Kk.II.21 reveal some physical signs of use in the form of occasional *marginalia* in hands other than those of their main texts and rubrication.

101. See Hardwick, *Catalogue of the Manuscripts in the Library of the University of Cambridge*, pp. 619–20. The focus appears to be the regular Benedictine life, the teaching and learning of monks and other religious, the inner life of the soul, and the spiritual progression through *confessio* and *conversio* of the Christian individual, namely Augustine.

102. On the contents of MS Ii.III.10, including a number of tracts concerning the controversy over the *Visio Beatifica* between Pope John XXII and Thomas Waleys, see Hardwick, *Catalogue of Manuscripts in the Library of the University of Cambridge*, pp. 416–18. Both MSS Kk.II.21 and Ii.III.10 were probably written by a professional scribe, as were so many thirteenth- and fourteenth-century volumes at Norwich: see Ker, "Medieval Manuscripts from Norwich," pp. 250–52, who discusses the scribes hired to produce books at Norwich during this period; and see also H. C. Beeching and James, "The Library of the Cathedral Church of Norwich and Priory Manuscripts now in English Libraries," *Norfolk Archaeology* 19 (1917), pp. 69–70.

From Professional to Private Readership: A Discussion and Transcription of the Fifteenth- and Sixteenth-Century Marginalia in *Piers Plowman* C-Text, Oxford, Bodleian Library, MS Digby 102

Tanya Schaap

Until recently, little scholarly attention has been paid to the marginalia found in *Piers Plowman* manuscripts despite their potential as a valuable source for the study of medieval reader response.[1] Understandably, most of the recent scholarship on *Piers* marginalia has tended to focus on the better known *Piers* manuscripts: Oxford, Bodleian Library, MS Douce 104; London, British Library, MS Additional 35157; and San Marino, California, Huntington Library, MS HM 143. Some of the less studied manuscripts, however, offer much to enhance our understanding not only of how contemporaries received Langland's work but also how sixteenth-century readers responded to it. Oxford, Bodleian Library, MS Digby 102 in particular offers layers of marginalia not often found in *Piers* manuscripts: it contains marginalia contemporary with the creation of the manuscript in the mid-fifteenth century, and a more substantial layer written in the early sixteenth century. Digby 102 is, in fact, quite a good copy of the C-text but unfortunately due to its imperfect beginning, commencing in the middle of Passus II, has been given little attention by most *Piers* scholars.[2] However, the marginalia of Digby 102 is worth considerable attention.[3]

Digby 102 is dated from the mid-fifteenth century and was later owned by Sir Thomas Allen, 1540–1632, a renowned Oxford scholar.[4] There are a total of 480 written annotations in Digby 102 compared with 208 in HM 143 and 257 in Douce 104. Of these 480, however, 381 were written more than half a century after the creation of the manuscript. These later annotations are written in an early tudor secretary hand which was in use roughly between 1485 to the late 1540s. The annotator's version of the hand dates around the turn of the century, the most common features of the hand being the single-loop "a," the double-loop "v" (clearly distinguishing itself from the "u"), the "m" with the final minim below the line, the long "r," the long "s" (like a long staff), and a spread-out "w." If in fact this annotator (hereafter referred to as the sixteenth-century annotator) was writing at the turn of the century, his annotations would have been added sixty-five to seventy-five years after the earlier ones.

Only 97 annotations are scribal, that is, they are the annotations produced at the time the manuscript was created. Two different scribes were responsible for copying the body of text; they used an anglicana formata hand of medial quality and wrote in a rather untidy, cramped style. A third scribe rubricated the text, adding the Lombard initials, the rubrics (sometimes partially in the margin), the red underlining of Latin text, and the red and blue strokes dividing the lines of poetry. The rubricator is also responsible for the bulk of the scribal annotations.[5]

As Paul Saenger and Michael Heinlen explain, it was the duty of scribal annotators to correct the punctuation, add the foliation and rubrics if needed and, depending on the text, to provide annotations as finding notes for readers.[6] Medieval annotations were "provisions for the reader, and not necessarily, as is often thought, evidence of reader use."[7] The primary concern of the scribal annotators was for future readers; it was their duty to enhance the readability of the poem, to provide marginalia which would clarify the meaning of the text and expedite the retrieval of information. Kathryn Kerby-Fulton describes the scribal annotator as a "professional reader" whose work "is not the stuff of a quill-happy owner, but real scriptorium slog-work." She explains that *Piers* annotators were concerned with the edification of readers and paid special attention to mnemonic devices: "medieval annotation appears to have been, at its best, a labor of love stimulated by the conviction of working for the corporate, social good."[8] So if scribal annotations are evidence of a reading administered at the professional level, one motivated not so much by personal convictions as by a concern for the reading and comprehension of others, what can we make of the 381 annotations in Digby 102, written nearly three-quarters of a century after the manuscript's creation? Are these annotations evidence of reader use? Are they the stuff of a quill-happy owner? Through a comparison of the scribal annotations and those of the sixteenth-century annotator, it becomes clear that these later annotations are indeed evidence of a private rather than professional reading of *Piers,* and as such, offer a rare glimpse into the historical context within which Langland's text was received.

Approximately 60 percent of the 97 scribal annotations in Digby 102 are *notas* which are intended to highlight key passages of religious, social, moral, or political significance rather than to draw attention to plot or dramatis personae. The implications of this annotation pattern are interesting; it suggests that scribal, or professional, readers of *Piers* regarded the text more as a polemical work than as a work of fiction. One rare occasion in which a scribal *nota* does draw attention to the plot may be found at Passus VII:182, fol. 23v; it is significant, however, in that it marks the point at which Piers himself first enters the action of the poem.[9] Many of the scribal *notas* highlight passages censuring the sinful behaviors of friars. Typical examples of this kind of note may be found at Passus II:219, fol. 1v (the point at which Falsness flees to the friars), Passus VI:299, fol. 19r (Repentaunce's advice that friars must make restitution), and Passus IX:249, fol. 33v (a description of friars). Other scribal *notas* draw attention to passages on religious doctrine, biblical authorities, and Christ's death and resurrection. One of the most significant concerns for the scribal annotators is poverty, not surprising considering its thematic significance in the poem. Issues of particular concern include the disadvantages of poverty, the importance of patience, and the dangers of wealth. Instances of these *notas* occur at Passus XII:221, fol. 47r (a warning to the rich), Passus XIII:115–16, fol. 49r (a passage on priestly poverty), and Passus XVI:117, fol. 60r (Actif's confusion over the Latin definition of poverty.)

The remaining scribal annotations consist of no more than one or two words, almost all of which are written in Latin. Most of these annotations are designed to highlight key figures in the poem. A number of annotations, however, supply more information than is given in the text and aim to paraphrase a number of lines of text. In his work on the annotations of HM 143, Carl Grindley identifies this type of annotation as the Textual Extrapolation Summation annotation, a subtype of the Narrative Reading Aid Summation annotation and the rarest type of Summation annotation found in HM143.[10] An instance of the Textual Extrapolation annotation in Digby 102 occurs at Passus XVIII:202, fol. 71v:

That thre bilongeth to
a lord that leiaunse claymeth / Might and a
Trinitas mene to se his owne myhte / Of hym sulue *and*
his s*er*uant and what soffreth hem bothe.

These few lines are part of a longer passage beginning at line 179 in which Faith attempts to explain the triune nature of God to the dreamer. Nowhere in this entire passage, however, does Faith specifically refer to the Trinity. Instead, Faith makes an analogy to a lord in power: the three aspects of his position are his power, an instrument of that power, and that which allows them both to exist. It is quite possible that the annotator recognized the complex and somewhat confusing nature of this analogy and, out of a concern for future readers, provided "Trinitas" in the margin as a helpful tool for understanding.

One of the most fascinating scribal annotations occurs at Passus IX:106, fol. 31v:

Ac ʒut ar ther other beggares in hele as hit semeth
lollard Ac hem wanteth wyt men *and* wommen bothe / The whiche
aren lunatyk lollares and lepares aboute / And madden
as the mone syt more other lasse / Careth they for no
colde ne counteth of noon heete.

In this instance, the scribe has interpreted Langland's discussion of the "lunatyk lollares"—those physically able but mentally unstable beggars—as a subtle reference to Lollards, a pejorative term which came to be associated with the followers of the heretical teachings of Wyclif at the end of the fourteenth century. If this scribe was working during the mid-fifteenth century, as his handwriting suggests, his negative reaction to the word "lollare" is entirely appropriate. On folio 33 at lines 213–14 of the same passus, the fifteenth-century annotator highlights the use of the "lollare" vocabulary again, in this case noting the word "lolleth." Directly below his annotation, the annotator of the early sixteenth century marks the passage with "lollard*es*."

Kyndeliche
be crist ben suche ycald lollares/As by the engelisch
of oure eldres of olde mennes techyng/he that lolleth — nota
is lame or hys leg oute of ioynte/Or y maymed
in sum*me* membre for to meschyef hit souneth — lollard*es*
Riht so sothly suche man*ere* heremytes/lollen aȝen
the byleue and the lawe of holy churche.

Both of these passages belong to a larger section of the poem in which Langland attempts to distinguish between false beggars and the needy poor. They are also part of an even larger section which is completely new to the C-text (IX:66–281). Both of these passages may reflect an attempt on Langland's part to reclaim the traditional definition of "lollare" as one of God's "priue disciples" (IX:118). In her study, Scase offers an explanation of the historical and etymological context of the word "lollare":

> Usage in the poem, and in contemporary and later writings, suggests that it was only possible for a short time in late fourteenth-century England to use "loller" as a satirical term for those who were defined by the law of Christ as the gyrovagues of the contemporary church. The evidence suggests that this definition was maintained despite (and most probably because of) the growing use of the near-homonym "lollard" for the heretics who followed the teachings of Wyclif, but that the "*Piers Plowman* sense" soon lost ground in competition with the other usage.[11]

Through an examination of various marginalia in *Piers* manuscripts, Scase concludes that despite Langland's efforts to divorce his work from Wycliffite tendencies, it did nevertheless become associated with Lollard sentiments. The annotations transcribed above are good examples of such evidence. Scase goes on to cite the annotator of Douce 104, who avoids using the "loller" vocabulary and instead, uses terms such as "Beggers and bidders" and "begers þat hath lemmonys." Scase cites Digby 102 as an example of a manuscript which shows a scribal interest in the etymology passage, that section in Passus IX which attempts to define "lollare" (p. 157). The two instances of the "lollard" annotation in Digby 102 are excellent examples of how readers, both early and late, were concerned over the etymological implications of the term and did indeed associate the "loller" vocabulary with "lollardy."

It is evident from the various scribal annotations in Digby 102 that the early annotators were concerned and interested readers of *Piers*. The rubricator, who was responsible for the bulk of the scribal annotations, was quite familiar with the poem and had a keen interest not only in the major themes such as the glorification of poverty but also in some of the more minor, yet interesting, characters, as well as with extrapolating some of the poem's more difficult metaphors.

The marginal notes made by the early-sixteenth-century annotator, the heaviest layer of marginalia in Digby 102, were most likely copied for very different reasons than the scribal annotations. Since these later annotations were not produced at the time the manuscript was created, they raise the question of whether this later annotator was a private owner of the manuscript rather than a professional reader. There is always the possibility, of course, that an early-sixteenth-century owner of the manuscript brought the book to a scribe for professional annotation, although this is highly unlikely. While the later annotator has no trouble reading Middle English and appears to be familiar with Latin, many of the Latin annotations comment on a section of the text written in Middle English and vice versa; the style in which the annotations are written suggest the annotator was either working for someone he knew very well, or he was annotating for personal reasons (as a private reader, perhaps as the owner of the manuscript).[12] The latter is likely for a variety of reasons.

In HM 143 and Douce 104, a number of annotations directly address the reader and usually begin with words and phrases such as "nota houu," "nota de houu," "hyere," "lo how," or "loke hyer." Of all the sixteenth-century annotations in Digby 102, only one appears to be an Address annotation and may be found at Passus V:124, fol. 13v: "nota hou oon shale com*me* to heven." All other sixteenth-century annotations are made up of words or phrases directly gleaned from the text, phrases which summarize the plot, or various instances of textual extrapolation. Of course, there are many plot-summary annotations in HM143 and Douce 104 as well; it is the absence of Address annotations in Digby 102 that is of importance here. With the exception of a single Address annotation, none of the annotations of the sixteenth-century read as though they were intended specifically for other readers.

Furthermore, while many of the annotations are helpful place-finders, annotations intended to guide the reader to particular themes, actions, and key figures in the poem, there are also several which would be meaningful only to the author of the annotations. Typical place-finders or annotations intended to guide a reader to key figures in the poem include "gyle" (II:156, fol. 1r), "Concyens" (II:203, fol. 1v), and "The kyng *and* mede" (III:131, fol. 4r). Typical examples of annotations which highlight plot action include "provisers shale s*er*ue p*re*lates" (II:182, fol. 1r), "lyar to Freris" (II:240, fol. 2r), and "a bille by pees a ȝenst wrong" (IV:47, fol. 9v). In amongst these somewhat typical place-finders are annotations which would seem meaningful only to a reader who was annotating for private study. One may be found at Passus III:250, fol. 5v:

	And that is
A conquero*ur*	the kynde of a kyng that conquereth on his enemys /To helpe hyeliche alle his host or elles g*ra*unte/Al that his men may wynne do therwith here beste.

If this note were intended as a place-finder for the reader, it should have read "a kyng that conquereth" or "kyng a conquero*ur*." Instead the annotator chose to note only the word which describes the king, making no marginal reference to the king himself. It would seem that such an annotation would be useful only for the person who wrote it or for someone who was very familiar with the poem.

Others also suggest that the sixteenth-century reader was annotating for himself rather than for future readers. At first glance, many of these marginal notes appear to be simple "Reading Aid" annotations which highlight key speakers in the poem. It is the point at which these speakers are being noticed which is of interest. The annotation which occurs at Passus XIV:202, fol. 54r is a good example:

Withouten bapteme as by here
bokes beth nat y saued/Con*tra* q*uo*d Ymagenatyf tho and
Imagynac*ioun* comsed to loure/And sayde.

Even though Ymagenatyf has been speaking for the last 198 lines, since the beginning of the passus, the annotator chooses to highlight his name at the point in which he is interrupted by the dreamer. Readers are told in the first line of the passus that Ymagenatyf is speaking, but are not reminded of this until line 202, when he begins speaking again after the interruption. If the annotator was concerned merely with highlighting the key figures of the poem, would he not have written this annotation at line 1, when Ymagenatyf first enters the action of the poem? There are two possibilities: either this particular annotation is evidence of an annotator writing for private benefit, a simple marginal reminder that it is Ymagenatyf who has resumed speaking, or it is at this point that Ymagenatyf has attracted the interest of the annotator. The latter is, of course, a possibility since this is where Ymagenatyf begins to explain the contrary side to the debate over the salvation of the righteous heathen.

Another example of an annotation which highlights the speaker's name directly after an interruption in the text occurs at Passus XVI:173, fols. 59v-61r:

Wher of s*er*ue//(fol. 61r)
ye y sayde sire liberum arbitrium/Of so*m*me tyme to fyhte
q*uo*d he falsnesse to destruye/And so*m*me to soffre
liberum arbitrium both tene and sorwe.

Liberum Arbitrium first enters the poem at line 157, where the annotator notes "actif had a leder that is liberum arbitrium" (fol. 61r), a typical annotation introducing the presence of a key figure. A few lines later at line 166, Liberum Arbitrium begins speaking, but is interrupted at line 172 by the dreamer. Once he begins speaking at line 173, the annotator notes his name in the margin for a second time. This type of annotation also occurs at Passus XXI:197–99, fol. 87v where the annotator notes "Concyence spake of criste *and* of the crosse," the first point at which Conscience has stopped speaking since line 26. Only eight lines later, the point at which Conscience begins again, the annotator notes his name once more.

All of these examples suggest that the annotator was reacting to the text in a way that is familiar to many modern readers, jotting down marginal notes as brief reminders to the action or characters in the poem. That these examples occur at passages in which the central speaker has been interrupted may suggest that the reader was suddenly reminded as to who was speaking. Perhaps out of an effort to aid reading in the future, the sixteenth-century annotator noted the names of some of the more important speakers, for reasons of authority, often more than once, in order to keep his reading and comprehension on track.

In addition to the somewhat typical annotations which aid in reading and comprehension, there are also a number of Textual Extrapolation annotations, those annotations which supply more information than given in the text and which aim to summarize by using words which do not appear there. In his study of the marginalia of HM 143, Grindley identifies this type of annotation as the rarest sub-type of the Summation annotation.[13] His study, however, focuses on scribal annotations, those notes supplied during the manuscript's creation for the benefit of future readers. In such a context, it is easy to understand why the Textual Extrapolation annotation is so rare: in order to avoid confusion for future readers, scribal annotators made an effort to stay as close to the text as possible, highlighting dramatis personae, summing up significant passages, and noting various moral and political concerns. The numerous instances of the Textual Extrapolation annotation in the hand of the sixteenth-century annotator suggest that no effort was made to avoid these types of marginal comments.[14]

Three examples of the Textual Extrapolation annotation, found one after another at Passus VII:292, 295 and 300, fol. 25r deserve particular attention. This passage describes those members of society who excuse themselves from the pilgrimage, choosing "Actif" life rather than "Contemplatif" life, thus rejecting the invitation to God's kingdom:

ȝe *villam emi* q*uo*d oen and now — vaynglory
y moste thyder/To loke how me liketh hit and toek
his leue at peres/An other anoen ryht nede he sayde
hadde/To falwe with fyue ȝokes for thy me byhoueth — Covetise
/To goo with a good wil and graytheliche hem dryue
/For thy p*ra*ye y ȝow peres p*a*raunt*er* ȝyf ȝe meten/Treuth
telleth hym this that y be excused/Thenne was oen
hihte actyf an hosbonde he semede/I haue wedded — lechery
a wyf wel wantowne of man*ner*es.

Clearly, the annotator was concerned with this issue as he glosses the passage with moral disparagement: "vaynglory," glosses the line, "ȝe *villam emi* q*uo*d oen and now y moste thyder/To loke how me liketh hit" (lines 292–93),[15] a striking attack on those who forsake the kingdom of heaven for their own personal gain and glory, and "covetise" glosses a reference to those who choose not to abandon worldly possessions for the kingdom of God. The passage goes on to describe Actif, a man whose married state prevents him from taking part in the pilgrimage. Shocked by Actif's rejection of the pilgrimage and perhaps more so by the qualities of his wife ("wel wantowne of man*ner*es"), the annotator writes "lechery" in the margin.

The issue of lechery is, in fact, a significant concern for this annotator. There are numerous occasions throughout the poem in which he annotates passages directly concerned with the issue of lechery and the pleasures of the flesh: at Passus III:57, fol. 3r, he writes "lechery" next to Mede's speech on the desires of the flesh; at Passus III:166, fol. 4v, he marks a *nota* next to a passage which describes Mede as "tikel of here tayl"; at Passus VI:170–71, fol. 17r, he writes "luxuria," the fourth deadly sin; at Passus X:283, fol. 39r, he writes "weddyng" next to a passage encouraging marriage and warning against lechery; and at Passus XI:173–74, fol. 42r, he writes *concupiscencia carnis et oculorum*, a reference to the two maids, "Lust-of-the-flesh" and "Lust-of-the-eyes." The sixteenth-century annotator is clearly concerned with topics of moral concern, in particular, those dealing with sexual immorality. It raises the question as to why he should be so diligent about offering moral verdicts on so many passages dealing with sexual impurity. Could this reader be annotating the text knowing that someone else would also be reading it, perhaps a spouse or family member? This is not to suggest that the annotator was a professional reader, but rather a private reader who knew that his marginal comments would be read by an impressionable family member.

There is also evidence in the sixteenth-century marginalia that the annotator may have had early Protestant leanings. A piece of this evidence may be found in the annotation at Passus XII:84, fol. 45r, which is again an example of the annotator's consistent use of the Textual Extrapolation annotation:

God of his godnesse y sey his grete wille/And withouten
mo bedes byddynge his bone was vnderfonge/And y saued as Iustice
ye may se withoute syngynge of mo masses/Loue withoute

lele byleue as my lawe ryhtfol/Sauede me sarrasyn soule
and body bothe.

In this passage, Trajan explains how he was saved despite not being baptized. In annotating this passage with "Iustice," the annotator is most likely referring to the salvation of Trajan as an exemplar for true justice. In Douce 104, the annotator annotates this same passage with "troian þe trew hempero*wr* and a pagan," another example of the Textual Extrapolation annotation. As Kerby-Fulton explains,

> [i]t supplies information (that Trajan was an emperor) not given in the text, but more importantly, it comes out in support of Trajan as "trew." Modern readers may perhaps not realize how troubling the issue of Trajan's salvation could be. In Douce 104 the other reader response we have, the illustrator's, is entirely negative. Trajan is represented as a pagan—and therefore grotesquely . . . Trajan's story was a crux for theologians debating issues of grace and salvation, and discreet writers seem to have avoided pronouncing upon it.[16]

As the Digby 102 annotation "Iustice" shows, the sixteenth-century annotator in Digby 102 appears to be supporting that side of the debate which defends salvation by grace; grace which offers consolation to the righteous unbaptized and contends with those who have placed all their security in baptism and following the law. Just as the Douce 104 annotator supports the "trewe" nature of Trajan and his story, the early-sixteenth-century annotator in Digby 102 hails its "justice." In siding with Trajan, the annotator reveals his liberal thinking on the subject and thus, early Protestant tendencies.

A number of the sixteenth-century annotations reveal an interest in legal issues, and one of the more interesting is found at Passus II:205, fol. 1v:

	now by crist
	q*uod* the kyng and y cacche myhte/Fals or Fauel or
Rex precipit	here felawe Lyare/y wole be awreke in the wreches
attachiare	and on here werkes alle/And do hem hange by the
falshede et	halse and alle that hem maynteyneth/Shal neu*ere*
alie	man on this molde maynprise the leste/Bote riht as
	the lawe loketh lat falle on hem alle/And comaundede

> a constable that kam at the furst/Go atache tho
> tyrauntes for eny tresor y hote.

Even though no Latin is present in the text, there is good reason for the annotator's use of Latin here.[17] In this passage, the King commands the arrest of Falseness and others. The legal term "attachen," which occurs in line 211, means "[t]o secure (somebody or something) for legal jurisdiction and disposal, to take or place under the control of a court; to arrest or seize by authority of a writ of attachment."[18] The king's commanded attachment of persons was an established procedure in English common law; the writ of attachment sent out under the king's name was a writ of *praecipe* and was always in Latin. To anyone who knew about English common law, the annotation, *Rex precipit attachiare falshede et alie,* would be recognizable and entirely appropriate, especially in its Latin form. In glossing the passage in such a way, the sixteenth-century annotator reveals a knowledge of legal language and process and an interest in a section of the poem dealing with legal procedures.

The sixteenth-century annotator's interest in legal issues is further revealed at Passus III:26, fol. 2v, where he notes the arrival of "Clerkes" in a passage in which they meet with Mede. He also marks line 34 of the same Passus with a *nota,* the point at which Mede assures the clerks of their profitable positions in the court. This concern over passages dealing with the law is also apparent in the annotations "mede ledith lawe" at Passus III:194–95, fol. 5r and "nota mede lettith lawes" in the same passus at line 450–51, fol. 8v. This attention to such passages suggests, of course, that the annotator may have been a lawyer or a legal clerk and so was familiar with legal language and process.

The early-sixteenth-century annotations also show a peculiar use of literary bilingualism. As shown by a few examples above, the annotator had the habit of occasionally annotating in Latin where no Latin appears in the body of the text. The Latin terms, however, would have been recognizable to someone who knew little Latin. There are also nine sixteenth-century annotations written in Middle English where the same word or phrase has been written in Latin in the body of the text. An example of this may be found at Passus XXI:204, fol. 87v:

> I wondred what that was and wagged Conscience
> The holy goste /And was afered for the lyhte for in fuyres liknesse
> /*Spiritus paraclitus* ouerspredde hem alle.

In translating *Spiritus paraclitus* into "The holy goste," the sixteenth-century annotator makes a simple translation from Latin to Middle English. If the annotator had an adequate knowledge of Latin, as revealed in his Latin marginalia, why would he gloss the text with such a simple translation? Could this suggest that the annotator was glossing the text for readers whose Latin was not as advanced as his own?

In addition to the translations from Latin to Middle English and vice versa, there are a few cases in which the early-sixteenth-century annotator comments on a Latin phrase in the text with a slightly different Latin phrase in the margin. One of these annotations occurs at Passus XVII:141, fol. 66r:

dilige deum propter deum id est propter veritatem/et inimicum tuum propter	
mandatum id est propter legem/et amicum propter amorem id est propter	nota de amore
caritatem /loue god for he is goed and ground of alle	dei et proxime
treuthe/Loue thyn enemy entierly godes heste to folfille	
/loue thy frend that folweth thy will that is thy faire soule.	

The annotator sums up the lengthy Latin phrase in the body of the text with a short Latin phrase in the margin, which translated reads, "note well concerning love of God and neighbour." It is interesting that the annotator excludes any reference to loving your enemy, which is clearly part of the message in the text.

This style of literary bilingualism occurs once more at Passus XIX:214, fol. 76r:

To alle vnkynde	nota de ingratitu
creatures as Crist hym sulue witnesseth/*Amen dico*	dine
vobis nescio vos.	

In this instance, the sixteenth-century annotator notes Christ's words, translated as "Truly I say to you, I do not know you" (Matt. 25.12), with *nota de ingratitudine.* The Latin word *ingratus* does appear four lines later so there is, of course, the likelihood that the annotator read the entire passage in full before annotating, but it is interesting that the annotator felt the need to mark this passage, which alludes to the parable of the wise and foolish virgins,[19] with the word *ingratitudine.* Other examples of this type of annotation occur at Passus XV:225a, fol. 57r, where he writes *nota bene de papa* next to a Latin quotation from Paul, refering to Paul as *papa,* and at Passus XVI:90, fol. 59v, where he writes *nota bene de paupertate* next to the line, "lasse boest hit maketh/To breke a beggares bagge then an yre-bounden coffre."

In an attempt to get closer to the identity of the early-sixteenth century annotator of Digby 102, it is helpful to compare his interests and concerns with those of the annotators of HM 143 and Douce 104. As Kerby-Fulton tells us in her comparison of the annotators of HM 143 and Douce 104, neither annotator shows much concern with issues of social domestic advice such as marriage and sexuality:

> the kind of interest [the Douce 104 annotator] takes in marriage is of a social and theological kind, such as one might expect from someone trained in pastoral care. Langland's extensive discussion of marriage in passus X provokes three notes from [Douce 104] (and none from [HM 143] whatsoever). [Douce 104's] notes betray no interest in property, sexuality, or romance (all topics covered by Langland), but rather in the social and moral ramifications of illegitimate children or ill-advised marriage.[20]

In contrast to these two annotators, Digby 102's early-sixteenth-century annotator shows considerable interest in social domestic issues. The Digby annotator's reaction to the discussion of marriage in Passus X is rather extensive and he remarks not only on the moral ramifications of illegitimate children and ill-advised marriage ("bastardes" at l. 210, fol. 38r and *nota bene* at l. 257, fol. 39r), but also shows an interest in advice given on widows and on the sexual behavior of married men ("wydowes" at l. 278, fol. 39r and "weddid men" at l. 287–88, fol. 39r). Perhaps this interest in domestic advice suggests that the annotator's goal in glossing the text was two-fold: to aid in personal reading and comprehension, and also to highlight passages of significant concern for a family member. With so much marginal emphasis on marriage, children and sexuality, this family member may very well have been a spouse.

The enthusiasm and consistency with which the sixteenth-century reader annotated the text suggest he was a concerned reader of

Piers. In many ways, Digby 102's sixteenth-century annotations are entirely unlike those of the more sophisticated HM 143. As Kerby-Fulton suggests, the annotator of HM 143 engaged in

> a certain kind of "professionalism"—"professional" slacking off on a commissioned job that the scribe sometimes apparently found tedious, especially toward the end of a passus or of the manuscript itself. Annotations were the first aspect of a text to suffer when professional boredom set in, because they were most disposable.[21]

The greatest number of annotations by the sixteenth century annotator in Digby 102, however, occurs in Passus XXII, clearly not evidence of a disinterested reader. Whether the sixteenth-century annotator was a paid scribe, annotating the text for someone else, or a reader of the poem, annotating for his own private use and perhaps for the use of a spouse and other family member, the annotations offer a glimpse into a sixteenth-century reading of *Piers.* One might expect the content of the annotations of the sixteenth-century reader to differ radically from those of the scribes working sixty-five to seventy-five years earlier, but this is not the case. The manner in which the later annotator marks up the text does indeed differ from that of the scribes; the abundant use of the Textual Extrapolation annotation and the enthusiasm and consistency with which he annotated support the argument that he may have been annotating more for private use and perhaps for the private use of someone familiar than out of a professional concern for public readership.

The content and meaning of many of the later annotations, however, have much in common with the scribal annotations; were it not for the handwriting of the later annotator, which clearly places him in the early sixteenth century, it would often be difficult to distinguish many of the later annotations from those copied many years prior. With the exception of the sympathy for Trajan, which is vaguely anti-ecclesiastical, the later annotator shows no signs of overt Protestantism, nor does he have any difficulty understanding Middle English or reading the various scribal hands.

Whether they are the product of a scribe in the early-fifteenth century or a reader in the early-sixteenth century, marginal annotations do indeed provide evidence of the early influence of *Piers Plowman* on its readers. Despite its fragmentary beginning, Digby 102 is a fascinating

Piers Plowman manuscript as it offers scholars an opportunity to study the influence of Langland's text on an early-sixteenth-century reader, a reader who, in all likelihood, was reading for private, family use, commenting freely on those passages of the most interest. In any discussion of the early responses to *Piers*, it seems a mistake to perceive the manuscripts as a reflection of the work and interests of one man alone, William Langland. When trying to recreate the historical context in which a text such as *Piers* was first read and received, it is better to view the text as one which was ultimately produced from more than one hand. As Jerome McGann points out, modern editors of *Piers* have tended to ignore the historical context available through manuscript study: "the dynamic social relations which always exist in literary production—the dialectic between the historically located individual author and the historically developing institutions of literary production—tends to become obscure."[22] In attempting to discover something of the historical impact a text such as *Piers* exerted on its readers, it is necessary to recognize the concerns and interests of everyone who left a mark on the manuscript, perhaps especially its annotators.

A Note on the Transcription

This transcription presents the complete marginalia of Oxford, Bodleian Library, MS Digby 102. The folio numbering used is based on the following collation: ii (modern) + ii; 1–4; 5: three leaves; 6–128; 138 (lacks 8); 14–188; 198 (lacks 5–8). The passus and line numbering used is based on Derek Pearsall's 1978 edition of the C-text. The original spelling as well as the distinctions between "u" and "v" and "i" and "j" have been preserved. Capital letters are used only where they occur in the manuscript. Both English and Latin words which are divided by lineation have been silently restored and all Latin abbreviations have been silently expanded. All expansions of English abbreviations, however, have been italicized. All notations written in hands other than the hand of the sixteenth-century annotator appear in boldface type.[23]

Apparatus

The transcription which follows is set out according to the format recommended by Malcolm Parkes,[24] and the following symbols have been used:

[ ] enclose words and letters which have been deleted by the scribe by means of crossing out, erasure or expunctuation.

{ }	enclose letters which have been supplied in the transcription where the manuscript is deficient through damage, or where letters have been hidden by the binding. Where traces of the letter are still visible in the manuscript, the supplied letter has been printed in roman type. Where no traces of the letter remain, the supplied letter has been italicized. Where it is not possible to determine the nature of the missing letters from the context, dots have been supplied to indicate the number of letters which would fit into the space available.

For Digby 102 in particular, the following symbols have been used:

I_	indicates the presence of a combination bracket and underline.
o~	indicates the annotation has been circled in the text.

Passus II:

Folio	*Line*	*Content*
1r	156	gyle
1r	169	lawe
1r	177–78	mede ridit on a shiref
1r	182	provisers shale s*er*ue pr*e*lat*es*
1v	200	Sothenesse
1v	203	Concyens
1v	205	Rex precipit attachiare falshede et alie
1v	219	**nota**
1v	220	Falshede to the frerys *and* gile to m*er*-chaunt*es*
1v	227	lyar to p*ar*don*ers*
2r	231	p*ar*don for pe{ns}
2r	233	leches
2r	240	lyar to Freris
2r	246	Nota de regno

Passus III:

Folio	*Line*	*Content*
2r	2	mede brought to the kyng
2v	14	Ioy the iustice cam to mede
2v	26	Clerk*es*
2v	34	nota
2v	38	A confesso*ur* to mede
2v	46	shrifte shameles
3r	55	Syngyng for mede
3r	57	lechery
3r	61	nota
3r	68–69	Nota of g*r*auyng in wallys
3r	77–78	pyllery for misdoers
3r	82	Regrato*urz*
3v	88	**nota**
3v	95	gylours
3v	113	vsurers *and* reg*r*ato*urz* be not enf*r*aunchised
4r	119	mayres
4r	131	The kyng *and* mede
4r	143	loue treuthe *and* councell of reson
4v	154–57	concyens is desired to wedde mede
4v	166	nota
4v	179	mede copith the co*m*missary
5r	194–95	mede ledith lawe
5r	202–03	mede *and* religion
5r	210	clerk*es* *and* couetise
5r	218	concyens accusid mede to the kyng
5v	244	**nota**
5v	250	a conquero*ur*
5v	258	nota
6r	267	mede maketh loue
6r	293	**nota**
6r	296	a difference bytwene hyre *and* mede
6v	315–16	nota de adnullacione doni
6v	323	nota de salamone
7r	342	Relacio recta
7r	351	hope
7r	362	Relacio indirecta
7r	373	ryghtfull custom

7v	383–84	nota of comens
7v	402–03	Charitie
7v	406	o~**nota**
7v	408	what hurte is by mede
8r	435	nota
8v	450–51	nota mede lettith lawes
8v	453	love shall make lawe a laborer
8v	462	nota
8v	475	Nota
9r	488	Nota

Passus IV:

Folio	*Line*	*Content*
9r	8–9	reson to rule the realm*e*
9r	17–19	nota
9v	28–29	wytty man *and* wyly man
9v	45	I_{.}**billa**
9v	47	a bille by pees aȝenst wrong
10r	72	nota
10r	73–74	wisdom witte *and* mede
10r	89	nota
10v	95–97	mede agreid pees with wrong*e*
10v	101	nota
10v	107	Nota bene
10v	122	o~**nota**
11r	133–36	wrong*e* to be punyshyd for any mede
11r	158–59	maryage for good*es*
11v	168–71	mede *and* men of lawe muche treuthe lettith
11v	184–88	reson chaunceler to the kyng *and* concyens be Iuges in co*ur*t*es*
11v	189–91	vnfittyng sufferaunce

Passus V:

Folio	*Line*	*Content*
12r	16	idelnes
13r	83	prayers *and* penaunce is god labo*ur*
13r	111	reson revest as a pope concyens his crosier
13v	114	pestilence for synne
13v	124	nota hou oon shall com*me* to heven
13v	141	p*re*lat*es*
13v	147	religion
14r	151	o~**nota**
14r	158	I_**monachi etcetera**
14r	180–82	the kyng to love his comens
14v	188	vnitee
14v	196	nota pylgrymag*es*

Passus VI:

Folio	*Line*	*Content*
14v	3	Repentaunce
14v	20	I_**Superbia**
15v	64	I_**Inuidia**
16r	102	I_**Ira**
16v	147	o~**nota bene**
17r	166	nota
17r	170	[o~**luxuria**]
17r	170–71	luxuria
17v	196	covetise
18r	239	I_**Auaricia**
18r	256	nota bene
18v	257a	Restituc*io*u*n*
18v	287	o~**nota**
18v	290	nota bene
19r	299	o~**nota bene**
19r	300	of tithes
19r	309	A walssheman didde restituc*io*un
19r	315	**q*uar*t*us***
19r	323	nota for theym that haue not to restore
19v	350	o~**Gula etc**
20r	376	o~**nota**
21r	437	Abstinence

Passus VII:

Folio	*Line*	*Content*
21r	1	**media**
21r	3	Accidia
22r	70	**nota**
22r	84	sage foles
23r	152	**Spes**
23v	164	pylgryme
23v	176–79	pilgrymes knowith not trouthe
23v	182	**nota**
23v	183–84	ploughman sayd trouthe
23v	194–95	p*ro*pertees of trouthe
24r	205	wey to trouthe
24r	208	mekenes
24r	211	love god *and* thy neybur
24r	216	hono*ur* thy fad*er* *and* mod*er*
24r	222	**X precepta**
24v	229	Nota bene
24v	246	Grace
24v	255	trouthe
24v	262	nota
25r	269	grace
25r	270	vij sust*er*s that s*er*ue trouthe
25r	274	largitas
25r	284	cuttepurse
25r	288	mercy
25r	292	vaynglory
25r	295	Covetise
25r	300	lechery
25v	304	contemplacyon

Passus VIII:

Folio	*Line*	*Content*
25v	8	occupac*io*n for women
25v	22–23	knyghthode *and* ploughman
26r	36	nota bene
26r	40	take no yeft*es* of pore
26r	45	chorles bonys in charnell ar not knowen fr*o* lord*es*
26r	51	speke not agenst co*n*cyens n*e* holy chirche right
26v	68–72	Al treu crafty men *and* true laborers doo folowe trouth
26v	77–78	no tithes of dysers *and* suche unla*u*full getyng*es*
26v	81	piers ploughman is wyfe *and* his children
26v	85	nota bene
26v	96	pers testament
27r	128	lorels *and* fayto*u*rz
27v	150	waster
27v	161	knyght
27v	168	hunger
27v	bottom	**tertia pars**
28r	183	heremytes
28v	221–23	punyshe stray beggers with hunger
28v	232–33	wikkydly wonne wysly to be spente
29r	271	nota de dieta salubri
29r	287	nota almes to moste nedy
29v	295	leches
29v	316	piers mete
30r	333	wast*er*s mete
30r	339	vacabund*es* curse the kyng *and* his lawes
30r	345	Famyne to chastise wasters
30r	350	nota bene

Passus IX:

Folio	*Line*	*Content*
30v	15	byshoppis
30v	23	m*er*chauntz
30v	45	**nota**
30v	45	menne of law
31r	61	beggers
31r	73	nota almes
31v	98	nota bene
31v	106	**lollard**
32r	127a	**nota**
32r	129	mynstrellys
32r	140	heremytez
32v	167	nota
32v	190	holy heremytz
33r	199–200	heremyt*es* vnthryfty
33r	213–14	o~**nota**
33r	216	lollard*es*
33v	232	holy dayes to be kepte *and* fastyng dayes vnd*er* payn of dedly synne
33v	249	**nota**
33v	255	bisshops
34r	257	nota
34r	261–62	nota bene
34r	284	p*ar*don of pers
34v	291	doo well *and* haue well
34v	293	he that evyll lyvith evill he shale dye
34v	311	**nota**
34v	323	dowell passith pardon *and* pilgrymages to rome
35r	331	trentals is not so goode as doo welle
35r	344–45	p*ar*don auayleth lytell w*ith* out doo well

Passus X:

Folio	*Line*	*Content*
35r	4	doo welle
35v	31	nota bene
36r	74	**Thought**
36v	79–80	doo welle
36v	88–89	doo bettyr
36v	92	doo beste
37r	114	witte
37r	131–32	corpus et Anima
37r	136	Kynde
37r	143–44	In witte
37v	146	vij kep*ers* of the soule
37v	151–52	discripc*io*u*n* of kynde
37v	164a	nota bene
38r	200	love god
38r	210	bastard*es*
39r	255	**nota**
39r	257	nota bene
39r	276	**matri*monium***
39r	278	wydowes
39r	283	weddyng
39r	287–88	weddid men

Passus XI:

Folio	*Line*	*Content*
39v	1–2	witte wyfe is studye
39v	14–15	witte mengid w*ith* couetise is vsed
39v	19–20	o~**nota**
40r	37	**nota**
40r	38	of spekyng dyvinyte at bord*es*
40v	59	**nota**
41r	106	**nota**
41v	132	clergy
41v	154	**nota**
41v	160	**Trinit*e***
42r	173–74	concupiscencia carnis et oculorum
42r	189	Age
42r	196	Rechelesnesse
43r	242	nota bene
43r	249	**nota**

Passus XII:

Folio	*Line*	*Content*
44r	10–11	pena pecuniaria
44r	23	**nota**
45r	74	I_**Troianus**
45r	84	Iustice
45r	93	love and leaulte
45v	top left corner	**medius**
45v	115	lawe of love
45v	131	o*ur* lord in pore apparell
46r	140–42	pou*er*te is beste if pacyence folowe
46v	171	**paupertas**
46v	175–77	pacyent pou*er*te prynce of all vertues
47r	182	**nota**
47r	221	o~**nota**
47r	226	couetise

Passus XIII:

Folio	*Line*	*Content*
47v	32	**nota**
48r	40	m*er*chaunt
49r	115–16	o~**nota**
50r	180–83	mankynde is worse than best*es*
50r	195–95a	o~**nota**
50r	202–03	nota bene
50v	223a	**nota**

Passus XIV:

Folio	*Line*	*Content*
51r	18a	**imprecare**
51v	63	nota bene clergye
52r	73–74	Astronomy
53r	154–55	nota bene
53v	177	pecok
53v	197–98	nota of salamon *and* od*er*
54r	202	Imagynac*io*u*n*
54r	203	**nota**

Passus XV:

Folio	*Line*	*Content*
54r	9	Freres
54r	13	covetise ou*er*cam all sect*es* lered *and* lewde Curates
54v	26	Concyens *and* clergye *and* Resou*n*
54v	33	pacyence
54v	34	o~**nota**
55r	56–7	penau*ns*
55r	60	nota bene
55r	65–7	nota a doct*our* of dyvinte drank wyne
55r	76–7	Freres
55r	83	nota
55v	94	**nota**
55v	96	nota of the frere
56r	123–27	do well is as docto*ur* p*re*cheth do beste is to p*re*che *and* doo beste is to doo as he p*re*-cheth
56r	133	nota bene
56r	144–45	nota to get loue of thyn enemy
56r	149	nota
56r	154	o~**nota**
56v	158	pacientes vincunt
56v	170	nota
56v	179–80	**nota**
56v	185–87	pacyence sobrietas *and* sothffast byleve
56v	193	A mynstrell actiua vita
57r	225a	nota bene de papa
57v	250	voluntas dei to fynde al men
57v	255	sobrenes in the v wittes
58r	274–75	what is p*ar*fite pacience
58r	301	nota bene

Passus XVI:

Folio	*Line*	*Content*
58v	25	nota
58v	34–5	nota bene
59r	47–8	**nota**
59r	58	pride is in Riches
59v	90	nota bene de paupertate
59v	106	nota of maryage
60r	116	quid est paupertas
60r	117	o~**nota**
60r	127a	I_**paupertas**
60v	157	actif had a leder that is lib*er*um arbitriu*m*
61r	172–73	lib*er*um arbitriu*m*
61r	183–86	the differens of anima *and* animus sensus et cetera
61r	200a	**Anima**
61r	200a	nota bene
61v	204–05	**nota** bisshipis haue diu*er*se namys
61v	211	lucifers knyght*es*
61v	216	nota bene
61v	222–25	connyng to knowe scienc*es* put Eve oute of paradyse
61v	237	nota bene
62r	242–49	As all goode co*m*myth of holy chirche by p*re*stehode so oute of evyll prestis all evyll co*m*myth
62r	263	ypocrysy
62r	271a	nota bene
62v	271a-274	goodis ill geten wikked men shall have
62v	295	Charite
63r	312	Charite
63v	340	mery at mete
63v	363	Auaricia

Passus XVII:

Folio	*Line*	*Content*
64r	3	irascimur et nolite peccare
64r	18	**nota**
64r	19	holy heremit
64v	42–3	take that right wylle
64v	47	**nota**
64v	52	Mesure
64v	53–54	Mortmayn
64v	61–62	to helpe thy kyn is charite
65r	69–72	Clerk*es* kepe crist*es* tresire that pore me*n* shold have
65r	90	nota bene
65r	92	if men doo well all thyng*es* shalbe plente
65v	106	science is not had nowe p*er*fitely
65v	111	**nota**
65v	126	charite is to loue god *and* doo aft*er* his lawes
66r	141	nota de amore dei et proxime
66r	164	macomete
66v	195–96	nota bene
67r	206–07	couetise shall cause the chirche to be lowed
67v	214	**nota**
68r	281	norma presulis
68r	285a	o~**nota**

Passus XVIII:

Folio	*Line*	*Content*
68v	10	nota
68v	14	Caritas
69r	28	sancta trinitas
69r	31	thre wynde the world the Flesshe *and* the devyll
69r	40	**nota**
69r	61–64	nota why sume appils be grett*er* than odyr
69v	76	I_**nota**
69b	83	vita Actiua et contemplatiua
70r	123	**Anunciacio**
71v	198	nota
71v	202	**Trinitas**
71v	214	**3 quartus**
71v	216	nota bene
72r	257	nota bene

Passus XIX:

Folio	*Line*	*Content*
72v	1	Spes
73r	18–19	dilige deum and proximum
73v	59	hope w*ith* Moises com*m*aundement*es*
73v	64	Samaritauns
74r	83–84	**nota**
74r	96	nota bene of the olde lawe
74v	127	newe lawe
75r	145	nota
75v	202	**nota**
76r	214	nota de ingratitudine
76r	227a	**mihi**
76r	229	diues
76r	235a	a nygard
76v	246–47	nota bene to dep*ar*te w*ith* yo*u*r good*es*
76v	252–53	that kynde dothe vnkynde fordothe
76v	262	peccatum in spiritum sanctum
77r	272–73	o~**nota**

Passus XX:

Folio	*Line*	*Content*
78r	22–23	**passio domini**
78v	53–54	de passione Christi
79v	115	Mercy
79v	123	Treuthe
80r	144–45	**nota**
80r	165	nota bene
80r	168	Rightwisnesse *and* pees
80v	204	**nota**
81v	272	o~**nota**
82v	322–23	it is not well goten there gyle is the rote
83r	340	nota bene
83r	355	mendacium
84r	419–20a	brodyrs in blode *and* in baptisme

Passus XXI:

Folio	*Line*	*Content*
85v	41–42	o~**nota**
86r	84–85	magi *and* their offeryng*es*
86v	115	diliges inimici
86v	128–29	Miracula Christi dobette
87r	154	o~**nota**
87r	156	Resurrectio cristi
87r	161a-62	that woman knowith may be noo councell
87v	182–83	dobeste perdon
87v	187	redde q*uo*d debes
87v	197–99	Concyence spake of criste *and* of the crosse
87v	204	The holy goste
87v	208	Concyence
88r	211–13	grace is w*ith* perse the ploughman
88r	215–16	diuisiones graciarum
88r	222	Antecriste
88r	223–24	False flat*er*ers shalbe curate3
88r	233	nota bene
88r	234	diuersitatem graciarum

88v	255	nota bene
88v	256	concyens to be kyng *and* crafte to be stiward
88v	276	iiij cardynall vertues
89r	304	nota bene de iusticia
89v	326	Mercy
89v	330	vnite all holy chirche
89v	334–35	pers goth to tylye trouth
89v	338–39	pride *and* his s*eru*a*u*nt*es* to lette pers
90r	347	**nota bene**
90r	349	colourid confessioun
90r	359	grace
90r	361–62	kynde witte
90r	370	Iiuro*ur*ȝ
90v	375–78	holynes to growe *and* to stinde eu*ery* man helpe
90v	385	sacramentum altaris
90v	390	Redde q*uo*d debes
90v	407	nota a brewer
91r	410	o~**nota**
91r	411	a curate
91r	417	cardynals
91r	425–26	nota of the pope
91r	435–37	the ploughman tilleth for gode *and* bad
91r	442	nota
91v	443	nota de papa
92r	479a	nota bene

Passus XXII:

Folio	*Line*	*Content*
92r	10–11	nede hath noo lawe
92r	26–27	nota bene
92v	46	necessitas
92v	53	**nota Antecristus**
93r	70–72	pryde bare antecrist*es* baner
93r	80	I_ **natura**
93r	84	o~**nota**
93r	85	kynde
93r	89	Elde age
93r	91	kynde
93r	92	dethe
93v	104	kynde
93v	110	I_ **Fortuna**
93v	111	lecherye
93v	121–23	covetise ou*er*cam concyence *and* all cardynall vertus
93v	126–27	Symony suyd covetise
93v	132	nota bene
94r	135	Iugys
94r	137	I_ **Arches**
94r	138	Syvile t*ur*nyd in to symony
94r	143	I_ **vita**
94r	157–59	lyfe *and* his leman Fortune
94r	160–62	Sleuthe weddid wanhope
94r	166	I_ **nota Senex**
94v	171	lyfe
94v	178	Age made man balde
94v	191–93	Age takith awey tethe *and* bryngith gowtys
94v	198	o~**nota**
94v	200–01	kynde drewe a way *and* dethe drewe nere
95r	204	vnyte
95r	218	I_ **nota sacerdotes**
95r	221	nota bene
95r	223–26	vices had vnyte *and* concyens down
95r	228	**nota**
95r	228–30	conciens callid clergy to helpe
95r	230	I_ **Fr*er*es**

95r	233	freris cam for couetise to haue cure of soule
95v	240–42	let freris lyve like beggers or by aungels fode
95v	256a	o~**nota**
95v	269–70	freris be withoute nombre
96r	275–76	all thyng*es* in comen
96r	278–79	non concupisces rem proximi tui
96r	282–83	I_**nota**
96r	288–90	confession of iurro*ur* *and* od*er* false
96r	299	concyens was w*ith* vnite
96r	302	Ipocrisy
96v	306–08	gode shrifte wolde haue sharpe salue redde q*uo*d debes
96v	315	Frere flater
96v	331	o~**nota**
96v	334–36	contric*io*u*n* hurte with Ipocrisye
97r	340	frere penitrans domos
97r	347	nota
97r	362–63	the frere gaue contriciou*n* a plastyr of a pryvy payment
97v	369	nota bene
97v	379–80	no drede of synne
97v	383–86	concyence is gone to seke pers plough man *and* grace

University of Victoria

Notes

1. General discussions of marginalia found in *Piers Plowman* manuscripts include: George Russell, "'As They Read It': Some Notes on Early Responses to the C-Version of *Piers Plowman*," *Leeds Studies in English 20* (1989), 173–89; George Russell, "Some Early Responses to the C-Version of *Piers Plowman*," *Viator* 15 (1984), 275–303; and Wendy Scase, *Piers Plowman and the New Anti-clericalism* (Cambridge, 1989). Kathleen Scott offers a detailed discussion of the marginal illustrations in Oxford, Bodleian Library, MS Douce 104 in "The Illustrations of *Piers Plowman* in Bodleian Library MS Douce 104," *Yearbook of Langland Studies* 4 (1990), 1–86; and in "The Illustrations of MS Douce 104," in *Piers Plowman: A Facsimile of Bodleian Library, Oxford MS Douce 104*, eds. Derek Pearsall and Kathleen Scott, (Cambridge, 1992), pp. xxvii-xciv; and Derek Pearsall discusses the written marginalia of MS Douce 104 in the introduction of *Piers Plowman: A Facsimile of Bodleian Library, Oxford MS Douce 104.* Carl James Grindley discusses a method of classification for late medieval insular marginalia in "Reading *Piers Plowman* C-Text Annotations: Notes toward the Classification of Printed Marginalia in Texts from British Isles 1300–1641," *English Literary Studies* 85, forthcoming

2001. For complete transcriptions and discussions of *Piers* marginalia, see Tanya Schaap, "From Scribe to Reader: A Study of the Marginal Annotations of Piers Plowman C-Text, Oxford, Bodleian Library, Digby 102," MA thesis, University of Victoria, 1996; Carl James Grindley, "From Creation to Desecration: The Marginal Annotations of Piers Plowman C-Text HM 143," MA thesis, University of Victoria, 1989; Carl James Grindley, "The Life of a Book: British Library Additional Manuscript 35157 in Historical Context," PhD diss., University of Glasgow, 1997; Kathryn Kerby-Fulton's and Denise Despres's transcription of the written marginalia of MS Douce 104 in *Iconography and the Professional Reader: The Politics of Book Production in the Douce Piers Plowman* (Minneapolis, 1999); Marie-Claire Uhart's transcriptions of Oxford, Bodleian Library, MS Digby 145, British Library, MS Additional 35287, MS Douce 104, and British Library, MS Additional 35157 in "The Early Reception of *Piers Plowman*," PhD diss., University of Leicester, 1986 and C. David Benson and Lynne S. Blanchfield's transcriptions of the marginalia of the B-text manuscripts in *The Manuscripts of Piers Plowman: the B-version* (London, 1998). In "'As They Read It,'" Russell offers transcribed extracts from MS Douce 104, British Library, MS Additional 35157, and MS HM 143.

2. See Schaap, "From Scribe to Reader"; Janet Coleman's brief discussion of Digby 102 in *English Literature in History, 1350–1400: Medieval Readers and Writers* (London, 1981), pp. 98–110; and J. Kail's complete transcription of the political poems found in Digby 102 in *Twenty-Six Political and Other Poems* (Digby 102), EETS o.s. 124 (London, 1904).
3. I should like to thank Dr. Kathryn Kerby-Fulton for her many helpful suggestions and encouragement during this study.
4. For information on Thomas Allen and his manuscripts, see Andrew G. Watson, "Thomas Allen of Oxford and his manuscripts," in *Medieval Scribes, Manuscripts, and Libraries: Essays Presented to N.R. Ker*, eds. M. B. Parkes and Andrew G. Watson (London, 1978), pp. 279–314.
5. There are two annotations in Digby 102 ("Thought" at fol. 36r and *imprecare* at fol. 51r) which are neither scribal nor in the hand of the sixteenth-century annotator. They are copied in an even later hand and are perhaps additions made by later owners of the text such as Sir Kenelm Digby or Sir Thomas Allen.
6. Paul Saenger and Michael Heinlen, "Incunable Description and Its Implication for the Analysis of Fifteenth Century Reading Habits," *Printing the Written Word: the Social History of Books, circa 1450–1520*, ed. Sandra L. Hindman (Ithaca, 1991), p. 239.
7. Saenger and Heinlen, "Incunable Description," p. 244.
8. Kathryn Kerby-Fulton, "The Professional Reader as Annotator," *Iconography and the Professional Reader in the Douce Piers Plowman*, p. 69.
9. All passus and line numbering are taken from *Piers Plowman by William Langland: an edition of the C-text*, ed. Derek Pearsall (Berkeley, 1978). All quotations from *Piers Plowman* are transcribed directly from Digby 102.
10. Grindley, "From Creation to Desecration," p. 56 and Grindley, "*Reading Piers Plowman*," forthcoming.
11. Scase, *Piers Plowman and the New Anticlericalism*, p. 155.
12. Since the identity of the sixteenth-century annotator is unknown, there is no sure way of knowing whether the annotator was male or female. On the basis of content,

one might assume the annotator was male: the annotator is familiar with Latin (commenting in Latin on sections of the text where no Latin is present) and also shows a keen interest in those sections of the poem dealing with legal issues; the annotation *Rex precepit attachiare falshede et alie* on fol. 1v, in particular, reveals the annotator's knowledge of legal language and process, suggesting that he was perhaps trained as a lawyer or legal clerk. The marginalia in the hand of Anne Fortescue in MS Digby 145 provide evidence of a female annotator using Latin in her annotations, so despite the use of Latin, there is a possibility that the annotator here was female. As well, the annotator's interest and concern over domestic issues such as marriage and sexuality may support the argument that she was female. At the present time, there is no way to know with certainty. For convenience, I will refer to the annotator using the masculine pronoun.

13. Grindley, "From Creation," p. 56.
14. Various instances of the Textual Extrapolation annotation include "heremytes vnthryfty" at Passus IX:199–200, fol. 33r (a passage on providing food for the hermits), *corpus et Anima* at Passus X:131–32, fol. 37r (a passage describing how Dowell lives with Anima; there is no mention in this section of the body, or *corpus*), "coueltise" at Passus XII:226, fol. 47r (a passage describing the greed of rich men), "Astronomy" at Passus XIV:73–74, fol. 52r (a passage describing men of natural intelligence who lack the revelation of the Christian faith), an annotation which occurs at the same location in the text in both HM 143 and Add. 35157; and "nota bene of the old lawe" at Passus XIX:96–98, fol. 74r (a passage describing the Trinity as Abraham taught) and "newe lawe" at Passus XIX:127–31 (a passage describing the Trinity as Christ taught).
15. *Villam emi*, 'I have bought a field' (Luke 14.18), see Pearsall, *An edition of the C-text*, p. 144. Pearsall explains that "[i]n lines 292–304 (added in C), dealing with those who excuse themselves from the pilgrimage, L[angland] paraphrases the answers of those who decline the invitation to the great supper (i.e. refuse to participate as Christ's disciples in the kingdom of heaven) in the parable of Luke 14.16–24."
16. Kerby-Fulton, "The Professional Reader," p. 85.
17. I should like to thank Professor Tim Haskett for his helpful observations on the implications of this annotation.
18. John A. Alford, *Piers Plowman: A Glossary of Legal Diction* (Cambridge, 1988), p. 11.
19. See Pearsall, *Piers Plowman*, p. 52, n. 185 and p. 314, n. 214a.
20. Kerby-Fulton, "The Professional Reader," p. 89.
21. Kerby-Fulton, "The Professional Reader," p. 85.
22. Jerome J. McGann, *A Critique of Modern Textual Criticism* (Chicago, 1983), p. 81.
23. All of the annotations in boldface type, with the exception of "Thought" on fol. 36r and *imprecare* on fol. 51r, are scribal, that is to say, they are all written in hands contemporary to the manuscript's creation.
24. Parkes, *English Cursive Hands*, pp. xxviii-xxix.

The Vernacular Reader: Three Case Studies of the Transmission of Latin Texts into Vernacular Contexts

Introduction by Nicholas Watson

The three articles collected here throw light on disparate aspects of the hugely complex history of vernacularization in late-medieval England and Ireland. Collectively, they testify far more strongly to the variety of forces and processes involved in the movement of Latin thought and texts into the English and Anglo-Norman vernaculars, or the circulation of vernacular texts by Latinate clerics, than they do to that movement's coherence. At a time in Middle English studies when the vernacular has acquired some of the cachet that presently accrues everywhere to underdogs and margins—and in which the emergence of English into prominence is often understood in terms of a simple dichotomy between the rebellion of 1381 on the one hand and "Lancastrian language policy" on the other—this is surely more of an advantage than the opposite. Indeed, the one substantial thing the articles have in common, which itself demands that I describe them separately here, is their demonstration of the importance of the detailed work they represent: the kind of work which, so often in the history of medieval studies, has been as powerful an agent of change in our perceptions of the field as the at first sight more ambitious arguments of generalists. Once a lot more detailed work like this has been done, our map of late medieval English literary history, and the place of various types of Anglo-Norman and Middle English written discourse within that history, will become far more lucid than it is at present. Of course, it may also become too complex ever to be quite clear again; and even if it does become clear, it will not be the map we have now.

Although Patricia Baer's article "Cato's 'Trace': Literacy, Readership, and the Process of Revision in *Piers Plowman*," traverses ground I had imagined to have been criss-crossed thoroughly already, it finds new landmarks there. The putative author of a set of *Distichs* used in elementary instruction for much of the Middle Ages, Cato is one of those classical figures whose ethical pronouncements were so fully adopted by medieval Christendom that his "pagan" past was sometimes quite forgotten. Dante positions him, with characteristic precision, at the very foot of the mountain of Purgatory, that giant school for souls, where he must remain throughout time to aid those who come to learn there, an old man worthy of the reverence shown a father (*Purgatorio* I.32–33)—but from whence (at least according to Virgil) he will rise up at the last day in the bright garments of the saved (I.75). Around 1483–84, William Caxton, with characteristic business acumen, published a translation of the *Distichs* into English, at about the same time he produced the first printed edition of Chaucer's *Canterbury Tales.* Yet despite these completely different commendations of Cato by two of Langland's near-contemporaries, his role in *Piers Plowman* has previously been analyzed, by Andrew Galloway and others, as though his wisdom were considered both rudimentary and ultimately not quite Christian: a candidate for what Galloway sees as a systematic excision from Langland's final revision. Baer shows that Cato mattered to Langland, and that the *Distichs* were never left behind by a poet who, if he knew anything for sure, knew that rudimentary instruction contains all the seeds of moral and intellectual progress, and must be returned to again and again by those who cannot enter the kingdom of heaven as wise doctors, only as children. Indeed, as Baer notes, in pursuit of this vision of the faith, Langland's C-text "elevate[s] Cato from the role of a pedagogue to that of a prophet." Following Cato's "trace" through the versions of *Piers Plowman,* and by way of the controversial questions of Langland's audience (elite, vernacular, or mixed?), and even of the order of the versions, Baer makes a compelling case for the seriousness with which Langland took a medieval school-text and its author: as a bridge between all the audiences he can have hoped to address, all the levels of learning his great poem incorporates.

In their study and edition "Recommended Reading: Defining the Medieval Visionary. A Facing-Page Comparison of the Middle English and Latin Texts of the *Epistola solitarii ad reges* of Alfonso of Jaén," Arne Jönsson and Rosalynn Voaden give us the wherewithal to make a detailed analysis of the vernacularization of one, potentially contentious, religious text: the treatise Bridget of Sweden's chief promoter wrote in defence of the validity of her visions and mission as a writer. Where Baer finds an ambitious vernacular writer enthusiastic about his connection with a grammar school-text, which he seems to see as enhancing, rather than compromising, the dignity of his project, Jönsson and Voaden present a Middle English translation which, despite the accuracy of what it does contain, appears to have severely excised the very passages its putative female readers might most have wanted to read: those passages that might have given validity to their own visionary experiences and ideas about recording them. The late fourteenth-century compiler of *The Chastizing of God's Children* rounds off his version of portions of the *Epistola solitarii* with the blithe assertion that "Many men and wymmen haue hadde and haue reuelacions and visions," the "spirite of profecie," "deuocion" or "grete plente of teeris," as a result of which they comfort and convert others "either with deuout speche or prechyng, or with hooli teermes in writyng and makynge of bookes in Latyn or in Ynglisshe" (*Chastizing* 182.15–183.1): a statement that seems to welcome the process by which vision turns into book, even if the author does then add that such things "preuen nat a man ne womman hooli ne parfite" (183.2). Yet, although the surviving manuscript of the Middle English *Epistola* was copied at about the same time *The Book of Margery Kempe* was being written, in the same county of Norfolk, this version of Alphonse's treatise seems to imply a far less enthusiastic response to the prospect of English visionary women turning their hands to this particular form of imitatio Birgittae than does *The Chastizing.*[1]

All the same, how much is left here for the persistent vernacular reader, not simply of pointers to how the discourse of discretio spirituum works, but of evidence for the seriousness with which women's visions—and the claims they have historically made for themselves as prophets and writers—have been taken by the doctors and auctores of the Church! While the main representative of Bridgettine spirituality in fifteenth-century England, Syon abbey, persisted for more than a century without producing a single known visionary or, perhaps, writer, Bridgettine material was not read thus either by Margery Kempe in the 1430s or by Elizabeth Barton, welcomed at Syon in the 1520s for her stand over Henry VIII's divorce, and another powerful prophetic reader of Bridget. It seems unlikely that anyone who would undertake the translation of a text so potent as the *Epistola solitarii*, in however attenuated a form, into the vernacular spoken and read by would-be visionary women, could have been unaware of what he might be letting loose on the world. Caution in a translation like this may be little more than the ostentatious bolting of the stable door after the horse has fled.

Finally, Kathryn Kerby-Fulton's and Ruth Horie's "The French Version of the *Modus tenendi parliamentum* in the Courtenay Cartulary: An Introduction and Transcription"—the one political work in this group—we have an example of a vernacular translation that is unquestionably radical and that, just as unquestionably, builds on, or fulfills, the radicalism of its Latin original. The intended audience of the Latin *Epistola solitarii*—clerics charged with deciding on Bridget's candidacy for sainthood, and then spiritual directors charged with discerning the spirits at work in the women in their care—is ostensibly entirely different from that of its vernacular versions; indeed, a visionary woman with theoretical knowledge of *discretio spirituum* is potentially already debarred from passing Alphonse's test, which seems to depend on the inner simplicity of the candidate for authorized vision-making. By contrast, never did a Latin work seem to insist on its vernacularization more loudly than does this daring attempt to elevate "the constitutional power of the lower orders of parliament." A text in which the role of parliament and the way it works are redefined in such rebarbaratively unrealistic terms—from the process by which parliament is to be summoned to that by which transcripts of parliamentary records are to be made available "a chescun qi ceo demaunde" at reasonable cost—can only have force as it rubs hard and sharp against the actual practice of parliament-making. Rather like much medieval law—from the civil law that gestured grandly at a nation run from the center to the canon law that demanded the laity rule out about three quarters of their nightly opportunities for sex—the *Modus* is a wish-list, a castle in the air. But again like medieval law, it was not thereby without real power in the world: power that the owner of the cartulary from which this transcription of the Anglo-Norman *Modus* is taken, Philip de Courtenay, evidently wanted to exercise for his own ends in the trying role of King's Lieutenant of Ireland. As Kerby-Fulton and Justice show in the *Traditio* article that lies behind this transcription (see Horie and Kerby-Fulton's note 1), the London and Dublin civil servants who read and copied the *Modus*, and among whom the text may originally have been written, knew the world of actual parliamentary politics—it was their world—and thus knew the impact a text like this could, and apparently did, have. Since one of the text's avid readers may have been Langland, that arch-purveyor of visionary writing that seeks to modify the real world, it may not be stretching things too much to suggest that the *Modus* is itself a kind of visionary text, product of an apocalyptic as much as a political imagination, and that in its translation into Anglo-Norman and Middle English it can be read as seeking a kind of incarnation, a more intimate self-realization in national affairs. As with research into Bridgettine writing, much of which has so far been focussed on the establishment of correct Latin texts of Bridget's visions, work on the *Modus* has, nonetheless, generally ignored its vernacular versions to this point. The shift of emphasis this article will help bring about is bound to cause further reflection not simply on this text but on the wider issues involved in the passage of audacious political and theological sentiments out of and into Latin.

Harvard University

Notes

1. On the enthusiasm of at least one of the scribes of the Kempe manuscript, see Kelly Parsons, "The Red Ink Annotator of *The Book of Margery Kempe* and his Lay Audience," *English Literary Studies* 85, 2001.

Cato's 'Trace': Literacy, Readership, and the Process of Revision in *Piers Plowman*

Patricia A. Baer

One of the Middle English paraphrases of the *Disticha Catonis* opens with a prologue which, although it acknowledges that Cato was a pagan, still offers the prayer: "gode grante vs grace./to folow catouns trace."[1] The 'trace' that the *Disticha* itself left from its undeniably pagan origins, through to the determinedly Christianized editions of the Middle Ages, to the purified classical editions of the Renaissance, is indeed an interesting literary trail. One short phase of Cato's metamorphosis can be seen in the three versions of *Piers Plowman*,[2] and his Christian persona can shed some light on the evolution of *Piers* itself as well as reveal something of the nature of Langland's readership. Langland's use of maxims from the *Disticha* has been noted before, but unfortunately, their function within the poem and Cato's role as well have frequently been misconstrued. Recent criticism has often been biased by the presentation of the *Disticha* as a classical pagan text in "'purified' renaissance and modern editions" carefully stripped of their medieval commentary and glosses.[3] Since Cato and the *Disticha* no longer enjoy the status accorded to them in Langland's era, I will begin by reviewing briefly what is known about the *Disticha* and its circulation in the Middle Ages, as well as the vexed question of literacy in general, before returning to the main issues of readership and revision.

John Alford observes that Langland uses quotes from the *Disticha* more frequently than from any of the other seven works which were often bound with it in a school text known as the *Auctores Octo.*[4] The *Auctores* was frequently used as a first reader for students of Latin. However, the designation of the *Disticha* as a "reader" or "primer" suggests unfortunate connotations in our era, although such terms are technically correct. As Richard Hazelton has pointed out, "however unsophisticated the text of Cato may be, and despite the fact that the book was utilized as a first reader, it is not by any means to be thought of as a child's book."[5] The study of Latin was seen as a necessary first step in preparation for reading Scripture, and the act of reading and memorizing the *Disticha Catonis* would have had a long-lasting effect on its students: "Here in their first reader the *scholarii* encountered for the first time the amalgamation of classical and Scriptural lore that is characteristic of mediaeval literature. Here, perhaps, they first learned many verses from the pagan poets that memory would retain as tenaciously as it retained popular Scriptural quotations." [6] Indeed the amalgamation of pagan and Christian material often obscured the pagan roots of didactic texts such as the *Disticha.* In Cato's case, the Christianization was so effective that at one extreme, a few readers even thought that Cato had been a Christian.[7] At the very least, even when Cato was acknowledged to have been a heathen, his distichs were usually viewed as having been compatible with Christian virtues and morals. Medieval pedagogues, such as John of Salisbury, were optimistic that "young people using the *Distichs* for their first lessons became so imbued with the virtuous principles that these would linger with them just as an earthenware vase is long redolent of the perfume of the first liquid it contains."[8] Thus for Langland, as well as for his readership, the essence of the distichs was ingrained within the very act of becoming literate, and the spiritual emphasis of their education insured that the distichs were not regarded merely as pedagogical material. Viewed in this way, the *Disticha* was a foundational text which would have remained active in the reader's mind, maturing with age and reflection.

Langland's choice of texts such as the *Disticha* over more learned Latin texts has confused the issue of his own literacy as well as the level of literacy that he expected of his readership. Brian Stock notes that between "the eleventh and fourteenth centuries a literate was one who could read, write, and perhaps also speak Latin."[9] Applying such a definition to the author and readership of a largely vernacular poem embedded with unsophisticated Latin quotations does not grant Langland and his readership much status as far as literacy goes. Anne Quick has defended Langland's reputation with the suggestion that "the quotations in *Piers* show the lower and not the upper limits of the poet's learning."[10] She comments that for "a good writer, and particularly for so obviously didactic a writer as Langland, what determines the level of difficulty at which he writes is his intended audience."[11] Quick envisions this readership as a group which was comprised of "the higher clergy: benefice-holders in major orders who had studied at a university or *studium general*, for instance, monks and friars whose orders funded their education there, teachers at the same institutions, men who had access to the libraries of cathedrals and religious houses, and so on."[12] She believes that *Piers Plowman* likely reached a wider audience than this highly literate group but is confident that the poem "though it can be appreciated and understood in part by people who cannot read Latin, was aimed at those who could."[13]

Anne Middleton also envisions a highly literate audience and believes *Piers* "was received as a work of literature by a heterogeneous and attentive readership, and that this was the kind of reception it actively and consciously sought by its choices of genre and form, and by the manner in which its intentions are declared."[14] For Middleton, the heterogeneous audience of *Piers* consisted of clerical and lay readers who were united "by a common social location, and range of activities and interests. Whether laymen or ecclesiastics, their customary activities involve[d] them in counsel, policy, education, administration, pastoral care—in those tasks and offices where spiritual and temporal governance meet."[15]

Neither Quick nor Middleton seems willing to entertain, at least for very long, the notion of a purely vernacular readership for *Piers*. And yet, as Eamon Duffy observes, when contemplating the use of primers by the laity, "even for those with little or no Latin, there were degrees of possible comprehensions of the texts. Much of their contents, especially those liturgical or quasi-liturgical sections which made up their central core, would have been familiar even to lay people, and their meaning well understood.''[16] Cato and the distichs would also have been familiar to those with little or no Latin, due to the fact that maxims such as the distichs tend to enjoy an oral as well as a written tradition. Thus the proverbial nature of the *Disticha* insured that even the illiterate would have been familiar with many of the distichs. For the literate, Latin manuscripts of the *Disticha* of English provenance were extant from the ninth century on and there are many such manuscripts dating from the thirteenth and fourteenth centuries.[17] The vernacular tradition of *Disticha* manuscripts began in the late eleventh and early twelfth centuries with three Anglo-Saxon manuscripts followed by a series of Anglo-Norman and Middle English manuscripts dating from the twelfth to fourteenth centuries. The Latin manuscripts and their commentary illustrate the Christianizing process which made the *Disticha* acceptable to the clergy and others literate in Latin. The vernacular manuscripts demonstrate the manner in which the Christianized Cato was presented to a lay audience. Cato in *Piers* speaks to both audiences whether he uses the voice of the Latin lines, vernacular translations, or their contextual echoes.

Although critics have frequently suggested that the poem had a ''mixed'' audience, they have not always been clear as to whether ''mixed'' refers to both the literate and illiterate or whether it merely indicates different levels of education and literacy.[18] A literate audience would have appreciated the deeper significance of the inter-relationship between the Latin and Middle English. An illiterate audience listening to the poem would have focussed on the vernacular. The notion of a mixed audience is intriguing because the figure of *Piers Plowman* was mentioned in the letters of the rebels involved in the Peasants' Revolt of 1381. As Steven Justice remarks, it is also an elusive possibility: ''For one thing, it is not clear which of the rebels might have known Langland's poem, or what they, or she, or he knew of it: was *Piers Plowman* (at one absurd extreme) the bedtime reading of a thousand insurgents or (at the other) John Ball's distant memory of an evening's conversation?''[19] Such speculations aside, there is no doubt that by choosing quotations such as the distichs which reflected the cultural literacy[20] of the majority of the populace and by linking the Latin quotations with the vernacular, Langland reached out to a wider audience than that composed exclusively of the literate élite who were fluent in Latin.

The importance of Cato and the distichs to Langland and his readership is underscored by the fact that they are quoted or referred to more often than any other single secular authority in *Piers*. However, scholars differ in their tallies as to the number of quotations contained in the poem, and this issue must be clarified before dealing with the role of the distichs in the revising of *Piers*.[21] Alford cites *Piers* as containing ten quotations from the *Disticha*,[22] but Nicholas Orme cites *Piers* as containing twelve references because he is also counting allusions to Cato in which there is no direct quotation.[23] However, Orme appears to have counted a distich twice if his reference to A.XI.**45** (where there is not a quote from the *Disticha* or mention of Cato) is a typographical error and should read A.XI.**145**,[24] since A.XI.145 refers to the same distich as B.X.189.[25] Orme's count likely should stand at eleven and it should be noted that he misses C.XIII.223a, a distich which Alford lists.[26] Except for this particular distich, all of the other nine distichs which Alford counts are cited in *Piers* as being by Cato. In summary, Alford's estimation that there are ten quotations in total from the *Disticha* used in the three versions of *Piers* initially stands up to scrutiny. However, Quick identifies a distich unmentioned by Alford, as lying behind the Latin quotation of B.XI.416a and C.XIII.223a.[27] Moreover, both Walter W. Skeat and Jill Mann consider that the proverb *Pacientes vincunt*,[28] which is quoted on six occasions in the B-text, and on three occasions in the C-text, appears to have originated from a distich.[29] Indeed, it is likely that not all of the distichs represented in *Piers* are quoted in Latin. R. M. Hazelton estimates that eleven distichs are represented in *Piers* because Reason's vernacular lines of B.XI.378ff (C.XIII.207ff) may have brought *DC* I.3 to mind.[30] J. A. Burrow associates *DC* II.24 with the vernacular description of the belly-band which girds Reason's horse in the C-text.[31] Burrow's contribution, along with that of Skeat and Mann, and Hazelton would bring the total number of distichs used in *Piers* to thirteen. Possibly there are also other instances in *Piers* where the vernacular, or Latin for that matter, would have suggested the echo of a distich to the audience.

These statistics are of interest due to Andrew Galloway's contention that there appears to have been a "seemingly programmatic excision of Cato from the final C-text."[32] I have sorted out the quotations from the *Disticha* and references to Cato as follows: the A-text has one reference to Cato, and three quotations where Cato is cited; the B-text has one reference to Cato, eight quotations where he is cited, and nine where he is not (six of the latter are repetitions of the same quote

Pacientes vincunt); the C-text has three references to Cato, four quotations where he is cited, and nine where he is not (three of the latter are repetitions of the aforementioned *Pacientes vincunt*). Of all of these quotations, *DC* III.2 which appears in A.X.98 does not occur in the other versions of *Piers*; *DC* IV.4 in B.X.343a and *DC* III.6 in B.XII.22a do not occur in the A- or C-texts; and *DC* I.2 in C.XIII.223a-b and *DC* II.24 in C.IV.21 do not occur in the earlier versions of the poem. In the final tally, the C-text includes all the distichs that the B-text does except for two (and it quotes *Pacientes vincunt* three times as opposed to six in the B-text). Moreover, in the C-text, Langland has changed B.VII.155–56 from a direct quotation of *DC* II.31 to a mention of Cato as an authority on the subject of dreams; suggested *DC* I.12 with a Latin phrase in C.XIII.224b; and suggested *DC* II.24 by an added vernacular phrase in C.IV.21. Taken altogether in all three texts, the total references to Cato and the distichs (cited, uncited, and counting repetitions) from the *Disticha* stand at thirty-seven if all three versions of *Piers* are taken into account; at four if we are only looking at the A-text; at eighteen if we are only looking at the B-text; and at fifteen if we are only looking at the C-text. The repetitions of *Pacientes vincunt* skew the totals somewhat in the B- and C-texts. Moreover, *DC* I.26 also affects the total numbers because the B-text quotes it as a whole in B.X.195–96 and in part as a portion of the Redemption hymn in B.XVIII.162a; while the C-text only retains it as the latter occurrence in C.XX.165a. Contrary to Galloway's reckoning, the frequency of Langland's use of Cato and the distichs attributed to him is scarcely diminished in the transition from the B- to the C-text.

The problem with Galloway's perception that Langland set out to excise Cato from the C-text is that it casts Cato, and indeed Langland's opinion of him, in an unfavourable light which runs counter to the internal evidence in the *Piers*.[33] Faced with this dilemna, Galloway suggests that Langland was ambivalent. On the one hand, he remarks that in saddling Reason's horse, Cato is "made responsible for 'the instruction and ornamenting of the soul', an appropriate preliminary for carrying Christian Reason, as well as providing the eloquence to help deploy that weighty baggage ('curteis of speche')."[34] On the other hand, when Galloway compares the manuscript variations of the priest, Sloth's confession: "Ac in canoun ne in the decretales I can nouȝte rede a lyne," in the B-text which in the C-text appears as "Ac y can nat construe Catoun ne clergialiche reden" (B.5.428, C.7.34), he considers the change in this line from what Sloth cannot read (from "canoun" to

"Catoun") as an "instance of the doubt surrounding Cato's authority, not just in Langland's mind but also in the minds of his contemporary readers and scribes."[35] It is possible that the change from 'n' to 't' might merely have been an instance of scribal error which crept into the received C-text.[36] However, it is much more likely that Langland intended to highlight the inadequacy of Sloth's abilities to read a simple school text, let alone the more sophisicated canon laws and the papal decrees concerning them.[37] After all, a large part of the social tension in the poem revolves around the question of the ability of figures such as Piers and Sloth to read Latin. Latin literacy was an issue of concern in the fourteenth century because of the growing suspicion that many priests were so illiterate that they could not properly minister to the needs of their parishioners. Therefore in the C-text "what Sloth cannot read" makes him truly illiterate and this revision does not cast the slightest aspersion on Cato, but rather points to him as a remedy for Sloth's deficiencies.

The progression of composition in *Piers* from the A- to B- to C-texts, from the shortest text to the longest, from the text with the least Latin to that with the most, has been generally but not universally accepted by scholars. Jill Mann is among the latest to raise a challenge to this "alphabetical" sequence, and she does so on the grounds that Langland abridged the B-text to A in an effort to achieve a "wider circulation among the laity, especially among the young."[38] Mann does not simply reverse the alphabetical sequence but rearranges it so that the B-text comes first, and she suggests that Langland's revision strategy was twofold. Thus while the A-text becomes a condensed version for a non-Latinate or unsophisticated audience, the C-text turns into an augmented text presumably for the academic elite. Mann envisions the younger audience as being "non-Latinate (or perhaps in the very elementary stages of education)." She suggests that Langland systematically cut out passages containing Latin lines and phrases, and sporadically provided translations of the remaining Latin content, in deference to a perceived lack of Latin literacy in this youthful group. Moreover, she also considers that Langland excised vernacular passages on the basis of a desire to "tone down sexual content," to eliminate social criticism of the status quo, to exclude "undesirable criticism" of the Church, and to remove other miscellaneous lines "not directly relevant to the laity."[39] However, it seems strange that in addressing these audiences, Langland would choose to keep the content from the *Disticha* relatively unchanged in the B- and C-texts, and yet cut it so drastically in the A-text. After all, the *Disticha* was used, both before and after Langland's day, specifically to teach those "of tender age" not only the fundamentals of Latin grammar, but also the fundamental Christian virtues.

Mann seems at somewhat of a loss to explain why in the process of revision, as she sees it, Langland did not simply stick to removing Latin but instead at times inserted new Latin content. This question is especially pertinent to Langland's use of the *Disticha* in *Piers*. Although the distichs comprise only a small part of the revising process throughout the three texts, nonetheless, they offer a useful sampling for the purpose of examining Mann's proposed revision sequence. For example, the A-text includes the full quotation of Dame Study's use of *DC* I.26, which is also present in the B-text, but completely missing from the C-text in this context. Similarly, the A-text contains the first line of *DC* II.31 concerning dreams just as the B-text does, but the C-text merely alludes to the subject without supplying the actual quotation. Lacking in both the B- and C-texts, and present only in A, is Wit's use of the first line of *DC* III.2:

Ac ȝif þou werchist be godis word I warne þe þe beste,
Whatso men worden of þe wraþþe þe never;
Catoun counseilliþ—tak kep of his teching—
Cum recte viuas ne cures verba malorum,
But suffre & sit stille & sek þou no ferþere,
And be glad of þe grace þat god haþ Isent þe.
(A.X.95–100)

The basic sense of the quotation is paraphrased in the lines preceding it, but it is obviously not a clearly signaled translation aimed at a barely literate audience.[40] What is evident in this instance is the Christianized context of the distich in its compatibility with "godis word." If the momentum of composition and revision, as I think it more likely, moves from A to B to C, then this is an example of a distich which was omitted from the B- and, of course, the C-text. A possible reason for the excision of this particular distich, and the vernacular lines supporting it, is that Langland replaced it with *DC* II.14, which expresses similar sentiments concerning spiritual fortitude, at a more momentous occasion in the poem, the Founding of Holy Church (B.XIX.296a, C.XXI.297). Mann's proposed progression would make the revising of

Piers into a haphazard paring down from the B- to the A-, and an elitest augmentation from the B- to the C-text, rather than a process of eclectic creative growth. I think that the distichs in *Piers* offer support for the latter view as does the changing perception of the figure of Cato and his role within the poem.[41]

Despite the fact that there is very little change in number of quotations and references to Cato from the B- to the C-texts, there is a change in the perception of Cato. One of the names for the *Disticha* in the Middle Ages was *Disticha de Moribus ad Filium,* and in the B-text, Langland appears to have been aware of this traditional view of Cato:

> I seiȝ wel he seide me sooþ, and somwhat me to excuse
> Seide, 'Caton conforted his sone þat, clerk þouȝ he were,
> To solacen hym som tyme; [so] I do whan I make:
> *Interpone tuis interdum gaudia curis.*[42]
>
> (B.XII.21–22a)

When Langland revised this section of the B-text and deleted these lines, he omitted the only portrait of Cato as a quasi-historical figure contained in *Piers.*[43] Moreover, Middle English paraphrases of the *Disticha,* such as those found in Rawlinson MS. G.59 and Sidney MS.ΔIV.i, frequently address the reader in terms of "mi swete sone dere," "my fayre sone," and so on. Langland, however, chose not to utilize this aspect of the conventional characterization of Cato in the C-text. By casting Cato as Reason's knave, and by concentrating on that aspect, Langland portrayed him as a personification of wisdom whose words were directed to an entire society and not merely to the young.

The image of Cato as a teacher undergoes a further change in the revising process from the A- and B-texts to the C-text which moves him beyond the role of simple pedagogue. The pedagogical imagery first appears in the A-text, when Wit admonishes Will:

> Catoun counseilliþ—tak kep of his teching
> *Cum recte vivas, ne cures verba malorum.*
>
> (A.X.97–98)

In the B-text, the verbs "kennyng," "techyng," and "lereþ" are used to convey the pedagogical tradition identified with Cato's advice, however, these terms are conspicuously absent in the C-text. Both the A- and B-texts introduce *DC* I.26 with the pedantic comment "I sai ȝ it in Catoun" (A.XI.146/B.X.194), but only the B-text adds "This is Catons **kennyng** to clerkes þat he **lereþ**" (B.X.199).[44] The B-text is alone in including *DC* IV.4, which is also introduced with a teaching metaphor:

> And Caton **kenneþ** vs to coueiten it nau ȝt but as nede techeþ:
> *dilige denarium set parce dilige formam.*[45]
>
> (B.X.343–43a)

The A-text lacks distich Sententia 17, which is introduced in the B-text as:

> Caton **kenneþ** me þus and þe clerc of stories
> *Cui des videto* is Catons **techyng**.
>
> (B.VII.72–73)

while the C-text merely notes "Catoun acordeth therwith: *Cui des videto*" (C.IX.69). The C-text does not use 'kennyng,' 'techyng,' or 'lereþ' in connection with Cato, and in this instance changes the B-text "Caton **kenneþ** me þus" to "Catoun **acordeth** therwith" (C.IX. 69). The last image of Cato in the C-text, as in the B-text, is that of the stoical Christian covering himself "vnder consayl of Caton the wyse" (C.XXI.296), and it is this aspect which Langland chose to focus on in the C-text:

> The thridde seed that Peres sewe was *Spiritus fortitudinis*
> And ho-so ete of þat seed hardy was euere
> To soffre al þat god sente, seeknesse and angeres.
> Myhte no lyare with lesynges ne losse of worldly catel
> Makyn hym, for eny mornynge, þat he ne was murye in soule,
> And bold and abidynge busmares to soffre;
> And pleded al with pacience and *Parce michi, domine,*
> And keuered hym vnder consayl of Caton the wyse:
> *Esto forti animo cum sis dampnatus inique.*
>
> (C.XXI.289–97) (B.XIX.289–96a)

Thus, in the C-text, Langland has elevated Cato from the role of a pedagogue almost to that of a prophet.[46]

Changing the emphasis of the distichs from practical pedagogy to Christian counsel was in step with the Christianizing impetus of the era. By choosing to quote the *Disticha* in Latin, Langland retained its association with the Christianizing commentaries which accompanied it, and with Scripture. Hazelton has noted the similarities between the *Disticha* and the Books of Proverbs and Ecclesiasticus:

> and anyone familar with the *sententiae* of "Salomon" could not fail to recognize in the *Disticha* of Cato analogous and even identical ideas and sentiments . . . . But Proverbs was not the only Scriptural book that had affinities with Cato . . . . Ecclesiasticus . . . contains a significant number of sentences that in thought and tone are strikingly parallel to Cato's. The heavy emphasis on the quotidian in these Scriptural books, the admonishing tone, the use of the vocative formulae "*Fili, . . . ,*" "*Audi, fili, . . . ,*" and "*Audite, fili, . . . ,*" and the gnomic style were all to be found in the *Disticha Catonis.*[47]

Cato's position in *Piers* is such that Langland did not feel it necessary to rationalize or justify his presence as a "righteous heathen," as he so obviously did for Trajan (B.XI.140–56/C.XII.54–86). Hazelton notes that "as one of the *auctores* Cato spoke with *auctoritas,* and we need not wonder at finding him, without prejudice, in the company of Salomon, St. Paul, or the Fathers."[48] Moreover, Cato is cited in *Piers* to support these very authorities in the B-text, where Scripture cites St. Paul, Solomon, and Cato as being in accord:

> Poule preueþ it impossible, riche men [in] heuene;
> Salomon seiþ also þat siluer is worst to louye:
> *Nichil iniquius quam amare peccuniam;*
> And Caton kenneth vs to coueiten it nauȝt but as nede techeþ:
> *Dilige denarium set parce dilige formam.*
> And patriarkes and prophetes and poetes boþe
> Writen to wissen vs to wilne no ricchesse,
> And preiseden pouerte with pacience; þe Apostles bereþ witnesse,
> That þei han Eritage in heuene, and bi trewe riȝte,
> Ther riche men no riȝte may clayme but of ruþe and grace.
> (B.X.341–48)

The first line of Cato's distich *Dilige denarium, sed parce dilige formam*

(Love money, but have little affection for outward form) would have brought to mind the second line, *quam nemo sanctus nec honestus captat habere* (which no holy or honorable man strains to have).[49] In this instance, Cato is firmly situated in the company of patriarchs, prophets, and poets.

The difficulties that critics have sometimes had disassociating Cato and the distichs from their classical origins emerges in the criticism on the lines in B.VII.72–77b, when Truth ponders whether charity should be discriminatory or unconditional, and cites Cato, Peter Comestor, and St. Gregory as evidence while arguing both sides of the question. David Aers considers that Langland places the pagan views of Cato in opposition to the "impeccable orthodoxy" of St. Gregory.[50] However, Cato does not stand alone but is paired with Peter Comestor, the so-called "clerke of stories," who can by no means be considered a pagan or unorthodox.[51] Cato and Comestor are presented as being in such accord that the syntax makes it difficult to disentangle them, partly because Comestor is not named explicitly:

> Catoun kenneþ me þus and þe clerc of stories.
> *Cui des videto* is Catons techynge,
> And in þe stories he techeþ to bistowe þyn almesse:
> *Sit elemosina tua in manu tua donec studes cui des.*
>
> (B.VII.72–75)

There is nothing patently pagan concerning these injunctions "Look to whom you give"[52] and "Let your alms be in your hand while you study to whom you should give."[53] Aers himself points out that they represent a newer Christian ethos brought about by changing social conditions and "encouraged by convenient glossing of Jesus's hard sayings."[54]

The influence of glossing is especially pertinent in regard to *Cui des, videto* because most of the quotations from the *Disticha* in *Piers* are short phrases extracted from two line distichs, but this quote is a monostich and is given in its entirety. In classical times this brief sentence likely referred to the need for caution when currying favor in the process of forging business or political alliances. However, in the Christian commentary of the thirteenth century, these three simple words yield:

> *Cui des videto.* Dico quod tu des mutuum, sed videto cui des. Cum aliquis habet vicissitudinem, dandi videas si sit gratus aut non. Vel *cui des* bona tua, *videto* utrum sit dignum vel non. Unde scriptum est omnipotentis Dei: "Et retribue affectionis illius dignis, tunc precipit largiri et non[ne] dignis," quia "qui dat mimis et hystrionibus sacrificat demonibus."[55]
>
> (*Look to whom you should give.* I say that you should give money, but you should look to whom you give. When someone has trouble, thereupon you should look to see whether it is appropriate to give or not. For example *to whom you should give* your goods, *look to see* whether he is worthy or not. Whence it is written by God Almighty: "And give as due to those worthy of good will, then he admonishes to give abundantly and surely to the worthy" because "he who gives to mimes and actors sacrifices to demons.")

The gloss reveals the tendency of thirteenth-century Christians to see Cato's simple secular maxim in terms of a complex Christian moral dilemma which is in accord with Peter Comestor's judgemental *Sit elemosina tua in manu tua, donec studes cui des* (Let your alms be in your hand, while you study to whom you should give). The gloss also highlights the concern that the giver will be defrauded by undeserving beggars feigning misfortune.

The so-called "older Christian ethos" in the B-text is represented by St. Gregory, who reminds us once again not only of the debt we owe to Christ, but also of the limitations and fallibility of human knowledge:

> Ac Gregori was a good man and bad vs gyuen alle
> That askeþ, for his loue þat vs al leneþ:
> *Non eligas cui miser[e]aris, ne forte pretereas illum qui meretur accipere,*
> *Quia incertum est pro quo Deo magis placeas.*
> For wite ye neuere who is worþi ac god wote who haþ nede.
> (B.VII.76–78)

Gregory cites St. Jerome's commentary on Eccles.XI.6 (Do not choose whom you will pity, lest by chance you pass over the one who deserves to receive. Because it is uncertain by which deed you will please God more.) In Aers' opinion, "the tradition represented by Gregory in Passus VII is submerged in the ethos expressed by the non-Christian

Cato.''[56] And yet, Aers also considers that this passage represents a crucial turning point in the poem signaling "a dramatic disengagement from the newer ethos.''[57] Unfortunately, Aers focuses exclusively on the B-text so he does not comment on the C-text revisions where, as Justice notes, "Cato stays, Gregory disappears, but Gregory's conclusion remains, underwritten no longer by an authoritative text but by an extraordinary and compelling description of suffering poverty.''[58]

The most striking aspect of this passage in the C-text, which replaces Gregory's mini-sermon and is introduced by the *Cui des videto* quotation preceeding it, resides in its personal tone and in the vivid depiction of the contemporary social conditions. Gregory's observation "For wite ye neuere who is worþi, ac god woote who haþ nede" (B.VII.78) is replaced with "Woet no man, as y wene, who is worthy to haue;/Ac þat most neden aren oure neyhebores" (C.IX.70–161). In an authorial voice suggesting *propria persona*, Langland examines *Cui des videto* in Christian terms and pays special attention to the difficulty of assessing accurately who is truly deserving of charity. He moves from the plight of those who suffer "bothe afyngred and afurste" but are "abashed for to begge" (C.IX.85–86), to the undeserving able-bodied beggars "þe whiche brewhous ben here churches" (C.IX.98), to feeble-minded beggars who may be "in hele, as hit semeth," but lack the wits to care for themselves and so exemplify the spiritual ideal of Matt. 6.25 *ne soliciti sitis* (do not be concerned).[59] His main concern is to distinguish those who are truly needy and "bereth none bagges ne boteles vnder clokes'(C.IX.139) from those who take more than they need and wear "an hater to hele with his bonis" (C.IX.157).

Pearsall notes that these lines and the rest of the passage which Langland added in the C- text (C.IX.70–161) represent:

> a prolonged meditation upon the opposed injunctions of Cato and the gospels in relation to almsgiving. Having spoken earlier of a discriminating charity, L now makes it clear that charity must positively seek out the truly needy in order to fulfil the promise that God will provide whilst accepting the ban on beggary. Those who have must give so that those who have not need not ask.[60]

And yet the task of seeking out the "truly needy" remains a discriminatory task and the basic fear of being swindled by devious able-bodied beggars remains. The rhetoric denying alms to the fraudulent beggar betrays its anxiety by its self-righteous and defensive tone:

Ac Beggares with bagges, þe whiche brewhous ben here churches,
But they be blynde or tobroke or elles be syke,
Thouh he falle for defaute þat fayteth for his lyflode,
Reche ȝe neuere, ȝe riche, thouh suche lollares sterue.
(C.IX.98–101)

J. A. Burrow reacts strongly to this recommendation of a callous charity that would turn a blind eye while able-bodied beggars starved:

> Here the B Text cites authorities on both sides of the question: Cato and Comestor are in favour of discrimination in the dispensing of charity, but (*ac*) Gregory is against. B inclines to the latter view, with the proviso that the bogus poor who enjoy the benefits of indiscriminate charity will be held to account by God. The C Text quotes only Cato (*Cui des, videto*, IX. 69) and favours his view, even suggesting at one point that malingerers may be left to starve (IX. 101).[61]

The lines counseling a hard-hearted attitude towards such malingerers sound unduly harsh when they are taken out of the context of the poem as a whole; however, they should be read with the preceeding passus, the Ploughing of the Half Acre, in mind. The swiftness with which Hunger drove able-bodied beggars to work suggests that it is unlikely that such scoundrels would actually "sterve" to death. Moreover, the C-text addition reiterates that a beggar of this variety "can eny craft in caes he wolde hit vse,/Thorw which craft a couthe come to bred and to ale" (C.IX.155–56). Thus rich men need not worry because such beggars will find a way to provide for themselves if necessity drives them to it. Instead the rich are advised to save their charity for the "lunatyk lollares," or as Langland identifies them, "Godes munstrals and his mesagers and his mery bordiours" (C.IX.135), for "to vnderfongen hem fayre byfalleth for þe ryche" (C.IX.128). Langland's concern is not mean-spirited but rather a fervent desire to help the genuinely needy, and *Cui des videto* precipitates a soul-searching response. The discriminatory advice which remains at the heart of Cato's monostich does not automatically brand it as pagan or non-Christian. The fact that Cato's name remains while others were dropped in the process of revision does not suggest the triumph of pagan ideals, but rather the power of the *Disticha* to stimulate debate and the expectation that his wisdom was worthy of consideration in such matters.

At the Founding of Holy Church, Langland quotes only the first line of the distich *Esto forti animo cum sis dampnatus inique*[62] (Be of strong spirit when you are wrongly judged) which appears initially to be of little consolation. However, the unstated second line, *Nemo diu gaudet, qui iudice vincit iniquo* (No one rejoices long, who overcomes by means of an unfair judge), in a Christian context suggests the final "judgment day" when all earthly victories will be seen to be ultimately transitory. The commentary on the second line of the distich emphasizes that God as the final judge will reward the faithful and condemn the wicked whose mundane victory will prove to have been spiritually hollow:

> quia *nemo gaudet diu qui vincit aliquem iniquo iudice*; quasi diceret, adversarius tuus qui vincit, in iudicio Deo ille non gaudebit.[63]

> (because *no one rejoices long who overcomes anyone by means of an unfair judge*, that is to say, your adversary who overcomes, will not rejoice in the judgement of God.)

The patient will at last have their day and their victory.

In the process of revision from the A- text through to the C-text, Cato had become an authority whose opinion was to be valued alongside those of the Church Fathers. By pairing the *Disticha* as the largest secular source in *Piers* with the Bible as the largest single source, Langland suggests that the search for grace does not require Latin literacy at a sophisticated level. Nor did he feel compelled to write his poem predominantly in Latin but chose instead the mixed medium of the vernacular interspersed with Latin words and phrases. Stock remarks that "Although Christian authors from Augustine on studied and mastered rhetoric, they were constantly reminded that Jesus and the apostles spoke in the plain language of uncultivated men."[64] Langland surely considered that whether his readership had mastered only enough Latin to read the Bible or advanced to more rhetorically demanding texts, they had all the literacy necessary to pursue the road to salvation. Alford notes the fundamental importance of the *Disticha* to *Piers* in that:

> The proem to the *Distichs* derives the "cardinal" virtues from *cardo* (hinge), as does *Piers* B.Prol.103–04; and, more, it identifies these four virtues as "the material cause" of the work, just as *truth*, sown

from the four "seeds" of the cardinal virtues by Piers the Plowman (B.19.274 ff.), is the material cause of Langland's poem.[65]

The four virtues are present at the founding of Holy Church in *Piers*, and with Cato's help, Langland takes his readership back to the very beginning of the Church before institutional decay had started to set in. For Langland, as for many others in the Middle Ages, Cato's "trace" was a worthy path or example to follow in the company of Piers the Plowman in search of Christ.

University of Victoria

Appendix A

Distichs which are quoted (in whole or in part) or paraphased in *Piers Plowman.*

1) Sententia 17

cui des videto

"Watch to whom you give."
—used in *Piers* in B.VII.73, C.IX.69.

2) *DC* I.3

Virtutem primam esse puta conpescere linguam;
proximus ille deo est, qui scit ratione tacere.

"Consider control of your tongue the prime virtue; he who knows how to keep quiet at reason's call is very close to a god."
—suggested by the use in *Piers* of the phrase *Philosophus esses si tacuisses* in B.XI.416a and in C.XIII.223a;[66] or by Reason's vernacular lines in B.XI.378f and in C.XIII.207f.[67]

3) *DC* I.5

Si vitiam inspicias hominum, si denique mores,
cum culpant alios: nemo sine crimine vivit.

"Look into the lives and characters of people, when they find fault with others: no one lives a blameless life."
—used in *Piers* in B.XI.404, C.XIII.211.

4) *DC* I.12

Rumores fuge, ne incipias novus auctor haberi,
nam nulli tacuisse nocet, nocet esse locutum.

"Shun rumors, lest you begin to be considered another rumor-monger, for silence never hurt anyone, but talk is harmful."
—Suggested in *Piers* by the use of the phrase *Locutum me aliquando penituit, tacuisse nunquam* in C.XIII.223a-b.[68]

5) *DC* I.21

Infantem nudum cum te natura crearit,
paupertatis onus patienter ferre memento.

"Since nature created you a naked infant, remember to bear the burden of poverty patiently."
—used in *Piers* in B.VI.315, C.VIII.338.

6) *DC* I.26

Qui simulat verbis nec corde est fidus amicus,
tu qui fac simile: sic ars deluditur acte.[69]

"He who simulates friendship with words but is not a true friend at heart—you do the same to him; thus art is tricked by art."
—used in *Piers* in A.XI.147–48, B.X.195–96, B.XVIII.162a, C.XX.165a.

7) *DC* I.38

Quem superare potes, interdum vince ferendo,
maxima enim morum semper patientia virtus.

"From time to time, conquer one who is no match for you by bearing with him for patience is always the greatest moral virtue."
—suggested in *Piers* by the use of the proverb *pacientes vincunt* in B.XIII.135a, BXIII.171a, B.XIV.33c, B.XIV.54, BXV.268, B.XV598a, C.XV.138, C.XV.157a, C.XV.254.[70]

8) *DC* II.14

Forti animo esto libens, cum sis damnatus inique:
nemo diu gaudet, qui iudice vincit iniquo.

"Keep a brave and cheerful spirit, when you have been unjustly condemned: nobody who has won through a corrupt judge is happy for long."
—used in *Piers* in B.XIX.296a, C.XXI.297.

9) *DC* II.24

Prospice qui veniant casus: hos esse ferendos;
nam levius laedit quidquid praevidimus ante.

"Foresee future misfortunes and the need to bear them; for what we have foreseen harms us less."
—suggested in *Piers* by the use of the phrase "Auyseth-þe-byfore" in C.IV.21.[71]

10) *DC* II.31

Somnia ne cures, nam mens humana quod optat,
dum vigilat, sperat, per somnum cernit id ipsum.

"Do not worry about dreams, for what the human mind desires it hopes for when awake, but actually sees in sleep."
—used in *Piers* in A.VIII.134a, B.VII.156.
—alluded to in *Piers* C.IX.304–05.

11) *DC* III.2

Cum recte vivas, ne cures verba malorum,
arbitri non est nostri, quid quisque loquatur.

"When you are living right, do not worry what bad men say; we have no control over what individuals say."
—used in *Piers* in A.X.98.

12) *DC* III.6

Interpone tuis interdum gaudia curis,
ut possis animo quemvis sufferre laborem.

"Mix your business with occasional pleasure, so you can endure any labor with good cheer."
—used in *Piers* in B.XII.22a.

13) *DC* IV.4

Dilige denarium, sed parce dilige formam.
quam nemo sanctus nec honestus captat habere.

"Love money, but have little affection for outward form, which no holy and honorable man strains to have."
—used in *Piers* in B.X.343a.

Appendix B

Lines in *Piers Plowman* in which Cato is referred to but not quoted.

1) Cato referred to as Reason's knave—A.IV.17, B.IV.17, C.IV.17 (with a possible reference in the C-text to *DC* II.24).
2) Sloth's reference to Cato—C.VII.34.
3) Cato referred to as an authority on dreams—C.IX.305 (in reference to *DC* II.31).

Appendix C—Quotations from the *Disticha Catonis* in *Piers Plowman*

Disticha Catonis ed. Boas	A-text ed. Kane	B-text ed. Kane/Donaldson	C-text ed. Pearsall
DC II.24			C.IV.21
DC I.21 (cited)		B.VI.315	C.VIII.338
Sententia 17 (cited)		B.VII.73	C.IX.69
DC II.31 (cited)	A.VIII.134.a	B.VII.156	(see also C.IX.305)
DC III.2 (cited)	A.X.98		
DC I.26 (cited)	A.XI.146–47	B.X.195–96 (see also B.XVIII.162a)	(see also C.XX.165a)
DC IV.4 (cited)		B.X.343a	
DC I.5 (cited)		B.XI.404	C.XIII.211a
DC I.3		B.XI.378 ff.	C.XIII.207 ff.
		B.XI.416a	C.XIII.223a
DC I.12			C.XIII.223a-b
DC III.6 (cited)		B.XII.22a	
DC I.38		B.XIII.135a	C.XV.138
		B.XIII.171a	C.XV.157a
		B.XIV.33c	C.XV.254
		B.XIV.54	
		B.XV.268	
		B.XV.598a	
DC I.26[72] (see above)	(see also A.XI.146–47)	B.XVIII.162a	C.XX.165a
DC II.14 (cited)		B.XIX.296a	C.XXI.297

References to Cato in *Piers Plowman*

	A-text	B-text	C-text
Reason's knave	A.IV.17	B.IV.17	C.IV.17
Sloth's reference			C.VII.34
an authority on dreams			C.IX.305

University of Victoria

Notes

I would like to express my appreciation to Nicholas Watson for encouraging my interest in Langland's use of Cato in *Piers Plowman* in my M.A. thesis, and for reading and commenting on this article.

1. *Cursor Mundi A Northumbrian Poem of the XIVth Century,* ed. Richard Morris, Part V (Toronto, 1966), pp. 1669–74. This fragmentary version of the *Disticha Catonis* is located at the end of the *Cursor Mundi* in the Bodleian Ms. Fairfax 14, leaf 122. Although there were doubts concerning the authorship of the distichs, during the Middle Ages "Cato" was the name generally associated with them. This compilation of moral advice was variously known as the *Dicta Catonis, Dicta M. Catonis ad filium suum, Libri Catonis Philosophi, Dionysii Catonis Disticha de Moribus ad Filium, Disticha Moralia D. Catonis, Parvus Cato et Magnus Cato;* I will refer to it as the *Disticha Catonis* and abbreviate it in footnotes as *DC.* It was frequently used as a first reader for students learning to read Latin. Current scholarship concerning "Cato" generally stresses the fictive quality of this pseudonymous author by referring to him as "pseudo-Cato" as John Alford does in *Piers Plowman: A Guide to the Quotations,* (Binghamton, 1996), p. 26, or as "the supposed author" as Gerald Morgan refers to him in "The Meaning of Kind Wit, Conscience, and Reason in the First Vision of *Piers Plowman,*" *Modern Philology* 84 (1986), 357. However, I will refer to the author (or group of authors) responsible for the *Disticha* simply as Cato without qualifying adjectives or quotation marks.
2. For *Piers Plowman* citations, I have used *Piers Plowman, The A Version,* ed George Kane (London: The Athlone Press, 1960); *Piers Plowman, The B Version,* eds. George Kane and E. T. Donaldson (London, 1975); and *Piers Plowman by William Langland: An edition of the C-text,* ed. Derek Pearsall (Berkeley, 1978). For the distichs I have used *Disticha Catonis. Recensuit et Apparatu Critico Instruxit,* ed. Marcus Boas and Henricus Johannes Botschuyen (Amsterdam, 1952) cited by book and number. For the translations of the distichs, I have used Ian Thomson and Louis Perraud, *Ten Latin Schooltexts of the Later Middle Ages* (Lewiston, 1990). Thomson and Perraud have based their translations on Boas's Latin text. All other translations are mine unless noted otherwise.
3. Richard Hazelton, "Two Texts of the *Disticha Catonis* and Its Commentary, with Special Reference to Chaucer, Langland, and Gower," PhD diss., Rutgers U, 1956, p. 1.
4. Alford, *A Guide to the Quotations,* p. 26. See also Nicholas Orme, *English Schools in the Middle Ages* (London, 1973), pp. 103–04 and p. 126, for a discussion of the *Sex Auctores*

and the *Auctores Octo,* both of which contain the *Disticha.* He notes that the *Sex Auctores,* which was popular until the thirteenth century, was comprised of Cato, Theodulus, Avianus, Maximian, Claudian and Statius. However after 1300, the *Sex Auctores* was replaced by the *Auctores Octo* as a school text, and only Cato and Theodulus were retained from the earlier volume while the other *auctores* were replaced with poems from the twelfth and thirteenth centuries.

5. Richard Hazelton, "Chaucer and Cato," *Speculum* 35.4 (1960), 357.
6. Richard Hazelton in "The Christianizaion of 'Cato': The *Disticha Catonis* in the Light of Late Medieval Commentaries," in *Medieval Studies* (Toronto, 1957), p. 173.
7. Hazelton in "The Christianization of 'Cato'," 167, n. 27, remarks that "The *Expositio Remigii super Catonem* in MS 1433 (saec xi) of the Public Library of Lucca contains the following curious remark in reference to the author of the *Disticha: 'quidem eum christianum esse profitentur, alii vero paganum testantur,'* " Hazelton is quoting A. Mancini, "Un Commento Ignoto di Remy d'Auxerra ai *Disticha Catonis," Rendiconti della Reale Accademia die Lincei*: Classe di Scienze Morali, Steriche e Filologiche, Serie 5 (1902), p. 179. It was generally known of course that "Cato" was a pagan, but the comment here is an indication that a few, at least believed that he was literally a Christian. Ingrid Arvide Brunner notes in her dissertation, "The Anglo Saxon Translation of the *Distichs of Cato*: A Critical Edition," diss., Columbia University, p. 32, that "certain manuscripts indicate the ultimately close connection in the minds of medieval people between the originally pagan *Distichs* and Christianity. An edition of the *Latin Distichs* published in 1500 has a woodcut showing Christ on the Cross."
8. Brunner, "The Anglo-Saxon Translation of the *Distichs of Cato,*" p. 26.
9. Brian Stock, *The Implications of Literacy* (Princeton, 1983), p. 27.
10. Anne Wenley Quick, "The Sources of the Quotations in *Piers Plowman,*" PhD diss., U of Toronto, 1982, 40.
11. Quick, "The Sources of the Quotations," 38.
12. Quick, " The Sources of the Quotations," 40.
13. Quick, "The Sources of the Quotations," 40.
14. Anne Middleton, "The Audience and Public of *Piers Plowman,*" in *Middle English Alliterative Poetry and its Literary Background,* ed. David Lawton (Cambridge, 1982), p. 101.
15. Middleton, "The Audience and Public of *Piers Plowman,*" p. 104.
16. Eamon Duffy, *The Stripping of the Altars—Traditional Religion in England c. 1400–c. 1580* (New Haven and London, 1992), p. 220.
17. See Hazelton, "Chaucer and Cato," 359, n. 7, for a list of medieval Latin mss.
18. A. C. Spearing, in *Criticism and Medieval Poetry* (London, 1972), p. 125, remarks that *Piers Plowman* "seems to be directed at an audience of mixed intellectual capacity." He believes that Langland made provision for this within the poem and cites the occasion on which the Good Samaritan gives two separate analogies to explain the doctrine of the Trinity. However, Spearing doesn't discuss whether an audience of "mixed intellectual capacity" would have included the literate and illiterate.
19. Steven Justice, *Writing and Rebellion* (Berkeley, 1994), p. 119.
20. By "cultural literacy," I wish to indicate the texts which we might expect the average educated reader to have had contact with before reading *Piers.* I think that the reader response and reception theories of Wolfgang Iser and Hans Robert Jauss have interesting implications for the readership of *Piers.* See Robert C. Holub, *Reception Theory: A Critical Introduction* (New York, 1984), pp. 148–50.

21. See appendix A for a list of all the distichs which have been identified as playing a role (in whole or in part) in *Piers.* See appendix B for a list of the references to Cato where a distich is not directly quoted or paraphrased. See appendix C for summary charts of the information in appendices A and B.
22. Alford, *A Guide to the Quotations,* p. 26, n. 51.
23. Nicholas Orme, *Education and Society in Medieval and Renaissance England* (London, 1989), p. 251.
24. Orme is using Skeat's edition, *The Vision of William concerning Piers the Plowman, in Three Parallel Texts, together with Richard the Redeless, by William Langland,* ed. W. W. Skeat, 2 vols. (Vol I : Text, Vol. II: Introduction, Notes and Glossary, Oxford, 1886). Reprinted, with addition of Bibliography by J. A. W. Bennett (1954). (In Kane and Donaldson, A.XI.145 would be A.XI.146.) Emphasis of the arabic numerals is mine.
25. In Kane and Donaldson, B.X.189 would be B.X.195. This is *DC* I.26.
26. For the A- and B- texts, Alford uses the Athone editions of the poem: *Piers Plowman: The A Version,* eds. George Kane and E. Talbot Donaldson and *Piers Plowman: The B Version* eds. George Kane and E. Talbot Donaldson, and for the C-text, he uses *Piers Plowman: The C Version,* eds. George Russell and George Kane (Berkeley and London, 1997). In Pearsall's edition of the C-text, C.XIII.220 would be line C.XIII.223a. This is *DC* I.12.
27. Quick, "The Sources of the Quotations," 451. This is *DC* I.3.
28. This phrase is italicized in Pearsall's edition to indicate rubric in the ms.
29. Alford, *A Guide to the Quotation,* p. 145, does not acknowledge the source of the proverb as Cato. See Alford's alphabetical index for the proverb's occurrences in the poem. Skeat, *Piers Plowman,* p. 138, n. 195, suggests Langland was thinking of Cato's Sententia xl, and/or *DC* I.38. 195. Jill Mann in "Proverbial Wisdom in the Ysengrimus," *New Literary History* (1984), 108 n. 5, cites only *DC* I.38.
30. Hazelton, "Two Texts of the *Disticha Catonis,*" pp. xxxix-xl. Hazelton uses Skeat's edition for his line numbers, B.XI.378f (C.XIII.207 ff.) would be B.XI.376 ff in Kane and Donaldson (C.XIII.207 ff. would be C.XIII.204 ff. in Pearsall). Andrew Galloway in "Two Notes on Langland's Cato: *Piers Plowman* B I.88–91; IV.20–23," *English Language Notes* 25 (December 1987), 10 suggests that the same distich is "a plausible source" for Holy Church's lines in A.86–89, B.I.88–91, and C.I.84–87, because "The echoes in '*compescere linguam*' to Langland's 'trewe of his tonge' and '*proximus ille deo*' to 'He is a god' suggest that the distich's words have risen to Langland's concordance-trained mind, conflating with and altering similar passages from Luke."
31. J. A. Burrow, "Reason's Horse," *Yearbook of Langland Studies* 4 (1990), 141.
32. Galloway, "Two Notes on Langland's Cato," p. 11.
33. However, it should be noted that the Middle English versions of the *Disticha* are based on Everard le Moine's Anglo-Norman version, and include Everard's prologue which appears to protest too much when defending Cato's compatibility with Holy Scripture. For a complete text of Everard's *Disticha* with a Middle English paraphrase, see *The Minor Poems of the Vernon MS,* ed. F. J. Furnivall, EETS o.s. 117 (London, 1901), pp. 553–609.
34. Galloway, "Two notes on Langland's Cato," p. 11–12.
35. Galloway, "Two Notes on Langland's Cato," p. 11, n. 11.
36. The variants in Russell and Kane for C.7.34 are: catoun] canon PEVAQSKG. *Piers Plowman: The C Version,* eds. George Russell and George Kane (Berkeley and London, 1997), p. 329.

37. Galloway, "Two Notes on Langland's Cato," p. 11, n. 11, considers "canon" as referring to "the part of the Mass before Communion," but due to its pairing with decretals it must surely refer to canon laws.
38. Jill Mann, "The Power of the Alphabet: A Reassessment of the Relation between the A and the B Versions of *Piers Plowman*," *The Yearbook of Langland Studies* 8 (1995), 46.
39. Mann, "The Power of the Alphabet," 28, 34, 36–37, 40, and 41.
40. Mann, "The Power of the Alphabet," 34, passes over the fact that not all of the Latin is translated with the comment that it is "partly as if the redactor was tiring of his task or finding it too difficult."
41. See Kathryn Kerby-Fulton's review in *The Yearbook of Langland Studies* 8 (1994), 458, for further reasons which refute Mann's thesis in this article.
42. *DC* III.6.
43. Thomson and Perraud note in *Ten Latin School Texts*, p. 52 that medieval scholars expressed their reservations concerning either of the possible historical Catos as the authentic author of the *Disticha:*

    > John of Salisbury, for example, in his *Polycraticus* VII 9 cites one of the distichs, with the remark, "Cato or some other says this, for the author is uncertain." Similarly, the author of the Tegernsee *accessus* names Cato the Censor and Cato of Utica as possible authors, and reports that some take "Cato" in the title simply to mean "wise man." Conrad of Hirsau in his *Dialogus super auctores*, and Hugh of Trimberg in his *Registrum multorum auctorum* betray a similar confusion.

    However, despite their doubts, Cato's name remained as the author along with the sense that he had been a real historical figure.
44. Emphasis throughout this paragraph is mine.
45. *DC* IV.4.
46. Langland was not alone in assigning Cato spiritual roles. Dante cast him as the gatekeeper in the *Purgatorio* and as a symbol of God in the *Convivio*. See Robert J. Groar, *The Legend of Cato Uticensis from the First Century B.C. to the Fifth Century A.D.: With an Appendix on Dante and Cato* (Brussels, 1987), pp. 102–10.
47. Hazelton, "The Christianization of 'Cato'," pp. 163–64.
48. Hazelton, "The Christianization of 'Cato'," p. 171.
49. *DC* IV.4.
50. David Aers, *Community, Gender, and Individual Identity: English Writing 1360–1430* (London, 1988), p. 50. However, it should be noted that Gregory and Cato were often quoted as being in agreement. For example the fourteenth-century preacher's handbook, the *Fasciculus Morum*, ed. and trans. Siegfried Wenzel (University Park and London, 1989), cites Gregory and Cato concerning the sins of Wrath and Envy: see especially pp. 118 and 171.
51. Skeat, *B-text*, p. 121 describes Peter Comestor as the author of the *Historia Scholastica* which is "an account of all the chief events recorded in the Old and New Testaments."
52. *DC* Brevia Sententia 17.
53. This is an abridged version of Tobit iv.7–11.
54. Aers, *Community, Gender, and Individual Indentity*, p. 50. Also see pp. 34–35 for examples of Richard FitzRalph's glosses, such as concerns Luke 14.12–14 "pore men þat beþ stalworþe and stronge schulde nouȝt be cleped to þe feeste of beggers, for þei mowe quyte hit wiþ her travail."

55. Hazelton, "Two Texts of the *Disticha Catonis*," p. 10. The emendation of "non" to "nonne" is my suggestion due to the context; however, I have not had the opportunity to examine the manuscript to check whether "non" bears an abbreviation mark.
56. Aers, *Community, Gender, and Individual Identity*, p. 53.
57. Aers, *Community, Gender, and Individual Identity*, p. 53.
58. Justice, *Writing and Rebellion* , p. 242.
59. Alford, *A Guide to the Quotations*, p. 57, directs us to R. W. Frank, Jr., *Piers Plowman and the Scheme of Salvation* (New Haven, 1957), pp. 31–33; and Wendy Scace, *Piers Plowman and the New Anti-clericalism* (New York, 1989), pp. 61–64 and passim, for medieval interpretations of this important verse.
60. Pearsall, *Piers Plowman*, p. 163, n. 61.
61. J. A. Burrow, *Langland's Fictions* (Oxford, 1993), p. 42 n. 27.
62. *DC* II.14.
63. Hazelton, "Two Texts of the *Disticha Catonis*," p. 175.
64. Stock, *The Implications of Literacy*, p. 28.
65. Alford, *A Guide to the Quotations*, p. 27.
66. Quick, "The Sources of the Quotations," 451.
67. Hazelton, "Two Texts of the *Disticha Catonis*," pp. xxxix-xl.
68. Alford, *A Guide to the Quotations*, p. 78.
69. Boas uses *qui* in this line although *quoque* as in the commentaries transcribed in Hazelton, "Two Texts of the *Disticha Catonis*," pp. 48 and 155, makes better sense grammatically. Similarily *acte* should likely read *arte*.
70. Skeat, *Piers Plowman*, p. 138, n. 195, suggests that Langland was thinking of Cato's Sententia xl, and/or *DC* I.38. Mann in "Proverbial Wisdom," 108, n. 5 cites only *DC* I.38.
71. Burrow, "Reason's Horse," p. 141, n. 9.
72. This distich has been included twice in the table. In A.X.147–48 and B.X.195–96, Cato is cited and both lines of the distich are quoted. However, in B.XVIII.162a and C.XX.165a, the distich is suggested by the phrase *Ars vt artem falleret* from the Redemption hymn.

Recommended Reading: Defining the Medieval Visionary. A Facing-Page Comparison of the Middle English and Latin Texts of the *Epistola solitarii ad reges* of Alfonso of Jaén

Arne Jönsson and Rosalynn Voaden

Introduction

Shortly after the death of Bridget of Sweden in 1373, her spiritual director and editor, Alfonso of Jaén (1329/30–1389; also known as Alphonse of Pecha) added an eighth book, the *Liber celestis imperatoris ad reges,* to the collection of her visions and revelations, the *Sancta Birgitta Revelaciones*, which he had been largely responsible for organizing and editing. Alfonso was concerned at this time to amass all the documentation which he could so that a comprehensive account of Bridget's life and visions could be published in time for the opening of Bridget's canonization process. Some of the material in this eighth book was excerpted from the first seven; the remainder appeared here for the first time. All of the visions and revelations which it contains are concerned, as the name implies, with temporal rulers. To serve as a preface to this book, Alfonso wrote the *Epistola solitarii ad reges*, in which he defends Bridget's status as visionary and prophet by outlining how she conforms to the principles of *discretio spirituum*, the doctrine which establishes the criteria for distinguishing true visions and visionaries from those inspired by the devil. Demonstrated adherence to *discretio spirituum* was a very important factor in the successful journey toward sainthood.[1] The *Epistola* was divided into eight chapters, the last serving as the true introduction to the *Liber celestis imperatoris ad reges*.

Copies of the *Revelaciones* circulated in various forms; sometimes Book VIII was lacking in its entirety; sometimes all or part of the *Epistola* served as a kind of epilogue to the first seven books of revelations. In England there are six Latin manuscripts of the complete *Revelaciones*, which were executed in England. All these manuscripts are in one group; copies of fragments from later in the century reveal the influence of continental manuscript groupings.[2] There are two extant Middle English translations of substantially complete versions of the *Revelaciones*, entitled the *Liber celestis*: one is found in London, British Library, MS Cotton Claudius B.i, the other in London, British Library, MS Cotton Julius F.ii. MS Claudius B.i ends part way through Book VII and Julius ends after the seventh chapter of the *Epistola*. MS Cotton Julius F.ii is thus the only extant Middle English version of the *Epistola solitarii ad reges* of Alfonso of Jaén.

The Middle English Text: London, British Library, MS Cotton Julius F.ii Manuscript Description

"The Revelations of S. Bridget, princess of Nerike in Sweden," Bks. I-VII, translated into English; with the Prologue of Matthias, canon of Linkoping. Book VII is complete, and ends with chapter 31 on fol. 246v. It is followed immediately by the *Epistola solitarii ad reges*, beginning:

"O ȝe clere and bright kynges and wold to god . . . " The *Epistola* includes chapter VII, the Recapitulation, which ends on fol. 254r with the words: "And the seyinges of al doctours and holy fadris vpon this mateer diffusely and manyfold wise speking." It is followed by an epilogue giving a brief account of Bridget's death and canonization. The last page of the manuscript—fol. 254v—contains two Latin prayers to St. Bridget.
Paper: ff. 254. 12"x 8.5".
Date: Dr. Ian Doyle has suggested a date for the manuscript in the late 1430s or early 1440s.
Provenance: Norfolk.[3]

Editorial Method

Editorial emendations have been kept to an absolute minimum and are indicated by [square brackets].[4] Scribal errors are reproduced in {rounded brackets}. When the letters are legible, they are given, otherwise they are indicated by one period for each letter. Interlineations are enclosed in <angle brackets>. Abbreviations and suspensions have been expanded in *italics.* An apostrophe ' indicates an unexplained flourish. Where possible, expansions have been made consistent with the scribe's own expanded spelling; however, the scribe him- or herself is rarely consistent. In these cases, the expansion takes the most common form. Punctuation and capitalization have been maintained as far as possible as they are in the manuscript, as have word divisions. *i, j, u,* and *v* are as they appear in the manuscript. Yogh (ȝ) and thorn (þ) are reproduced. The scribe rarely uses thorn, preferring *y*, which is formed quite differently. He sometimes draws a stroke across the stem of *h* and *l*; this seems to be simply an otiose flourish. Obliques/and// reproduce the same symbols in the manuscript. Their purpose is not clearly apparent, although they are sometimes used in conjunction with hyphens to indicate the end of a chapter. Hyphens of varying length—and---also reproduce marks in the manuscript, which, again have no consistently discernible purpose, and may just be otiose. The suffixes for the ordinal numbers have been placed on the line and italicized, but have not been expanded. Half-bracketed Arabic numbers indicate lines in the manuscript. Note that these numbers do not appear in the manuscript itself, but have been inserted to convey the layout of the manuscript. In the manuscript, rubrics are in red ink, and set off from the body of the text on lines of their own. A two-line space has been left at the beginning of each chapter for an illuminated capital.

After Book I: 2, the chapters are not numbered. The same clearly legible hand is used throughout the *Epistola,* indeed, throughout the entire manuscript of Julius F.ii, for both text, corrections, and marginal glosses.

The Latin Text

As stated above, the *Epistola solitarii* was written by Bishop Alfonso as an introduction to the *Liber Celestis Imperator ad Reges* (Book VIII of St. Bridget's *Revelaciones*). Consequently it has been preserved in the manuscripts and printed editions of the *Revelaciones.* The present text is based on a collation of ten selected manuscripts, which have been proved to be of high quality. The examination showed that the *Epistola* was handed over in a fairly homogeneous way, so the manuscripts have had to be classified from a small number of variant readings. That analysis showed that the manuscripts can be divided into two main groups. A comparison of the hyparchetypes of these groups shows a number of cases where the one hyparchetype has another reading than the other. These variations (mostly transpositions of words or insignificant omissions/additions) as well as readings of individual manuscripts and of sub-groups have not been recorded here, since they do not affect the understanding of the text. For details about manuscript classification and a detailed report of variant readings, we refer the reader to Arne Jönsson, *Alfonso of Jaén: His Life and Works with Critical Editions of the Epistola Solitarii, the Informaciones and the Epistola serui Christi* (Lund, 1989).

Comparative Study

The Middle English translation of the *Epistola* is a considerably abridged version of the Latin text; material has been excised in sections, but outside of these sections, the Middle English is a faithful translation of the Latin. MS Cotton Julius F.ii is the only extant Middle English version of the *Epistola*; none of the Latin manuscripts executed in England is an ancestor of MS Cotton Julius F.ii. With the manuscript information available at present, it is impossible to tell whether Julius F.ii was an original abridgement made directly, or at a remove, from a copy of the Latin text or from a Middle English text; whether it was the only abridged version; and whether any Middle English versions were complete translations of the Latin.[5]

We felt that it would be useful to bring together the Latin and Middle English texts of the *Epistola*, both in order to make this important medieval treatise more readily available to modern scholars, and to facilitate comparison of the original and the translation. We must emphasise that the Middle English text is *not* a translation of the Latin text on the facing page. There is no extant Latin source for the Middle English translation. In this article the two texts have been set up on facing pages to make comparison easier and to call attention to the content of the abridged material.[6] A comparison between the most nearly complete version of the Latin *Epistola* that we have, and the abridged Middle English translation, is valuable in that the excised material could suggest a motivation for the abridgement; this in turn could indicate factors influencing the translator/scribe, and thereby enhance our understanding of the reception of treatises such as the *Epistola*.[7]

References to Bridget's *Sermo angelicus* and to its creation, are probably excised in the translation because the *Sermo* is not part of the *Revelaciones* proper, and does not appear in the manuscript of the *Liber celestis*. Apart from this, an initial survey of the excised passages suggests four possible motivations: (1) the obvious—to shorten and simplify the material, understandable after two hundred and fifty folios of exhaustive detail; (2) to suppress material giving practical advice about conformity to *discretio spirituum*, the discernment of spirits; (3) to suppress details of ecstatic behaviour; (4) to suppress material dealing with Bridget's authorization to write. The last three possibilities excite conjecture that perhaps the manuscript was destined for a female audience; in this case the suppression of material could result from a fear of women's alleged suggestibility in the area of visions, and a desire not to stimulate *imitatio Birgittae.*

Rosalynn Voaden
Arizona State University
USA

Arne Jönsson
University of Lund
Sweden

Notes

Thanks are due to Anthony Bale of the Centre for Medieval Studies at the University of York for his invaluable assistance in setting up the comparative text, and for his careful proofreading.

1. The influence of *discretio spirituum* on medieval women visionaries, in particular Bridget of Sweden and Margery Kempe, is examined by Rosalynn Voaden in *God's*

Words, Women's Voices: The Discernment of Spirits in the Writings of Late-Medieval Women Visionaries (York, 1999).

2. Roger Ellis, "*Flores ad fabricandam . . . coronam*: An Investigation into the Uses of the Revelations of St. Bridget of Sweden in Fifteenth-Century England," *Medium Aevum* 52 (1983), 165–66.
3. Richard Beadle, "Prologomena to a Literary Geography of Later Medieval Norfolk," *Regionalism in Late Medieval Manuscripts and Texts: Essays Celebrating the Publication of A Linguistic Atlas of Late Medieval English*, ed. Felicity Riddy (Cambridge, 1991), p. 104.
4. Any corrections that have been made are based on the critical edition of the Latin text of the *Epistola* in Arne Jönsson, *Alfonso of Jaén: His Life and Works with Critical Editions of the Epistola Solitarii, the Informaciones and the Epistola serui Christi* (Lund, 1989), pp. 115–71. Since Jönsson's text, which is based on a collation of extant manuscripts, does not diverge very much from the first edition, the Ghotan edition of 1492, we have chosen to use Gh as designation for Jönsson's text.
5. We are grateful to Dr. Roger Ellis for confirming that the abridgement almost certainly originated with the translator, rather than with a Latin source.
6. Because the Latin text is considerably longer than the Middle English, it has been necessary occasionally to leave considerable "white space" in the Middle English in order to keep the two texts aligned.
7. Rosalynn Voaden addresses this issue in "Rewriting the Letter: Variations in the Middle English Translation of the *Epistola solitarii ad reges* of Alfonso of Jaén," in *The Translation of the Works of St Birgitta of Sweden into the Medieval European Vernaculars*, ed. Bridget Morris and Veronica O'Mara (Turnhout, 2000). This article also considers the reworking of the *epistola* in *The Chastising of God's Children.*

Middle English and Latin Texts of the *Epistola solitarii ad reges*

fol. 246v] 16) In this booke yat followis here. yei are repr*e*uyd the whech on warys w*ith* 17) ought examynacou*n* preuys or repreuys. p*er*sonys seying them self to have 18) godly. visions and revelaco*u*ns,[1]/the ferst chappet*re*/19) o 3e cler and bright kynges and wold to god ye were very kinges in god 20) my*n* deer lordis derly be fore louyd w*ith* sympil and meke recome*n*dacou*ns* 21) before sent on to ye feet of 3oure regal maieste. ffor it is the man*er* of kinges 22) to wil discus {curuosly}<curiously>. and in discussinge to know the qualiteys of p*er*sonys to 23) them writyng*e*/ony onwont secret*es* of goddis wyl. And for yat now inyese 24) late dayes cloudid w*ith* a thik derkenes/As*er*teyne nobil woma*n* of body and soule 25) has resin callid. lady brigid the bewty of all wome*n* The whech as a bright 26) sterre. diffudis and yet*es* forth his shinyng bemys of holynes be diuers clymes 27) of the wyde word. The whech writ*es* now to vs be ye p*re*cept of most hy and [*fol. 247r*] 1) heue*n*ly empror this p*re*sent boke. w*ith*yn wrety*n* godly reuelat to hir as a bright merour 2) and a regal adornament*e*/and corepcou*n* or blamyng of oure maneris and sogett*is* 3) of the kingedom ¢ to be exsercisid ¢ holy gou*er*nans Therfore my lord*es* les yat no sodeyn 4) or on avisid indiscrete iugement of ony indiscret men./inducyng you to mys 5) beleue or incredulite. and the hardnes of Kinge pharao/as a whirle wynde. shuld 6) drawe ought fro youre h*er*tis the seed of beleue and feith./mekely taking and beleuy*ng* 7) this glorious boke wretyn/in ye h*er*te of the forseid lady/ w*ith* the fynger of all 8) m[i]ghty god. Therfore I haue decreyd yat 3e be not illudyd soche wyse . brefly and 9) plenarly. to schewe you the condicou*ns* and the qualite of the blissid soule of 10) the forseid lady. Brigid/and ye man*er* of wise yat she had the visions of god. 11) Also I intende to write and in writyng to teche boþe 3ou and odir a breff man*er* 12) of discernyng godly. visions fro the cursid illusiou*ns* of sathan the deule./Therfore 13) my*n* lordis I sey brefly. yat y*er* be many and diuers kendis of visiou*ns* And for yis 14) mateer is on knouyn as

Reprehenduntur hic illi qui ex arrupto et improuise nullo examine precedente approbant aut reprobant personas se asserentes habere visiones et reuelaciones diuinas.

Capitulum I.

1 Serenissimi reges et vtinam veri reges in Christo, domini mei precarissimi, supplici et humilima recommendacione premissa ante pedes vestre maiestatis regalis!

2 Quoniam moris regum existit velle curiose discutere et discuciendo cognoscere qualitates personarum eis scribencium aliqua insolita secreta voluntatis diuine **3** et quia in istis modernis temporibus densa caligine tenebrosis[2] surrexit quedam illustris generis et spiritus domina, domina Brigida de regno Suecie, decus omnium feminarum, **4** que velut stella clarissima sanctitatis radios fulgentes diffudit per diuersa climata vasti orbis, que nunc vobis scribit precepto celestis imperatoris altissimi presentem librum infrascriptum, ei diuinitus reuelatum, quasi quoddam preclarum speculum ad ornamentum regale et correpcionem morum vestorum ac subditorum regni sanctum regimen exercendum, **5** propterea, mei domini metuendi, ne subitum et improuisum aliquorum indiscretorum indiscretum iudicium, inducendo vos ad incredulitatem et duriciam Pharaonis, velut ventus turbinis euellat a cordibus vestris semen credulitatis et fidei accipiendi humiliter et credendi istum librum gloriosum, scriptum in corde predicte domine digito Dei viui,[3] **6** idcirco decreui, ne tali modo illudamini, breuiter et plenarie vobis ostendere condiciones et qualitatem anime prefate beatissime domine et modum, quo ipsa habebat visiones a Deo. **7** Intendo eciam vos et alios incautando scribere et scribendo docere modum breuem discernendi visiones diuinas ab illusionibus pessimis Sathane.

8 Dico igitur, domini mei, breuiter, quod visionum genera multa et diuersa sunt.

apilgrim {.} a mong men/for ye ignorau*ns* and on cu*nn*yng 15) of holy scripture. and experiens of mental p*ra*your and conte*m*placou*n* And of gostly 16) lyff/Therfore I have desirid oftyn sethis to eke w*ith* word*es* {. .} oon breff tretyse/the 17) wheche shuld be as <a> wenewyng scotyl to discerne visions for the gret perelis 18) the whech has happenyd to many p*er*sonys in my*n* tyme. for the onknoulache of 19) this so secrete and on vsid mateer And for yis blissid lady. to who*m* this p*re*sent 20) booke godlich was reuelat in vision/sche seis in the be gynnyng of yt/yat 21) sche sy. in Vision agret paleyce incomp*re*hensibil for gretnes/like the cler heue*n* 22) *et cetera*/Therfore now I haue decreyd the forseid tretysse & compile here be ye man*er* 23) wise of a epistyl/yat good and godly visions. shuld be excussid and dep*ar*tid fro 24) the deulys and wikkid visions as corn fro the chaff/And yat it may be pure 25) and clene corn./<and>in ye berne or lathe of sp*irit*ual holy me*n* may be leyd and wor 26) schepid.,. And the chaff of the deulys illusions be cast on the myddinge . . fer fro 27) the winde of goddis scripture blouyn'/Therfore <at ye> beginny*ng* in the name of crist 28) puttyng vndir alwey. ye thing*es* the whech I sey to ye correccou*n* of holy chirch [*fol. 247v.*] 1) and sad counsel./I sey. yat he yat wyl iuge discerne discusse or rightuosly to ex 2) amyn. the kendis of visiou*ns* or reuelacou*ns*/it be houys yat he haue the forseid holy 3) theorike of holy scripture/in and on the mateer of visiou*ns* the whech holy fadris 4) and doctor*es* clerly. has describid. And the practike of exp*er*iens of sp*irit*ual liff and 5) mental visiou*ns* sp*irit*ually or intellectually. godly infudid to them. And for 6) this theorike and pra{va}ctyke in fewe p*er*sonys this day of discerny*ng* the forseyd 7) thing*es*. or demynge visiou*ns* and sprit*es* are foundin/Therfore many <me*n*> erringe 8) as blinde men in this mateer {. .} ar turned to contempne sempyl and holy 9) p*er*sonys knet to god.

Et quia materia ista peregrina et quasi incognita est apud homines propter ignoranciam et impericiam sciencie Sacre Scripture et inexperienciam sentimentorum mentalis oracionis et contemplacionis et vite spiritualis, **9** ideo ego sepe desideraui epilogare vnum breuem tractatum, qui esset quasi quoddam ventilabrum ad discernendum visiones propter magna pericula, que multis personis meo tempore, proch dolor, euenerunt ex impericia istius tam secrete et tam inusitate materie. **10** Et quia ista beata domina, cui presens liber diuinitus reuelatus fuit in visione, dicit in principio eius, quod vidit in visione "palacium grande, incomprehensibile magnitudine, simile celo sereno", etc., **11** idcirco ego nunc decreui predictum tractatum seu ventilabrum hic per modum epistole compilare, quo visiones bone et diuine a dyabolicis et malignis, velut granum a palea,[4] excuciantur et subtiliter separentur, **12** vt sic granum purum et mundum in orreo spiritualium et catholicorum hominum recondatur et veneretur, palea vero dyabolica illusionum a vento flante Diuine Scripture longius in sterquilinium proiciatur et pedibus conculcetur. **13** Incipiens igitur in Christi nomine, semper subiciens omnia, que dixero, correccioni sancte matris Ecclesie et consilio saniori, **14** dico quod, qui species visionum seu reuelacionum iuste et discrete examinare et discutere ac discernere et iuste iudicare vult, **15** oportet quod habeat duo supradicta, scilicet theoricam sciencie Sacre Scripture in materia visionum, quam sancti patres et doctores subtiliter et lucide descripserunt, et practicam experiencie vite spiritualis et sentimentorum consolacionum et visionum mentalium, spiritualiter aut intellectualiter sibi diuinitus infusorum. **16** Et quia communiter hodie in paucis personis ista theorica et practica supradicta discernendi et iuste iudicandi visiones et spiritus, proch dolor, inueniuntur, **17** ideo multi velut ceci oberrantes per inuia in ista materia pocius ex arrupto ad condempnandum simplices et sanctas personas

The whech to discerne p*er*fitly and to p*re*ue or rep*re*ue tho — 10) thing*es* the whech suld be p*re*uyd or repreuyd/legginge no thinge resonabil 11) in yer on wysse iugement*es* and sodeyn seying*es* or rader det*rac*-cou*ns*/but that the 12) aungil of the deule oftyn tymes t*ra*nsfoormys him vnd*er* the spice and kende 13) of the aungil of light/and bringis foorth exsamplis of odyr sp*iri*tual p*er*sonys 14) the whech in tymis past {we}<was> deludid of the deule in yer visions not thinking 15) on the*m* y*at* where illumynid of god be visiou*ns* . And be tho thei have lightned 16) the chirch of god and odir men condempny*n*g namly simpil sp*iri*tual p*er*sonys 17) ydiot*es* and the kende of a woma*n* as ignorau*n*t/and of <a> light capacite a*nd* reputacou*n* 18) and y*er*fore to be taken on worthy. on to godly . visions or p*ro*fecyes/nat {.} 19) attendinge y*at* almighty god as weel in the old testame*n*t as in ye newe. 20) to shew his gret might has chosin to him as wel in woma*n*kende as 21) man kende . to confounde wisemen./whedir he made nat a p*ro*fete of 22) a scheppard and repleshid ȝoung ydiot*es* w*ith* sprith of p*ro*fecie/And whed*ir* 23) he chos nat/rude me*n* and fischer*es* in to apostolys and { . . } doughtor*es* hey 24) ar repleschid w*ith* the holy gost Also whedir mary the sust<*er*of> aaron . iudith . 25) and est*er* were geuen the sprith of p*ro*fecye/whedir nat Kinge Iosye. 26) was direct in his ded*es* be . oldam awoma*n* and a . profetisse/whedir not 27) thinkys and reme*m*bris yat delbora. the p*ro*fetyss gov*er*nyd the pepil of israel. 28) Also Anne the modir of sampson and odir wome*n* in y*e* old testament had. [*fol. 248r.*] 1) the sprith. of p*ro*fecye Also in the new testament Anne the dought*er* of fanuel 2) p*ro*fecied Elizabeth . Zacary . blissid lucye þ*e* v*er*gin as it is red in hir bokis Sibyl 3) tiburtyne and anod*er* Sibil and many odir of the whech y*ou* schal finde in holy 4) scripture and of seint*es* And for yat it is p*er*lous on avisid to condempne or to/re 5) p*re*ue sp*iri*tual visiou*ns*/ or the p*er*sonys seing that they haue dyuyn visions/or they

Deo coniunctas conuertuntur quam ad perfecte discernendum et iuste approbandum aut reprobandum ea, que pocius approbanda vel reprobanda forent, **18** nichil racionabile in suis improuidis iudiciis et subitaneis dictis seu pocius detraccionibus allegantes, nisi quod angelus Sathane sepe sub angeli lucis specie se transformat,[5] **19** et proferunt in medium exempla aliquarum personarum spiritualium, que preteritis temporibus in suis visionibus a dyabolo deluse fuerunt, **20** immemores tamen illorum, qui per diuinas visiones et infusiones a Deo illuminati fuerunt et per illas ecclesiam Dei et alios illustrauerunt et direxerunt, **21** condempnantes precipue simplices personas spirituales ydiotas et sexum femineum quasi ignarum et leuis capacitatis et reputacionis et ideo indignum ad visiones diuinas seu propheticas capescendas, **22** non attendentes, quod Deus omnipotens tam in Veteri quam in Nouo Testamento ad ostendendum omnipotenciam suam sepe infirma mundi elegit sibi tam in femineo sexu quam in masculis, vt confundat sapientes.[6] **23** Nonne de pastore fecit prophetam et iuuenes ydiotas repleuit spiritu prophecie? Et nonne non doctores sed piscatores et rudes homines elegit in apostolos, qui spiritu sancto repleti sunt? **24** Numquid non eciam Maria, soror Aaron, Iudith et Hester spiritu prophecie dotate fuerunt? Numquid non per Oldan mulierem prophetissam rex Iosias in agendis directus est? **25** Nonne recordaris, quod Delbora prophetissa rexit populum Israel, Anna quoque, mater Samuelis, Agar et vxor Manue, mater Sampson et alie femine in Veteri Testamento prophecie spiritum habuerunt? **26** In Nouo eciam Testamento Anna, Fanuel filia, prophetauit, Elizabeth Zacharie, beata Lucia virgo, vt habetur in libris suis, Sibilla Tyburtina, Sibilla Erictea et multe alie, de quibus in libris Sacre Scripture et sanctorum copiam magnam inuenies.

27 Et idcirco, quia periculosum est ex improuiso condempnare vel approbare spirituales visiones et personas asserentes se visiones diuinas habere, **28** antequam subtiliter

6) be examyned of the q*ua*lite of the p*er*sonys And also of ye man*er* of seinge and of 7) the q*ua*lite of the mater of visions. and all may be p*re*uyd be godd*es* scripture . and 8) of the writing*es* of holy doughttor*es* whedyr yei ar infudid or mynystred of illusiou*n* 9) or of the sprith. of treuþe./ffor we see y*at* pharao be leuyd not moyses yat he sy 10) god for he was a sympel man. And y*er*fore he not beleuyng {stodstille}[7] his vision 11) ne*n* his seing*es* and {.} rader the seinge of god/but stodstille frouardly in hardnes 12) of { . . } <hert and> mysbeleue. Therfore he was cast wrecchedly in ye red see w*ith* the 13) pepil of egipt. And also I haue sien ma<n>y moo in my*n* dayes. <the whech> ar mo[v]ed nout 14) to god counting*e* soche sp*iri*tual p*er*sonys sempil and ydiot*es* and yer sp*iri*tual visiou*ns*—15) veyne and feyned and fantasies. ffor the whech thei ar exspert wrecchidly. 16) the cruel sentens of god on them self and on þ*er* sogett*es* be the p*er*sonys and y*er* 17) visions p*re*nu*n*sid be fore to the*m*./Be exsampil in destruccou*n* of the kingedom of 18) cypris/for yat the prince beleuyd not the visions of blissid brigid to who*m* this 19) p*re*sent booke was shewid . as it is wretyn in y*e* last heue*n*ly boke xix chapet*er* 20) Also I haue seen and herd odir yat be levid illusions and fil p*er*lously. The—21) exsample of this see in y*e* vi boke lxviii chapet*er*./And in ye booke of collacou*ns* 22) of fadris. of John cassian . collacou*n* the ii chapet*er* w*ith* many like þ*er*fore it is more 23) {wid} wisdom to discusse w*ith* gret sadnes soche visions and p*er*sonys and yan the*m* 24) wel w*ith* deliberacou*n* and sadnes discussid and discretly iugid {awdir}<owdir> to preve p*re*uyd 25) or to <be> rep*re*ued/ The apostil seis preff whed*er* the sprit*es* be of god/and yan iff 26) it be foundin yat thei be of god we owe mekely to be leue the*m* and obey 27) them

examinetur de qualitate ipsarum personarum et eciam de modo videndi et de qualitate materie visionum et perspicaciter exprobentur ista omnia per Diuinam Scripturam et per scripta sanctorum doctorum, vtrum ab illusione vel an a spiritu veritatis infuse siue ministrate sint - **29** quia videmus quod Pharao non credidit Moysi, qui homo simplex erat et Deum viderat, et ideo eius visioni et dictis, vel pocius Dei, non credens, in duricia incredulitatis pertinaciter perstitit, propter quod in Mari Rubro cum populo Egypti miserabiliter precipitauit, **30** et multos alios eciam vidi temporibus meis, qui tales spirituales personas simplices et ydiotas et visiones earum spirituales vanas et quasi confictas aut fantasticas reputantes inobedientes Deo effecti sunt, **31** propter quod super se et subditos suos sentencias Dei crudelissimas, sibi per illas personas et earum visiones ante prenunciatas, miserabiliter experti sunt (**32** exemplum vide in destruccione regni Cypri, quia non credidit princeps visionibus beate Brigide, cui presens liber extitit reuelatus, vt habetur in vltimo Libro Celesti, XIX capitulo; **33** alios eciam vidi et audiui, qui credebant illusionibus et ex hoc periculose corruerunt, **34** exemplum huius vide in VI Libro Celesti, LXVIII capitulo et in libro Collacionum Patrum Iohannis Cassiani, collactione II, capitulo "Et vt hanc eandem" cum multis similibus) - **35** ideo consulcius est visiones et personas tales cum magna maturitate discutere et eas tunc bene et cum deliberacione et maturitate discussas et discrete iudicatas aut approbare aut eciam reprobare. **36** Ait enim apostolus: *Probate spiritus, vtrum a Deo sint.*[8] Et si tunc in examine inuentum est, quod a Deo sint, debemus humiliter illas credere et eis totaliter

holly. And yf thei be of the deule as wikkid illusions yan we owe to 28) dispise the*m* and noman*er* of wyse to geve feith to them//— // —29) The man*er* exsamynacou*n* is put here in theorike of ye qualite of the p*er*sone [*fol. 248v.*] 1) seinge visions and the man*er* of hauyng of them and of the q*ua*lite of mat*er* of visions 2) and of reuelacou*ns*//-/ the secunde chaptre ./3) holy fadris and doctoris of the chirche seis. yat a p*er*sone seinge visions shuld 4) be exsamynde on this wise. whe[d]i[r] it be a sp{*er*}*irit*ual p[er]sone or a wordly and 5) seculer whedir he leuys vnd*er* disciplyn and sp*irit*ual obediens of any discrete senior 6) or in his owne fre choise and wil . Also whed*er* he has put anoon his temptacou*ns* 7) and soche odir visions to examyni*ng* and doom of his sp*irit*ual fadir or odir discret 8) men w*ith* humilite bredinge to be illudid or alls he had hid the*m* or has p*re*sumyd 9) and <be> proud of the*m* and di[sp]isid odir men/Also y*is* p*er*sone shuld be examyned . seing 10) thos visions whedir he be of obediens humilite and cherite and tenting p*ra*your 11) or ded*es* of p*ri*de p*ro*cedis fro him for honouir or dignite . Also whedir this p*er*sone 12) be countyd among sp*irit*ual me*n* feithful and obedient to ye p*re*lat*es* and goue*r*nour*es* 13) of the chirche/or he be suspect of the feith or of obediens of p*re*lat*es* of ye chirch . 14) Also whedir he haue p*er*seu*er*yd <long> in sp*irit*ual liff v*er*tuosly or ell new begynner

obedire. **37** Si vero a dyabolo sint, vt illusiones pessimas illas debemus despicere et eis nullatenus fidem dare.

Ponitur hic in theorica modus examinis faciendi de qualitate persone videntis visiones et de modo habendi eas ac de qualitate materie visionum et reuelacionum.

Capitulum II.

1 Dicunt sancti patres et doctores Ecclesie, quod persona visiones videns debet tali modo examinari, **2** an scilicet sit persona spiritualis vel an sit mundana et secularis, **3** an eciam viuit sub disciplina et obediencia speciali, continua, spirituali alicuius senioris, discreti, virtuosi et maturi, catholici et experti patris spiritualis vel an in proprio arbitrio et voluntate, **4** item vtrum temptaciones suas et illas tales visiones, quas habet, statim supposuerit examini et iudicio sui patris spiritualis vel aliorum discretorum seniorum patrum spiritualium, cum humilitate timens illudi vel an eas occultauerit nulliusque examini et iudicio eas supposuerit, **5** aut ex illis de se presumpserit et se iactauerit vel se reputando alios despexerit. **6** Item examinari debet, vtrum ab ista persona vidente visiones resultent veri actus et virtutes obediencie, humilitatis et caritatis et intente oracionis, **7** vel an procedant ab ea actus reputacionis et iactancie aut superbie seu ostentacionis et elacionis vel appetitus laudis humane aut negligencia oracionis siue ambicio honoris vel dignitatis, **8** item vtrum ista persona apud viros spirituales reputetur vere catholica et fidelis et obediens prelatis et rectoribus Ecclesie, vel an sit suspecta de fide vel de obediencia prelatorum et rectorum Ecclesie, **9** item vtrum in vita spirituali virtuose et in penitencia et in habendo frequentes visiones humiliter et diu perseuerauerit, vel an in hoc sit recens et nouicia,

15) Also whedir he haue natural vndirstondinge and sp*iritu*al and veri discret. 16) doom of resoun/or he has but light vndirstonding*e* or sodeyn and fantastyk. 17) Gregory seis in his dyalogys yat holy me*n* discernys among illusions and . 18) reuelacou*ns* of visions ./voyces or ymagis w*ith* anInwardly . slombring[9]/yat 19) they may knowe what y*ei* sshal p*er*seyue of agood sprit/or what they schal 20) suffre of an illusor and whedir this p*er*sone was exsamynde <ony> odyr tyme 21) of the mat*er* and man*er* of visions be lettrid me*n* and sp*iritu*al or noo/And 22) these ar semyd to be sufficient as to examynacou*n* of the p*er*sone/ As to 23) the man*er* of seing and hering*e* sp*iritu*ally visions {and} <or> reuelacou*ns*/holy fadris 24) and doctoris of the chirch seis/yat it owis to be examynd. whedir this 25) p*er*sone seinge visions and hering the spechis of the*m*/whedir he se them 26) wakinge or slepinge <or dr[e]myng> or in bodily vision or ymaginacou*n* and gostly or 27) happili intellectual vision a boue nature . And whedir in y*at* me*n*tal ravesching 28) that is to sey . wha*n* he sees soche thing*es* . he felis su*m* me*n*tal suetnes . of godd*es* 29) love . or noo/And whedir than he seis and heris ony thing speking to him *[fol. 249r.]*1) any misteriis . or sheuyng ony godly douct*ri*nys or noo/And in what {h.} kende the 2) p*er*sone seis soche And whedir he fele than ony light of inteligens of manifestacou*n* of godly 3) mat*er* of y*e* visions or noo/Also he ought to be exsamyned whedir ye visions acordis w*ith* 4) diuyne scripture or discordis . And whedir yt induc*es* ony error or no/or ony newe thinge 5) that discordis fro resoun . Or if these visions be all wey trewe or su*m*tyme fals and lyes. 6) And whedir thei speke <of> honour*es* to come or riches or mannys loouyng*es* or humilite 7) in all thing*es* Or

10 item an ista persona visiones videns habeat bonum intellectum naturalem et spiritualem et verum et discretum iudicium racionis et spiritus, vel an sit leuis intellectus vel subita aut fantastica—**11** dicit enim Gregorius in Dyalogo, quod *sancti viri inter illusiones atque reuelaciones ipsas visionum voces aut ymagines quodam intimo sapore discernunt, vt sciant vel quid a bono spiritu percipiant vel quid ab illusore paciantur*—**12** et vtrum ista persona fuerit alias examinate de materia et modo visionum per viros litteratos et spirituales et approbata vel an non. **13** Et hec sufficere videntur quantum ad examinacionem persone.

Quantum vero ad modum videndi et audiendi spiritualiter et recipiendi reuelaciones seu visiones dicunt sancti patres et Ecclesie sancti doctores, quod debet examinari subtiliter, **14** vtrum ista persona videns visiones et audiens locuciones earum videt eas vigilando vel an dormiendo et sompniando **15** et vtrum in visione corporali vel an in visione ymaginaria et spirituali vel vtrum forte in visione intellectuali supernaturali **16** et vtrum in illo raptu mentali, qui extasis vocatur, scilicet quando talia videt, senserit aliquam mentalem supernaturalem dulcedinem amoris diuini vel an non, **17** et vtrum tunc videt et audit aliquem sibi aliqua misteria loquentem aut diuinas doctrinas et spirituales demonstrantem vel an non, et in qua specie tales personas videt, **18** et vtrum tunc sentit illuminacionem seu quandam illustracionem supernaturalis luminis intelligencie manifestacionis veritatis diuine illius materie illorum visorum vel an non.

19 De qualitate eciam et materia ipsarum visionum debet examinari, vtrum visiones ille concordant cum Diuina Scriptura vel an discrepant ab ea, **20** et vtrum visio illa sit ad humanorum actuum virtuosam direccionem et salutem animarum, vel an inducat in errorem catholice fidei vel an inducat aliquid monstrum et nouum vel aliquid, quod a racione discordet, aut a bonis, virtuosis et humilibus moribus nos auertat, **21** et an iste visiones semper vere sint an aliquando mendaces et false, scilicet quod illa, que predicunt, aliquando sint vera et aliquando non, **22** et an predicunt nobis futuros honores aut diuicias aut laudes humanas an humilitatem in omnibus, an eciam inducunt nos, quod extollamur aut quod presumamus et confidamus de aliquibus virtutibus nostris, an quod humiliemur, **23** item vtrum nos monent ad

mene vs ony thing to obey . v*er*tuos p*er*sonys/or co*n*trary . And be cause 8) of breffnes finally I sey . to make p*er*fit examinacou*n* in this mater as wel of the q*ua*lite 9) of the p*er*sone seinge this vision/as of the man*er* of seinge and of ye q*ua*lite of the mater 10) of visions . to discerne sprit*es* yat scheuys them or mynistris whedir thei be good sprit*es* 11) or ylle . Se moor pleynly . in y*e* heue*n*ly booke of reuelacou*n*s of god . to y*is* holy Brigid . 12) of suecy of the whech is wretyn in ye first booke . iiii*te.* chaptre . And in y*e* same booke. liiii*e* 13) chaptre And in y*e* iii*de* booke the {. . } x*o*/c*haptre* And in the iiii*te* booke/xxiii*o* c*apitulo*/and cx*o*{.} c*apitulo* 14) And in the vi boke/lii*o* c*apitulo*/and lxviii*o* c*apitulo*/ w*ith* many like where the forseyd lady . was 15) infoormyd plenarly of virgyn mary to discerne sprit*es* and visions of this mater 16) But if soche examynacou*n* goo be fore a perelous errore may happyn to come. And 3it 17) soche errour happenys offtyn tymes for defaute of discrete and sad examynacou*n* 18) The qualite of p*er*sone and of v*er*tuys of holi Brigid is conteyned her to whom y*is* 19) booke w*ith* in wretyn was schewyd and reuelat/. iii . chaptre. 20) These thing*es* sen in p*ra*ctisinge now to the mater of the qualite of the p*er*sone 21) to who*m* this p*re*sent boke was reuelat yt is to be knowin yat yis nobil 22) lady seynt brigid . ye whech sy. and herd .<sprit> visions of this p*re*sent booke and also of 23) y*at* gret heue[n]ly boke and many odir thing*es* and wrot the*m* to gedir . of be ye p*re*cept 24) of god as it is had in y*e* sext heue*n*ly booke/p*rimo* c*apitulo*/sprongin of the kende of the 25) kinges of gothis/and in the kingedom

obediendum eciam puris et simplicibus virtuosis personis spiritualibus et prepositis nostris an ad contrarium.

24 Et causa breuitatis finaliter dico, quod ad perfectam examinacionem faciendam in ista materia tam de qualitate persone videntis visiones quam de qualitate et modo videndi, quam eciam de qualitate materie visionum et de modo discernendi spiritus, qui illas ostendunt, infundunt seu ministrant, vtrum boni spiritus an mali sint, **25** vide plenissime in Libro Celesti Reuelacionum Dei ad istam beatam Brigidam de Suecia, de qua hic agitur, in libro I, IIII capitulo et eodem libro, LIIII capitulo et in III libro, X capitulo et in IIII libro, XXIII capitulo et CX capitulo et in VI libro, LII capitulo et LXVIII capitulo cum multis similibus, **26** vbi predicta domina a Christo et virgine Maria plene instruebatur de ista materia discernendi spiritus et visiones et mentalia sentimenta. **27** Nam si talis subtilis examinacio non precesserit, error periculosus poterit euenire in approbante vel reprobante indiscusse et ex arrupto talia videntem et eius visiones et reuelaciones, **28** quia forte iste subitus et indiscretus ex arrupto approbans talem videntem et eius visiones recipiet falsa pro veris, et vera vt falsa periculosissime reputabit, **29** et sic bone et vere visiones seu locuciones diuine respuentur et non credentur nec eis obedietur, eciam si veraciter a voluntate Dei processerunt, **30** falsis vero illusionibus fides prestabitur et obedietur in dampnum videntis et subito approbantis aut reprobantis indiscusse et ex improuiso, quod sepe contigit tam in Veteri Testamento quam in Nouo, et adhuc hodie talis error sepe contingit propter defectum discreti et maturi examinis.

Continetur hic qualitas persone et virtutum beate Brigide, cui infrascriptus liber extitit reuelatus.[10]

Capitulum III.

1 Hiis igitur in theorica visis, nunc iam practicando ad materiam qualitatis persone, cui reuelatus fuit presens liber, veniamus. **2** Sciendum ergo est, quod illustris domina sancte memorie beata Brigida, que visiones presentis libri et eciam illius magni Libri Celestis et alia multa in spiritu vidit et audiuit et ex precepto Dei illas conscripsit, vt habetur in VI Libro

of s[ue]cy . was born . the whech 3it leuyng 26) in wedloc/brougth. {to} hir husband to þe p*er*feccou*n* of chas[t]ite . yat yey leuyd 27) many 3er*es* w*ith*ought dede of the flesch . And so boye too went on pilgrimage to Seint Iamys in to galis w*ith* gret laboure*e* and exspensis and w*ith* gret deuocion . 29) And after ward ret*er*nyd hoom to yer owne cuntry of the kingedom of swecy. [*fol. 249v.*] 1) wher as hir husband died. and went to god Aftir yat sche was kendelid w*ith* the fyre of cher<i>te 2) she be toke hir self holly to crist the wheche toke hir benig[n]ly to his spouse . as it is had in ye 3) first heuenly boke/ii*o* c*apitulo*/And frothens forth sche be gan to haue more clerly. godly visions. the 4) whech anon sche put mekely to ye examynacou*n* of hir gostly fad*er* an holy ma*n* ye whech 5) was mast*er* in thologie callid mast*er* Mathie of suecy. achanon of licope*n*us chirch the whech 6) glosid the hol bibil/as it is wrety*n* in ye vi boke./lxxix*o* c*apitulo*/This lady expounyd these 7) visions mekely to exami*na*cou*n* and doom of odir prelat*es* and religious sp*iri*tual me*n* as it 8) is wretyn in ye iiii*te* heue*n*ly booke./lxxviii*o* c*apitulo* Aft*er* yat these p*er*fite me*n* in sciens and gostly 9) in lyff p*re*uyd these visions and re-u<e>lacou*n*s shewid to ye seyd lady . and gaff in sentens yat 10) thei p*ro*cedid fro ye sprith of treuye and not of an yllusor the sprith of falshed. Than 11) she beinge poore folowyd crist poor*e* and to folow his steppis/of all hir good*es* res*er*uid no 12) moore but sympil mete and drinke and cloth. And made distribucou*n* of all hir odir good*es* 13) amonge hir sonys and poore pepil. And be ye p*re*cept of crist went forth of hir cuntre 14) and knoulache. And so sche come to Rome on pilg*re*mage to ye staciou*n* and to vesite 15) pet*er* and poule . and odir seint*es* relikis whils y*at* crist bad hir do odyr thinge hauyng*e* 16) eu*er* w*ith* hir ii old men sad

Celesti, CI capitulo, **3** de genere regum Gothorum exorta et in regno Suecie, quod est ad aquilonem, nata fuit. Cuius parentes nobiliter et virtuose vixerunt. **4** Que adhuc in coniugio viuens maritum suum ad continencie perfeccionem adduxit, vt multis annis sine carnis copula viuerent, **5** et sic ambo ad Sanctum Iacobum de Galicia peregre profecti sunt in magnis laboribus et expensis et cum deuocione maxima, **6** et postea ad patrium suam regni Suecie redierunt, vbi tunc predictus maritus migrauit ad Dominum.

7 Ipsa vero tunc accensa perfecto castitatis amore totam Christo se totaliter tradidit, qui eam illico in sponsam suam benigne suis verbis amplectendo suscepit, vt habetur in primo Libro Celesti, II capitulo. **8** Et tunc ipsa incepit habere clarius visiones diuinas, quas statim supposuit humiliter examini cuiusdam sui patris spiritualis, sancti viri, qui erat magister in theologia, scilicet magistri Mathie de Suecia, canonici Lincopensis ecclesie, qui glosauit totam Bibliam, vt habetur in VI Libro Celesti, LXXXIX capitulo, **9** et exposuit eciam domina istas visiones suas humiliter examini et iudicio aliorum prelatorum et religiosorum spiritualium virorum, vt habetur in IIII Libro Celesti, LXXVIII capitulo et expressius in prologo Regule Saluatoris ei diuinitus reuelate. **10** Postquam vero predicti viri, periti in sciencia et spirituales in vita, visiones et infusiones et reuelaciones predicte domine reuelatas approbauerunt et sentenciauerunt eas procedere a Spiritu Sancto veritatis et non ab illusore spiritu falsitatis, **11** tunc ipsa, desiderans Christum pauperem pauper sequi et eius quodammodo vestigia imitari, de omnibus bonis suis nichil sibi nisi simplicissimum victum et vestitum humilem reseruauit. **12** Et sic, ceteris aliis suis bonis distributis inter filios suos et Christi pauperes habundanter et a mundi retinaculis se expediens, ex precepto Christi egressa est exemplo Abrahe de terra sua et de cognacione sua, vt patet in legenda vite eius, **13** et sic ad Romam peregrinando deuenit ad standum ibi in vita penitencie et ad visitandum humiliter limina apostolorum et reliquias aliorum sanctorum, donec Christus ei aliud precepit, **14** habens semper secum alios duos

and v*er*tuos and v*er*ginis and exp*er*t sp*irit*ual fadris . the whech 17) folwyd her til sche deyed ./yt was acording yat the most chast husband ye wheche 18) co*m*mendid his mood*er* to his discipyl being a virgin þ*at* he shuld comende his new 19) spowse to v*er*ginys and v*er*tuus fadris to be gou*er*nyd . Of the whech oon was a monke 20) religious and p*ri*or of cistens. a maydin in his flesch and sufficiently le<t>trid And for 21) that seide lady . wrot the revelacou*n*s as it is before seid be the p*re*cept of crist in hir 22) gotyk tunge. y*er*fore the seyd priour be ye co*m*maunde-ment of crist t*ra*nslatid all ye 23) bokis and yis p*re*sent boke. fro the moodir tunge in to latyn shouyd to ye seid lady . 24) Anodir gostly fadir of this lady was a prest of suecy . a virgin of venerabil liff/ye 25) wheche gou*er*nyd all the hous of the seid lady . and he taught hir and hir dought*er* 26) g*ra*mer and songe be *ye* p*re*cept of crist The whech fadris she as a meke monke 27) obeyed in all v*er*tuys/in someche yat sche durst nat left vp hir eyin fro ye ground 28) but yf sche had askid him ferst a special licens and g*ra*ntid . Eu*er*y day . sche was 29) shreuy*n* twis or thryes. And eu*er*y sonday sche and hir dought*er* reseyued w*ith* gret deuocou*n* 30) crist*es* body.

seniores, antiquos et maturos, virtuosos ac virgines et expertos patres spirituales, qui vsque ad mortem eam secuti sunt. **15** Congruum enim erat, quod ille castissimus sponsus, qui suam matrem virginem discipulo virgini commendauit, quod suam nouam sponsam eciam regendam virginibus et virtuosis patribus commendaret.

16 Quorum vnus monachus et prior Cisterciensis religiosissimus erat, virgo carne et satis sciencia litteratus. **17** Et quia ipsa domina reuelaciones scribebat, vt prefertur, ex precepto Christi in lingua sua Gothica, ideo ex eodem precepto Christi iste prior translatauit de illa lingua sua materna in Latinum omnes libros, et istum presentem, eidem domine diuinitus reuelatos. **18** De quo quidem religioso mencio fit in prologo Libro Celestis in fine. **19** Alter vero pater spiritualis istius domine erat quidam presbiter de Suecia, virgo eciam venerabilis et sanctissime vite, qui totam domum predicte domine regebat et eam cum filia sua gramaticam et cantum ex precepto Christi docuit et in viam virtutum paternalibus correccionibus virtuose corrigendo direxit.

20 Quibus patribus ipsa in tota vita sua in omnibus virtutibus ita humiliter obediuit, sicut verus monachus humilis obedire solet prelato suo, propter quod ipsa in tantam humilitatem et obedienciam et perfectam mortificacionem sue proprie voluntatis deuenit, **21** quod, quando ibat per indulgencias et sanctuaria, sociata semper cum predicto presbitero, suo patre spirituali, non audebat eleuare aspectum oculorum suorum de terra, nisi prius requisisset et obtinuisset ad hoc specialem licenciam eiusdem sui patris spiritualis. **22** Omni eciam die ipsa confitebatur bis et ter, et omni die dominica ipsa et predicta veneranda filia sua, que secum laudabiliter vixit et vsque ad mortem in penitencia et castissima viduitate honestissime perseuerauit, corpus Christi cum maxima deuocione et humilitate sumebant, **23** semper viuentes in magnis secretis penitenciis corporalibus, quas non oculis hominum ad vanam

And she was nat only meke owtuard*es* agenis men but also inwardly. 31) ageyn god countid hir self on worthi sinner as y*ou* may clerly see in ye secund 32) heue*n*ly booke ./ca*pitulo* xv*o* and in the sext boke ca*pitulo* lii*o*/And in the secund boke ca*pitulo* 33) xviii*o*/w*ith* many moo like/ what paciens she had . yow may see in y*e* iiii*te* heue*n*ly [*fol. 250r.*] 1) boke ca*pitulo* cxxiiii*o*/yat be gynnes thus Agnes spekis to ye spouse {di} seinge.[11] Come dought*er* 2) *et cetera*/and what hete of cherite sche had to crist and to virgin mary his moodir ./see 3) in ye iiii*te* boke / ca*pitulo* lxiii*o*/And in ye vi*te* ca*pitulo* lii*o*/And in the last boke/ca*pitulo* pr*i*mo/ *and* 4) the xiii*o* ca*pitulo*/Sche louyd hir neybours. w*ith* a modirly compassion . as it scheuys in þe 5) iii*de* boke./a*pitulo* xxiii*o*/On a tyme. wha*n* the kinge of Swecy wold haue greuyd his sogett*es* 6) w*ith* gret charg*es* <in> all his regne . yat they shuld pay . as*er*teyne q*ua*ntite of mony. in the 7) whech he was boundyn . to his borowis ./

gloriam sed soli Deo humiliter offerebant in simplicitate cordis et puritate spiritus sub predictorum duorum patrum spiritualium humili subieccione et continua obediencia spirituali. **24** Quibus patribus visiones, quas ipsa beata Brigida habebat, statim detegebat et omnia humiliter subiciebat eorum iudicio et discrecioni. **25** Et non solum ipsa erat humilis exterius apud homines, sed eciam intrinsecus apud Deum tam indignam et peccatricem se reputabat, quod in oracione sepe loquendo Christo, quasi de eo stupendo mirabatur et quodammodo eum redarguebat, **26** quia eam tam indignam ad videndum visiones diuinas et audiendum et scribendum sanctissima verba eius ipse sibi eam elegerat, vt clare videre poteris in secundo Libro Celesti, capitulo XV et in VI libro, capitulo LII in principio et "Tunc ego" et in II libro, capitulo XVIII cum multis similibus.

27 Qualem autem pacienciam et equanimitatem habebat prefata domina, non ego respondere volo, sed pocius respondeat tibi de hoc illa gloriosa virgo, Sancta Agnes, que de hoc testimonium perhibet in quarto Libro Celesti, CXXIIII capitulo, quod incipit: **28** *Agnes loquitur ad sponsam dicens: "Veni, filia, et impone tibi coronam factam ex septem lapidibus preciosis.*" Et de hoc vide lacius in legenda vite eiusdem domine, beate Brigide. **29** Qualem eciam ardorem caritatis habuit ad Christum et eius matrem virginem, vide in quarto Libro Celesti, LXIII capitulo et in VI libro, LII capitulo et in vltimo libro, capitulo I et capitulo XIII in fine cum multis similibus.

30 Proximos eciam ita materna compassione diligebat, quod, pro multis in specie et pro omnibus eciam in genere ad Christum orando, infinitas preces et lacrimas frequenter deuotissime effundebat, vt patet in libro III, XXIII capitulo et in multis aliis capitulis Libri Celestis. **31** Immo quodam tempore cum rex Suecie grauare vellet subditos suos in toto regno magnis exaccionibus, vt solueret quandam pecunie quantitatem, in qua tenebatur creditoribus,

ya*n* blissid Bregid seid to ye kinge./Sere do not 8) so/but take my*n* too sonys and put the*m* in plegge . wils y*ou* may pay. and offende not 9) god and thin sogett*es* as it is had moore clerly in hir legend.

32 tunc beata Brigida dixit regi: *Domine, noli hoc facere, sed recipe duos filios meos et pone eos obsides, donec soluere poteris, et non offendas Deum et subditos tuos,* vt hoc clarius habetur in legenda vite eius.

33 Omnibus autem aliis virtutibus predicta domina in tantum adornata et repleta erat, quod Christus eam in sponsam miro modo recepit et ipsam mirandis consolacionibus et diuinis graciis frequentissime visitauit dicens ei: **34** *Ego elegi te michi in sponsam, vt ostendam tibi secreta mea, quia michi sic placet.* 35 Et post paululum subiunxit dicens: *Propterea assumo te michi in sponsam et in meam propriam delectacionem, qualem decet Deum habere cum anima casta,* vt patet hoc in primo Libro Celesti, capitulo II cum multis similibus, que inuenies in libris, eidem domine diuinitus reuelatis.

36 De quibus quidem diuinis graciis ipsa numquam superbiebat, immo cotidie humiliando se, me teste, cum lacrimis et magis debitricem Deo se reputando grauius iudicium de hoc sibi superesse timebat. **37** Latere quidem ipsa et thesaurum istum diuinarum reuelacionum abscondere ob humilitatis custodiam maluisset, sed Christus eam imperio verborum suorum pluries astrinxit ad scribendum et loquendum verba sua diuina intrepide summis pontificibus, imperatori, regibus et principibus ac aliis gentibus, **38** vt ex istis diuinis verbis, scilicet Libri Celestis et presentis libri, homines peccatores ad Deum se conuerterent, boni autem et iusti in melius proficerent, **39** vt patet hoc clare in vltimo Libro Celesti, capitulo XXVII et in VI libro, capitulo CI cum multis similibus et in isto presenti Libro Celestis Imperatoris ad Reges in pluribus capitulis.

40 Quis enim talem vitam existimet ludibriis patere demonum Christumque tante impietatis arguere audebit, vt non tueretur in se sperantem et non se sed ipsum ex dileccionis eius plenitudine glorificantem? **41** Vel numquid bonus sponsus castam coniugem et fidelem exponit adultero illudendum?

10) Here it is sheuyd how many wysis blissid brigid had visions And reuelacou*ns* 11) fferderemore as I seide nowe be fore. and has made opyn to men not knowing*e* 12) su*m*thing*es* of the q*ua*lite of p*er*sone and of v*er*tuys of blissid bregid . And for yat now 13) many me*n* ar mervelid and doughte*s* of this g*ra*ce of seinge and herynge sp*irit*ual visions 14) geuy*n* to ye forseid blissid bregid . desiring to be s*er*tified of the man*er* yat she sy soche 15) thing*es* and herd ./oftyn tymes thei askid me/yat I shuld telle the*m* be rowe[12] of yat 16) and shuld testifie <the*m*> clerly . of the treuþ*e* . yat be ye infusion of <what> sprith. all <thes> thing*es* ar 17) reuelate*s* . Therfore I to ye honour of god and v*er*gin mary . and of the forseid blissid 18) lady. Shuld shewe first to the*m* to remeue all doughte*s* of *yer* h*er*tis how and what 19) man*er* of wise sche sy and herd the visions and reuelacou*ns* and aft*er*ward*es* I schal 20) p*re*ue be diuyne scripture ./yat thei procedid fro þe holy sprith . and nout fro ye 21) sprith of illusion./To ye ferst I sey . yat they may be certified/of yat maner 22) the whech sche sy . ye visions/not alonly be my*n* wordis but also be the wordis 23) of hir self blissid Bregid ./The whech sche hir self notifies clerly . in many chapetris 24) of ye bokis . And namly in ye iiii*te* boke/lxxvii*o* ca*pitulo*/And in ye vi*te* boke/ca*pitulo* lii*o*/25) where sche spekis w*ith* crist these wordis/O most dere god . and bestbelouyd of all 26) men yat y*ou* has made w*ith* me yis meruelous thinge {.} all me*n* heringe . And 27) so foorth.

Hic ostenditur qualibus modis beata Brigida habebat visiones et reuelaciones.

Capitulum IIII.

1 Preterea, quia iam dixi supra et patefeci nescientibus aliqua de qualitate persone et virtutibus beate Brigide, nunc autem, quia multi mirantur et dubitant de ista gracia videndi et audiendi visiones spirituales prefate beate domine data, **2** et certificari desiderantes de modo, quo ipsa talia videbat et audiebat, sepe requisierunt me, quod ego eis hoc seriose dicerem et de pura veritate eos clare certificarem et cuius infusione spiritus omnia ista reuelata existant, **3** ideo ego ad honorem Dei et virginis et predicte beatissime domine ac eciam ad remouendum dubium de cordibus predictorum dubitancium ostendam eis primo, qualiter et quibus modis ipsa visiones et reuelaciones videbat et audiebat, **4** et postea per ventilabrum diuine scripture probabo, quod a Spiritu Sancto hec et non a spiritu illusionis certissime procedebant.

5 Ad primum igitur dico, quod ipsi possunt de modo, quo ipsa visiones videbat, certificari non solum per mea sed eciam per verba ipsiusmet beate Brigide, que in pluribus capitulis librorum hec ipsa humiliter satis clare notificat et praesertim in IIII Libro Celesti, LXXVII capitulo et in libro VI, LII capitulo, vbi cum Christo loquitur ipsa in hec verba: **6** *O carissime Deus et omnium dilectissime, mirabile omnibus audientibus est illud, quod tu mecum fecisti. Nam quando placet tibi, tunc sopis corpus meum, non tamen sopore corporali, sed quadam quiete spirituali. Animam autem meam tunc quasi a sompno excitas ad videndum et audiendum atque senciendum spiritualiter.* **7** *O domine Deus, o quam dulcia sunt oris tui verba. Videtur vere michi, quociens verba spiritus tui audio, quod anima mea illa in se degluciat cum quodam sentimento ineffabilis dulcedinis sicut suauissimum cibum, qui cadere videtur, in cor corporis mei cum magno gaudio et ineffabili consolacione.* 8 *Mirabile tamen hoc esse videtur quod dum verba tua audio, tunc vtrumque efficior, scilicet saciata et famelica, propter hoc autem saciata, quia tunc nichil aliud michi libet nisi illa, propter hoc vero famelica, quia semper augetur appetitus meus ad illa,* etc. **9** Et de hoc in

Also I haue seen the forseid lady . oftyn sethis/god beying <my*n*> witness/su*m*tyme 28) sittinge and su*m*tyme to stonde in p*ra*your as sche wer*e* alyenat fro hir self rapt 29) in hir sprith. nothinge seinge ne*n* hering of yat was doon in y*at* place where as 30) sche was bodyly . The whech whan she was reu*er*tid to hir self she told me on worthy [*fol. 250v.*] 1) thou I were and ye forseid hir ./ii . confessor*es* . the visions the wheche sche had than 2) and gret secret thing*es* of god. Also the maner of visions seing is had . clerly I nough 3) in a s*er*teyne vision and secret reuelacou*n*/send ou*er* be þe seid lady . to lord pope gregory 4) xi*o* wher it is told how sche beinge inp*ra*your waking was rapt in sprith. And tha*n* 5) all the strenkthis of hir body was semyd . as to fayle/neuer the les crist and v*er*gin 6) mary has declarid . to hir seing yat ye mouy*ng* of hir herte was noo*n* illusion. 7) but the g*ra*ce of god And the holy gost op*era*cou*n* as it is had in the secund boke . xviii*o* ca*pitulo* 8) and in the vi*te* boke./lxxxviii*o* c*apitulo*/. Also knowe yat the seid lady brigid/ p*ra*yng waking*e* 9) sy in sprith kendis and foormys ne*n* <yei> were nat declared to hir what they shuld 10) signifie./but dought*es* <sche> remayned

prologo et eciam in fine Regule Saluatoris, eidem domine diuinitus reuelate cum aliis similibus.

10 Ego eciam, Deo teste, pluries vidi predictam dominam aliquando sedendo, aliquando prostratam stare in oracione totam absortam et quasi exanimem, alienatam a sensibus corporis, raptam in extasi spiritus, nichil videntem nec audientem de hiis, que agebantur in loco illo, vbi ipsa corporaliter erat. **11** Que quando reuertebatur ad se, narrabat michi indigno ad talia et prefatis duobus confessoribus suis visiones, quas tunc habuerat, et secreta magnalia et archana Dei. **12** Habetur eciam eius modus videndi visiones satis clare in quadam visione et reuelacione secreta, per ipsam dominam transmissa domino pape Gregorio XI, vbi narratur, qualiter ipsa existente in oracione, vigilando rapta fuit in spiritu. **13** Et tunc omnes eius corporis vires quasi deficere videbantur, sed cor ipsius inflammabatur et exultabat caritatis ardore, eiusque anima consolabatur, et quodam diuino robore confortabatur spiritus eius, ac eciam tota ipsius consciencia et intelligencia replebatur intellectu spirituali, vt ibi continetur.

14 Aliquando quoque ipsa sensibiliter senciebat cum ineffabili exultacione spiritus quendam sensibilem corporalem motum mirabilem in corde suo, quasi si ibi esset infans viuus se reuoluens, qui motus ab extra videbatur. **15** Et de hoc dubitans ipsa, an esset illusio dyabolica, ostendit suis patribus spiritualibus. Qui videntes et tangentes illud in stuporem admiracionis redacti sunt. **16** Hoc tamen dubium declarauerunt ei Christus et virgo Maria satis pulcre dicentes, quod ille motus cordis non erat illusio sed diuina gracia et operacio Spiritus Sancti, vt habetur in II libro, XVIII capitulo et in VI libro, LXXXVIII capitulo.

17 Item scias, quod aliquando ipsa domina Brigida orans vigilando in excessu mentis videbat in spiritu aliquas species seu formas, **18** nec tunc declarabantur ei, quid significarent,

and ins*er*teyne of tokenyng*es* of tho visiounys . As 11) it is had in the iiii*te* boke the secu*n*d chapt*re*. And w*ith* in ye same boke of the heue*n*ly 12) emprore {of} to ye kinges xxxi*o* c*apitulo* The whech visiou*ns* was declarid aftirward*es* 13) of crist as it is had in the seyde chappet*re* xxxi*o* and in the last chapt*re* of y*e* 14) iiii*te* booke./And su*m*tyme no thing was declarid to {the*m*} hir of þ*e* significacou*ns* of 15) the visions./but eu*er* she was ins*er*teyn of the*m* . But thou may spere how may 16) it be yat this blissid lady . vigilant in preyour might se . as she oftin tyme 17) sy . rapt in sprith./crist and his mood*er* and au*n*glis and seint*es* the wheche eu*er* 18) stondis in mutabilly and essencially . in heuen . And sodeynly . to see soulis to 19) be cruciat and also deulis speking in purgatori and in helle. And also—20) p*er*sonys ȝit leuyng*e* in this word all grese sche sy ordinatly in ye same 21) tyme speking to [g]edir/and whedir the seyd lady . soule was w*ith* in hir body 22) or w*ith* out wha*n* sche sy these thing*es* . To ye whech question . not I but sche 23) merore of all sapiens and {scr} sciens . mary the queen of heue*n* . schal ansuere 24) the/in ye vi*te* boke lii*o* c*apitulo*/

illa visa, sed remanebat dubia et incerta de significacionibus illarum visionum, **19** vt habetur in IIII Libro Celesti, II capitulo cum multis similibus et infra in isto presenti Libro Celestis Imperatoris ad Reges, XXXI capitulo. **20** Que visiones aliquando postea declarabantur ei a Christo processu temporis, vt habetur in dicto capitulo XXXI istius libri et in vltimo capitulo libri IIII. **21** Et aliquando nichil vmquam declarabatur ei de significacionibus illarum visionum, sed semper remanebat de illis incerta, vt habetur in aliquibus capitulis Libri Celestis. **22** Aliquando vero in spiritu videbat vigilans visiones in specie aliqua, et quasi semper statim in eadem hora declarabantur ei visiones ille a Christo loquente vel a sua matre virgine vel ab angelo vel ab aliquo sancto, **23** et manifestabantur ei tunc diuinitus in intelligencia sua significaciones illorum visorum, **24** vt habetur in IIII libro, VII capitulo et in VI libro, XXXV capitulo et LII capitulo et in isto libro presenti infrascripto, XLVIII capitulo cum multis similibus, que in Libro Celesti et in isto inuenies.

25 Sed poteris querere, quomodo potest esse, quod ista beata domina in oracione vigilante, poterat videre, sicut sepe videbat, rapta in spiritu, Christum et eius matrem virginem et angelos et sanctos, **26** qui semper immutabiliter et essencialiter stant in celo et in eodem instanti videre animas cruciari ac eas et eciam demones loquentes in purgatorio et in inferno et eciam personas adhuc viuentes in hoc mundo **27**—et omnes istos videbat ordinate in eodem instanti ad invicem et simul loquentes—et vtrum quando hec videbat dicta domina, anima eius erat in corpore vel an extra corpus. **28** Ad quam questionem non ego, sed illa, speculum omnis sapiencie et sciencie, regina celi, Maria tibi respondet valde pulcre in VI libro, LII capitulo in fine cum similibus, **29** vbi determinatur, quod hoc fiebat mira eleuacione et illustracione mentis et intelligencie eiusdem beate Brigide ad magnam vtilitatem tocius corporis Ecclesie cooperacione et ministerio Spiritus Sancti. **30** Aliquando quippe visa in extasi aliqua

And also soche wise she had the hol boke of questions 24) the whech is the V*te* boke in nu*m*byr amonge the bokis Also su*m*tyme sche 26) sy aunglis w*ith* hir bodily eyin And su*m* tyme oure lord ih*esu* crist and his 27) modir mary and namly in hir last ende . as it schal showe *with* Inne

specie Christi vel sanctorum, infundebantur in momento intellectui eiusdem beate domine aliqua magnalia, scilicet soluciones questionum, reuelaciones misteriorum et direcciones actuum virtuosorum et regula sancte vite per quendam influxum supernaturalis luminis diuini. **31** Et tali modo habuit quasi in momento totum Librum Questionum, qui est quintus liber in numero inter libros celestis voluminis, et Regulam eciam Saluatoris religionis monialium ei reuelatam, vt ibi habetur in fine regule, XXIX capitulo. **32** Aliquando eciam angelum corporeis oculis ipsa videbat, qui ex Dei precepto ei sermonem pulcerrimum satis prolixum paulatim et seriose dictabat, et ipso dictante in eodem instanti ipsa scribebat, **33** et sic fuit scriptus per interualla temporum ille excellentissimus Sermo Angelicus de excellencia Marie virginis, qui diuiditur per lecciones, que debent per ebdomadam nocturnatim legi a monialibus in matutinis in dicta religione monialium Regule Saluatoris.

34 Aliquociens quoque vidit predicta beata domina non solum in spiritu, immo eciam suis beatis oculis corporalibus dominum Iesum Christum et matrem eius virginem et presertim in fine vite sue, vt infra patebit. Quod tunc ipsa testabatur filie sue et suis patribus spiritualibus.

35 Pro maiori tamen parte ipsa neminem videns audiebat vocem Filii Dei vel virginis matris vel alicuius angeli vel sancti loquentis sibi verba mirabilia ad vtilitatem proximorum, direccionem morum, conuersionem gencium et reuelacionem misteriorum, vt patet in omnibus supradictis libris, vbi maior pars capitulorum incipit: "Filius loquitur" vel "Mater loquitur ad sponsam," etc. **36** Et aliquando tali modo predicebantur ei multa futura et prophetica de futuris et alia non prophetica per verba obscura, quorum significata ipsa nesciebat, an intelligerentur textualiter an figuraliter vel an spiritualiter vel per quem modum.

37 Immo sepe ipsa aliqua talia verba intelligebat textualiter, sicut fecit Beatus Franciscus, cum tamen Christus loquens vel mater eius illa volebant debere intelligi

28) here it is examyned be holy scripture vndir what kende of visions 29) the visions of this bo[k]e ar con{tynnyd}<teynid> and odir <thing*es*> reuelat to blissid bregid . *et cetera* [*fol. 251r.*] 1) Sethin the tyme I certified men doughtyng*e* of the q*ua*lite and v*er*tuys of the forseid 2) p*er*sone blissid lady brigid . and of diuers man*er*ys {the} and wyse/the wheche the seyd 3) lady sy . herd and felt visions and reuelacons of this pr*es*ent boke and of odir bokis . And for 4) that I haue touchid sufficiently of þ*e* qualite of the mateer of ye seid visions and reue 5) lacou*n*s as it is wretyn in c*apitulo* Also yat thing*e* And inye chaptre/ye*r*fore o ye {. .} empror*es* 6) ther fore I speke no moore of yat/but now it longis to examyn <and in> declaringe to pr*e*ue 7) aft*er* scripture . and the seing*es* of holy doughtors/vnd*er* what kende of visions commou*n*ly 8) hir forseid visiou*n*s and reuelacou*n*s ar co*n*teyned./

spiritualiter, **38** vt patet in IIII Libro Celesti, XV et LXXV capitulo et in presenti Libro Celestis Imperatoris ad Reges, XLVIII capitulo cum multis similibus capitulis contentis in dictis libris. **39** Et aliquociens loquebatur ei tali modo diuinitus verba clara, quorum veritas et significacio ei clare tunc pandebatur et aperiebatur, vt habetur in multis capitulis Libri Celestis, et vide de hoc in libro infrascripto ad reges, XLVIII capitulo prope principium.

40 Scias tamen, quod, prout ego indignus sepe audiui ab ore eius, semper in omnibus istis supradictis modis visionum maximam dulcedinem amoris Dei et ineffabilis consolacionis diuine ipsa senciebat in anima et mente sua in tantum, quod quasi nullatenus nisi cum suspiriis aut lacrimis hoc michi referre poterat.

Hic examinatur per sacram scripturam, sub qua specie visionum contineantur visiones istius libri et alie reuelate beate Brigide.

Capitulum V.

1 Ex quo igitur iam certificaui dubitantes de qualitate et virtutibus persone prefate, domine Brigide beatissime, et de modis diuersis, quibus ipsa domina visiones et reuelaciones presentis libri et aliorum librorum videbat et audiebat atque senciebat, vt supra patet, **2** nunc autem restaret videre de qualitate materie ipsarum visionum et reuelacionum, **3** sed quia satis de illa tetigi supra et tangetur infra in "Hoc eciam" et in "Ergo, o vos imperatores" et eciam ex preiacente huius libri materia et aliorum librorum suorum patet euidenter, ideo non figo plus pedem in hoc. **4** Sed iam michi restat nunc examinare et declarando probare secundum Scripturam et dicta sanctorum doctorum, sub qua specie visionum communiter predicte sue visiones et reuelaciones contineantur.

It is to be knowin ferst/yat Austyn] 9) in ye xii boke of genesis to y*e* lettir And Jerom in his prolog of yapocalips./iii p*ri*ncepal 10) kendis of visions ar describid ./that is to sey ./bodily. gostly. and intellectually./ Abodily 10) vision is whan we see ony thinge w*ith* oure bodily eyin/ Gostly or ymaginary vision 12) is seid whan we see sleping or waking ymagis of thing*es* in sprith . be the whech 13) sumodyr thinge is be tokenyd/As pharao sy eris of corn And moyses sy the buske bren 14) he sleping and his wakinge. Intellectual vision is whan ama*n* <or ap*er*-sone>[13] sees the treuþe of ye 15) misteryes the holy gost scheuyng*e* w*ith* the vndirstonding of mynde/As John sy the thing*es* 16) the whech ar told in the booke of thapocalips. he sy not only figur*es* in sprith but he 17) vndirstod in mynde the tokenyng*es* of the*m* . The ferst kende of visions the wheche is 18) corporal or bodyli towchis not gretly owre mater/Alþow the seyd blissid Brigid su*m* 19) Wylis. sy. the modir of god and hir sone w*ith* hir bodily eyin/yat is for to sey whan 20) she was a maydin/Also sche sy an awter and the modir of god . sitting vp on the 21) wheche callid hir and set a croun on hir hed . And a nodir tyme wha*n* she was in perel 22) of childing*e* And the moodir of god come yn to hir/Alle the ladyis seing*e* yat were 23) ther p*re*sent and sche touchid hir membris And anoon she was delyuerid./as it is wrety*n* 24) in hir le{n}gend. And ageyne wha*n* she sy feer descende fro heue*n* on the awter and in 25) the p*re*st*es* hand se<y>inge messe and <a> host/and in yat host a lamb . and ye face of a man 26) in the lomb. and a lombe in ye face/And also {.} sche sy a quyk child in y*e*{.} host/in 27) the p*re*st*es* hand . the {.} <whech> blissid the*m* stonding a bought w*ith* the signe of the cros seinge .I. 28) blisse yow beleuyng./I shal be the iuge to the*m* yat beleue nat//Se this in vi 29) boke lxxxvi*o* ca*pitulo* And wha*n* sche lay in extremys/sche sy ageyn bodily . crist comfortinge 30) hir *et cetera.* Soche a vision is to be beleuyd yat it was scheuyd to ye seid spouse of crist 31) in to hir comfort/and not mynistrid of an illusore tho yll sprith./And yat shewis clerly

5 Sciendum est ergo de primo, quod Augustinus in libro XII Super Genesim ad Litteram et Ieronimus in prologo Apocalipsis tria principalia genera visionum describunt, scilicet corporale, spirituale et intellectuale. **6** Visio enim corporalis est, quando videlicet corporalibus oculis aliquid videmus. **7** Spriritualis seu ymaginaria visio dicitur, cum videlicet dormientes vel vigilantes in spiritu ymagines rerum cernimus, quibus aliquid aliud significantur, sicut vidit Pharao spicas et Moyses rubum ardere, ille dormiens et iste vigilans. **8** Intellectualis autem visio est, quando videlicet Spiritu Sancto reuelante intellectu mentis veritatem misteriorum, sicut est, capimus, quo modo vidit Iohannes illa, que in libro Apocalipsis referuntur. **9** Non enim figuras tantum in spiritu vidit, sed et eorum significata mente intellexit.

10 Primum namque genus visionum, scilicet corporale, non multum tangit materiam nostram, licet tamen aliquibus vicibus ipsa beata Brigida gloriosam matrem Dei et eius filium corporalibus oculis viderit, scilicet quando erat puella. **11** Vidit enim altare et matrem Dei supra sedentem, que vocauit eam et imposuit ei coronam, et iterum quando periclitabatur in partu et mater Dei intrauit ad eam et videntibus dominabus cunctis, que aderant, tetigit membra eius et statim liberata est, vt hoc habetur in legenda vite eius, **12** et iterum quando vidit ignem descendere de celo super altare et in manu presbiteri celebrantis hostiam et in ea agnum et faciem hominis in agno et agnum in facie, et iterum vidit in manu presbiteri in hostia infantem viuum, qui signando astantes signo crucis dixit: **13** "Benedico vos credentes; non credentibus ero iudex." Vide hec in VI Libro Celesti, LXXXVI capitulo. **14** Cumque eciam ipsa iam ageret in extremis, vidit iterum corporaliter Christum eam consolantem, vt supra dicitur. **15** Talis enim visio, credendum est, quod ab ipso Christo eidem sponse sue Spiritus

[fol. 251v.] 1) for ye seyd lord ih*esu* crist told before to hir the day of hir passinge .v. dayes be foore she 2) deyed bidding hir take the sacramentes of the chirche. The whech. pr*e*cept the deule wold 3) not bid hir to take at hir deynge. Therfore it was preuyd yat that vision was of 4) god. in as moche as at the last poynt of hir liff sche reseyued the holy comunyng 5) and last anoyntinge*e* . deuowtly. many personys beinge pr*e*sent/the whech reseyued 6) sche sy crist comforting*e* hir w*ith* hir bodily eyin/come*n*ding mekely her sprith in to 7) his handis ./as it schewis in ye last booke. and the last chappet*re*/In this man*er* of 8) wyse of seing*e* visions yat is to sey bodily. I leue now/. Of the secu*n*nd kende of 9) visions yat is to sey. sp*irit*ual or gostly . or ymaginary. of sleperis we speke nat ffor 10) thes dremys ar countid be gregory most susspect i*n*n the iiii*te* boke of dialogis xlviii*o* ca*pitulo.* 11) Alþough su*m*tyme dremys ar trewe and good and of god./as it is seid . y*er*/where 12) thou owis to knowe./wha*n* soche dremys happenys . And in sleping*e* soche wise./yis 13) blissid lady . sy whan she was amaydin/onys sche sy crist as <he was> crucified . a[n]d fro y*at* 14) oure she was hertily set on his passion. This sompnial vision touchis nat oure 15) mateer/for yat lady s[e]y all hir visions in pr*a*your wakinge and not slepynge. 16) Now to come to ye yis secund kende . of sp*irit*ual vision . or ymaginary . of wakinge 17) p*er*sonys the whech touchis owre mateer/Blissid austyn seis thus in y*e* xii booke 18) vp on genesis to ye lett*er* whan the intencou*n* of mynde . is turnyd and takin 19) fro the witt*es* of the body . yan it is wont to be callid ought of mynde. Than 20) in ony wise what someuyr bodyes ar pr*e*sent and ar no*n* seen w*ith* opyn eyin/

Sancti ministerio in eius consolacionem fuerit ostensa et non a maligno spiritu illusorie ministrata. **16** Et hoc pater clare, quia ipse Dominus Iesus Christus predixerat ei diem sui exitus quinque diebus, antequam ipsa expiraret, precipiens ei sacramenta Ecclesie suscipere et de factis suis et monasterii sui aliqua per eum tunc reuelata disponendo ordinare. **17** Quod preceptum in fine vite dyabolus ei non dedisset, si illa visio dyabolica extitisset. **18** Probatur eciam, quod illa visio fuerit a Deo ex hoc, quia in illo extremo puncto vite ipsa communionem sanctam et extremam vnccionem presentibus personis multis deuote recepit. **19** Quibus susceptis et ipsum Christum oculis corporalibus tunc eam consolantem vidit et in eius manibus spiritum humiliter commendando expirauit, vt hoc patet in vltimo Libro Celesti, capitulo vltimo et in fine legende vite eius. **20** In hoc tamen modo videndi visiones, scilicet corporaliter, non figo pedem pro nunc, quia ipsa domina paucis vicibus videbat visiones corporalibus oculis.

21 De secundo autem genere visionis, scilicet spiritualis seu ymaginarie dormiencium non loquamur, quia ista sompnia suspectissima reputantur per Gregorium in quarto libro Dyalogorum, XLVIII capitulo. **22** Et habetur eciam idem in Libro IIII Celesti, XXXVIII capitulo, quamuis aliquando sompnia sint vera et bona et a Deo, vt ibi dicitur. Et ibi in Libro Celesti vide modum, quem debes tenere, quando talia sompnia eueniunt. **23** Et tali modo dormiendo vidit eciam ista beata domina, cum adhuc puella esset, semel Christum quasi tunc temporis crucifixum, et ab illa hora semper affecta fuit cordialiter ad passionem Christi. **24** Nec talis visio sompnialis tangit materiam nostram, quia ipsa domina quasi omnes visiones videbat in oracione vigilando et non dormiendo, vt in multis capitulis predicti Libri Celestis hoc patet euidenter.

25 Sed veniendo modo ad istam secundam speciem, quam dixi, scilicet visionis spiritualis seu ymaginarie vigilancium, que tangit materiam nostram, dicit sic Beatus Augustinus in libro XII Super Genesim ad Litteram: **26** *Quando autem penitus auertitur atque arripitur animi intencio a sensibus corporis, tunc magis dici extasis solet.*

nen 21) vttirly voyc*es* ar not herd for all the be holdinge of the mynde owdir it is in 22) ymagis of bodyes be sp*irit*ual vision or in thing*es* w*ith* ought bodies not figuryd . w*ith* 23) ony ymage of a body . be intellectual vision/. Therfore it shewis opinly . yat 24) whan the seid lady . stood in vision sopit w*ith* joye and sopoor of suetnes of goddis loue . alienat . fro hir bodily . witt*es* yat than she stood outh of hir mynde alienat 26) a boue hir self The deule may nat yete in soche swetnes of goddis loue in þe 27) mynde of ony p*er*sone As it shal showe w*ith* ynforth .{.} for that the deul has nat he 28) may nat geve to odyr me*n* ffor he may nat geue illumynacou*n* or illustracou*n* 29) of mynde. in no man*er* of wise./ to ony p*er*sone/for in intellectual vision/the soule 30) may neu*er* be illudid . of the deul . as it sheuys be Austyn and Thomays de alquino [*fol. 252r.*] 1) And all doughtoris acordis on yat/

Tunc enim omnino quecumque sunt presencia corpora eciam patentibus oculis non videntur, **27** *nec vlle voces prorsus audiuntur, quia totus animi contuitus aut in corporum ymaginibus est per spiritualem aut in rebus incorporeis nulla corporis ymagine figuratis per intellectualem visionem.* 28 Ex istis ergo verbis patet manifeste, quod quando dicta domina stabat in visione, sopita gaudio et sopore dulcedinis amoris diuini, alienata a sensibus corporis, vt supra ipsa narrat, quod tunc stabat in extasi alienata supra se, **29** nec talem dulcedinem et ebrietatem amoris diuini in alicuius mente dyabolus infundere potest, vt infra patebit, quia, quod ipse non habet, aliis infundere nequit. **30** Cum vero ipsa dicit supra et in libris, quod Deus animam suam tunc quasi a sompno excitabat ad videndum et audiendum atque senciendum celestia, diuina et spiritualia, et quod tunc ipsa visiones videbat et vocem loquentis audiebat in spiritu, **31** tunc ostenditur clare per istud dictum Augustini suprascriptum, quod ipsa tunc stabat rapta in spiritu per spiritualem seu ymaginariam visionem, **32** quia scilicet videbat in spiritu illas ymagines seu species et audiebat locuciones illorum visorum.

33 Quando autem ipsa dixit, vt supra habetur, quod tota consciencia et intelligencia eius in illo raptu extasis replebatur et illuminabatur quodam intellectu spirituali **34** et quod in momento erant, Christo loquente, infusa in intellectu eius multa, vt scilicet tota Regula Saluatoris et Liber Questionum et multa alia per quendam influxum luminis intellectualis supernaturalis, **35** ecce quod per hoc clare ostenditur nobis, quod ipsa tunc stabat rapta in illo extasi,[14] et tunc illuminabatur et illustrabatur mens et intelligencia eius diuinitus per supernaturalem, intellectualem visionem. **36** Et scias, quod hanc illuminacionem seu illustracionem mentis dyabolus nullatenus potest infundere alicui, quia in visione intellectuali numquam potest anima illudi a demone, vt infra clarius patebit per Augustinum et Thomam de Aquino, et in hoc omnes doctores concordant. **37** Cum eciam ipsa dicit, quod, in illo raptu seu

Pages 194, 202, 210, and 222 are blank to accomodate the facing pages; the Latin text is considerably longer than the Middle English. These pages, and others with obvious gaps, reflect that textual difference as well as occasional deletions in the Middle English text.

extasi ea existente, filius Dei vel virgo Maria vel aliquis angelus vel sanctus sibi loquebantur ea, que supra in Libro Celesti continentur et infra in presenti libro quasi per totum, **38** tunc per hoc clare colligimus, quod ipse miserator Deus ad ipsius domine et nostram vtilem direccionem consciencias nostras per verba doctrine sue dignatus est illustrare, **39** et quod de secretis misteriis suis ac de rebus futuris et aliis documentis sanctissimis sua quadam diuina, interna locucione per intellectualem visionem instruere nos per ipsam dominam voluit et docere.

Blissid gregory . seys in ye xxviii boke of morall 2) the secund chapt*er* yat ii man*er* of wisis the speche of god is vndirstoud/oure lord 3) spekis be him self/or be an aungil creature . word*es* ar schapin to vs But whan 4) god spekis be himself alonly . streinkthe of inwardly inspiracou*n* to vs is openyd. And 5) whan god spekis be him self he spekis of his word w*ith* ought word*es* and sillablis 6) the hert is taught for his inwardly v*er*tu is knowe*n* be as*er*teyn lefting vp to ye 7) whech the ful mynd is left vp and voyd mynde as heuyed./thus seys gregory. 8) Soche an ynwardly . godly speking*e* this holy lady . was taught and informyd . of 9) these thing*es* yat ar conteyned in this celestial boke to sp*iri*tual doctrine . as it scheuys 10) be þe hool booke. Also gregory . seis in the chapet*er* be fore yat su*m*tyme god spekis 11) to vs be aungelis at a tyme assumpt of the eyer be fore oure bodily eyin. 12) As abrah*a*m the whech myght not only see iii men but also to take and 13) reseyue the*m* in his erdly hous./And seys also/But if su*m* aungelis telling vs 14) inwardly thing*es* shuld take {.} bodyes of the eyer at atyme and apere to oure sit*es* 15) thus seis gregory.

40 De qua quidem locucione Beatus Gregorius in XXVIII libro Moralium, capitulo II plene et pulcre nos instruit in hec verba: **41** *Sciendum,* inquit, *preterea est, quia in duobus modis locucio diuina distinguitur. Aut per semetipsum namque Dominus loquitur aut per creaturam angelicam eius ad nos verba formantur.* **42** *Sed cum per semetipsum Deus loquitur, sola in nobis vis interne inspiracionis aperitur. Cum per semetipsum loquitur, de verbo eius sine verbis et sillabis cor docetur,* **43** *quia virtus eius intima quadam subleuacione cognoscitur, ad quam mens plena suspenditur, vacua grauatur. Pondus enim quoddam est, quod omnem animam, quam replet, leuat.* **44** *Incorporeum lumen est, quod et interiora repleat et repleta exterius circumscribat. Sine strepitu sermo est, quia et auditum aperit et habere sonitum nescit.* **45** Et subdit: *Spiritum enim Dei quasi quedam nobis verba dicere est occulta vi ea que agenda sunt intimare et cor hominis ignarum, non adhibito strepitu et tarditate sermonis, peritum repente de absconditis reddere.* **46** Et postea subiungit dicens: *Dei enim locucio ad nos intrinsecus facta videtur pocius quam auditur, quia dum semetipsam sine mora sermonis insinuat, repentina luce nostre ignorancie tenebras illustrat.* Hec ille Gregorius. **47** Tali enim interna diuina locucione ista sancta domina de hiis, que continentur in hoc libro et in Libro Celesti, ad spiritualem doctrinam imperatorum et regum et summorum pontificum ac prelatorum et omnium gencium et eciam ad conuersionem infidelium a sponso suo Christo loquente docebatur et instruebatur, vt patet per totum Librum Celestem et per presentem. **48** Subdit eciam Gregorius in preallegato capitulo dicens, quod *aliquando ymaginibus et ante corporeos oculos ad tempus ex aere assumptis per angelo nobis loquitur Deus,* **49** *sicut Abraham, qui non solum tres viros videre potuit, sed eciam habitaculo terreno*

Soche man*er* wise god spac oftyn tymes {spac} be his aungil to 16) his forseid spowse. And austyn seis in ye xii boke on genesis/and thomais de 17) alquino/and odir doughtor*es* That a p*ro*fete vndirstondis nat alwey right yat ar 18) seid and sheuyd to him in vision//

suscipere. **50** Et subdit dicens: *Nisi enim angeli quedam nobis interna nunciantes ad tempus ex aere corpora sumerent, exterioribus profecto nostris obtutibus non apparerent.* Vsque hic Gregorius. **51** Tali eciam modo Deus sepe per angelum loquebatur sue sponse predicte, et presertim quando in Roma ipsa existente, angelum, qui sermonem de excellencia virginis dictaret, ei misit. **52** Quem ipsa eciam corporeis oculis cotidie vidit, et ipso illum dictante per interualla temporum ipsa sermonem eundem conscripsit, vt patet supra.

53 Sed poteris querere, quare verba Dei aliquando ita obscure ab ipso dicuntur, quod diuersimode interpretari possunt, et quandoque aliter a propheta audiente et ab aliis hominibus et aliter a Deo loquente intelliguntur, **54** vt patet in Beato Francisco, quando ei dictum fuit a Christo: "Vade et repara ecclesiam meam"[15] et in multis aliis, qui verba, que spiritualiter intelligi debebant, materialiter et textualiter intellexerunt. **55** Respondeo secundum quod dicit Augustinus in libro XII Super Genesim et Thomas de Aquino in secunda secunde in titulo "De prophecia" et alii doctores, quod non semper propheta recte intelligit, que sibi in visione dicuntur et reuelantur. **56** Et super hoc vide solucionem, quam dat isti beate domine gloriosa virgo Maria in isto presenti libro infrascripto, scilicet Imperatoris ad Reges, capitulo XLVIII quasi in principio, "Sed poteris querere" et vide in IIII Libro Celesti, XV et LXXV capitulo cum multis similibus. **57** Et tali modo dicta domina Brigida aliquando intelligebat verba visionum corporaliter seu litteraliter, et tamen Christus vel mater eius loquentes intelligebant illa spiritualiter aut figuraliter, vt supra patet in proximis allegacionibus. **58** Liquet ergo ex predictis euidenter et ex preiacente materia librorum isti venerande domine diuinitus reuelatorum, quod ipsa habuit a Deo singularissimam graciam spiritus prophecie per internam Dei locucionem et per spiritualem et intellectualem visionem, ei diuinitus gratis datam, **59** quia vera et propria prophecia et reuelacio ac sciencia et doctrina causantur ex visione spirituali seu ymaginaria aliquorum corporum seu signorum **60** accedente tunc ibi influxu luminis

fforsoye I dar sey boldly. Aft*er* Thomays of alqu*ny* s*ecunda* s*ecundo* q. clxxiii*de* 19) and aft*er* od*er* doctor*es* yat yis gre of p*ro*fecy was geuy*n* to this blissid lady . godly . among*e* 20) odir greis of p*ro*fecy and is iugid hier whan ap*ro*phete sees not only the tokenys 21) of wordis or of ded*es* but also he sees wakynge su*m* bo[d]y spekinge to him ar su*m*what/hit/ 22) scheuyng*e* And namly yf yat spekis or scheuys./be in the kende of god. ffor 23) they sey . yat be yat thinge the p*ro*phet drauys ner moore to the cause sheuynge 24) than yf he yat spekis or sheuys/shuld sheue him in ye kende of a man or in ye 25) kende of an aungil. Aft*er* the seying' of ysay ./vi*o* c*apitulo*/I sy god sittyng/etc ffor nycholas 26) de lyra in ye prolog on the sawt*er* and odir doughters seis the same. That ye 27) degre of p*ro*fecie is moor excellent wher to odir like the vndirstondinge is clerer 28) her it is preuyd be go[d]ly scripture . that the visions and reuelacou*ns* of this 29) boke and of odir of blissid bregid has procedid of the holy. sprith. and not of y*e* 30) illusion of the deule and yat is p*re*vyd be vii tokenys or vii resounys co*n*teyned her [*fol. 252v.*] 1) Therfore now we shal see aft*er* the seing*es* of holy men . whedir the visions and 2) reuelacou*ns* has ben mynstrid of the holy spright of treuþ*e* of {of} the illusore þ*e* 3) sprith of falshed . Therfore I sey that y*er* ar many diffrens[*es*] in ye whech . clerly . reuelacou*n* 4) or vision may be discernyd of agood sprith or an yll . as wel in ye q*ua*lite of the 5) p*er*sone seinge soche thing*es* as in sencibil inwardly thing*es* of yat sowle . as in man*er* 6) of leuyng*e*/here folowys vii signis tokenys or resounys w*ith* in wretyn be ye whech 7) the vision of agod . sprith is discernyd fro ye deulys illusion./

intellectualis et supernaturalis veritatis diuine, vt patet ex modis et sentimentis supradictis, quibus ipsa visiones videbat, et ex dictis Augustini in libro XII Super Genesim ad Litteram, **61** vbi est textus clarus de hoc, quia ymagines corporales in spiritu eius expresse sunt et quasi semper earum intellectus diuinitus reuelatus in mente. **62** Immo audacter dico secundum beatum Thomam de Aquino in secunda secunde, questione CLXXIII et secundum alios doctores, **63** quod iste gradus prophecie isti beate domine diuinitus gratis datus inter omnes alios gradus prophecie alcior iudicatur, quando scilicet propheta non solum videt signa verborum vel factorum sed eciam videt vigilando aliquem sibi colloquentem aut aliquid demonstrantem, **64** et presertim si ille loquens vel demonstrans sit in specie Dei, quia dicunt, quod per hoc magis ille propheta appropinquat ad causam reuelantem, **65** quam si ille loquens vel demonstans se ostenderet in specie hominis vel in specie angeli secundum illud Ysaie, VI capitulo: *Vidi Dominum sedentem* etc **66** et maxime ex eo quod inter omnes scripturas omnium prophetarum clariori modo intelligendi a Deo scriptura ista prefate domine, quam alie scripture aliis prophetis, fuerit reuelata, **67** quia dicit Nicolaus de Lira in prologo super psalterium et alii doctores idem dicunt, scilicet quod ille gradus prophecie est excellencior, vbi ceteris paribus est intelligencia clarior.

Hic probatur per diuinam scripturam, quod visiones et reuelaciones istius libri et aliorum beate Brigide emanauerunt et processerunt a Spiritu Sancto et non ab illusione dyabolica, et hoc probatur ex septem signis siue racionibus hic contentis.

Capitulum VI.

1 Sane quia iam supra proximo clare ostensum est subtiliter intuenti, sub quo genere visionum contineantur iste presens liber et alii, reuelati prefate beatissime domine Brigide, **2** idcirco nunc videamus secundum dicta sanctorum, an a Spiritu Sancto veritatis vel an ab illusore spiritu falsitatis visiones et reuelaciones istorum librorum illi fuerint ministrate. **3** Dico igitur, quod multe differencie sunt, in quibus clare potest discerni reuelacio vel visio boni

Pages 194, 202, 210, and 222 are blank to accomodate the facing pages; the Latin text is considerably longer than the Middle English. These pages, and others with obvious gaps, reflect that textual difference as well as occasional deletions in the Middle English text.

spiritus a malo tam in qualitate persone talia videntis quam in sentimentis interioribus anime ipsius, quam eciam in modo videndi et in materia visionum **4** discuciendo subtiliter ad quid illa visio nos promouet et inducit. **5** Ad quorum noticiam et practicam discernendi, ne illuderetur, ista prefata domina beatissima pluries et satis clare diuinitus fuit edocta et per visiones et documenta diuina plenius informata, **6** vt habetur in primo Libro Celesti, LIIII capitulo et in II libro, XIX capitulo et in III libro, X capitulo. **7** Et vide de hoc septem differencias, que assignantur isti domine Brigide, sponse Christi, a virgine Maria inter visiones boni spiritus et mali satis pulcre in IIII libro, XXIII capitulo et CX capitulo et in VI libro, LXVIII capitulo et LXIX et XCII capitulo cum multis similibus.

8 Et licet tam clara et notorie manifesta est ista gracia diuina prefate beate domine diuinitus gratis data, **9** quod nulla suspicione fallacis spiritus valet obfuscari, maxime cum iam ipsa de hoc alias fuerit in regno Suecie diligenter examinata per prelatos ac viros spirituales et magistros in theologia, **10** et licet per eos fuerit determinatum, quod ista gracia sit diuina et a Spiritu Sancto diuinitus et data, vt supra dixi, **11** et licet eciam iterum in Neapoli in presencia domini Bernardi archiespiscopi et trium magistrorum in theologia et aliorum plurium militum et peritorum virorum me teste ista gracia fuerit approbata, **12** immo quedam reuelacio, quam tunc ipsa domina eis presentauit, per vnum dictorum magistrorum ex precepto domine regine et archiepiscopi coram toto populo ciuitatis ad hoc vocato specialiter fuerit in ecclesia cathedrali publicata et solempniter predicata, **13** nichilominus tamen ad maiorem habundanciam et vt mordacibus detractoribus et calumpniatoribus silencium imponatur et pie de hoc dubitantibus plena satisfaccio impendatur, volo probare per dicta doctorum Sacre Scripture et sanctorum patrum, **14** quod ista sint a Deo infusa et data prefate domine ad informacionem et vtilitatem tocius corporis Ecclesie et direccionem omnium electorum et non a spiritu maligno

The ferst most s*er*teyn 8) sygne . is yat ye vision is of god . whan yat p*er*sone seing visions is really meke 9) and levis undir obediens of su*m* sp*iri*tual fadir v*er*tuos and exp*er*t in sp*iri*tual lyff And 10) the p*er*sone yat s[e]is p*re*sumys not on him self nen is not left vp w*ith* pr*i*de nen 11) desir*es* no man*ny*s p*ra*ysing*es* nen hydis not the visions . but leuys w*ith* v*er*ry humilite 12) And anoon*e* tellis his visiou*ns* and te*m*ptacou*ns* And expounys it mekely to ye examynacou*n* 13) and iugeme*nt* of his sp*iri*tual fadir and odir old sp*iri*tual fadris . And takis it approbat 14) that he or they p*re*uys/I sey that soche asoule may nat be illudid./As the cler text 15) of this is in ye boke of collacou*ns* of fadris in ye collacou*n* of John cassian ca*pitulo* ii*o* 16) the whech spekis of a monke deludid of adeul vndir the kende of an aungel of light 17) And in ye same collacou*n* Than moyses . *et cetera* where ye seid abbot moyses spekis on y*is* 18) these word*es* In no man*er* of wise aman schal be desseyued . the wheche leuys not 19) only in his owne doom but be ye exsampil of his bett*er*/ Therfore whan the forseid 20) lady brigid leuyd alwey . vndir special obediens and doctrine of sp*iri*tual old fadris 21) and v*er*tuos/*et cetera.* y*er*fore clerli it is co*n*cludid of the forseid det*er*mynacou*n* of yat holy 22) fadir moyses and odir holy fadris/yat al thing*es* þat <was> reuelat to the*m* in bokis was 23) of the holy gost and not of the deul/illusor/

illusorie ministrata, **15** et hoc probo per septem signa seu raciones infra scriptas, quibus discernitur visio boni spiritus ab illusione dyabolica.

16 Primum signum certissimum est, quod visio sit diuina, quando scilicet illa persona visiones videns est realiter humilis et viuit sub obediencia et disciplina continua alicuius patris spiritualis discreti, senioris et virtuosi et experti in vita spirituali, **17** et quando non presumit de se iste persona videns nec extollitur nec se iactat nec appetit laudes humanas nec occultat visiones, **18** sed cum humilitate vera viuens omnes visiones et temptaciones suas statim detegit et exponit humiliter examini et iudicio sui patris spiritualis aut aliorum seniorum patrum spiritualium **19** et tunc vt approbatum recipit, quod ille vel illi approbant, et vt reprobata repudiat illa, que illi reprobanda diffiniunt. **20** Talis enim anima, dico, quod non potest illudi, et de hoc est textus clarus in libro Collacionum Patrum Iohannis Cassiani, collacione secunda, capitulo "Et vt hanc eandem", que loquitur de illo monacho sub specie angeli lucis deluso a dyabolo, **21** et eadem collacione, capitulo "Tunc Moyses", vbi idem abbas Moyses de hoc loquitur in hec verba: *Nullatenus enim,* inquit, *decipi quisque potest, qui non suo iudicio sed maiorum viuit exemplo, nec valebit ignorancie eius callidus hostis illudere,* **22** *qui vniuersas cogitaciones corde nascentes perniciosa verecundia nescit obtegere, sed eas maturo examine seniorum vel reprobat vel admittit.* **23** *Illico namque, vt patefacta fuerit cogitacio maligna, marcescit, et antequam discrecionis iudicium proferatur,* **24** *serpens teterrimus velut a tenebroso, subterraneo specu virtute confessionis protractus ad lucem et traductus quodammodo ac dehonestatus abscedit.* **25** *Tamdiu enim suggestiones noxie dominantur in nobis, quamdiu celantur in corde.* Hec ille Moyses. Et vide ibidem in capitulo sequenti. **26** Igitur cum prefata domina, beata Brigida, viuebat semper sub speciali obediencia et doctrina patrum spiritualium seniorum et virtuosorum etc et habuerit in se profundissimam veram humilitatem **27** et omnes visiones et temptaciones suas ac eciam alia facienda humiliter

The secund signe of godly visiou*ns* is 24) in ye whech a soule may not be disceyuyd wha*n* the soule in y*e* tyme y*at* it sees ye 25) vision felis him self yan holly to be repleschid and inflamyd w*ith* the fyre of infusiou*n* 26) of godly cherite and savor of goddis love/the whech the deule has not in ony wise27) And ye*r*fore it is co*n*cludid yat he yat werkys soch thing*es* {god is} in his soule is god

supposuerit obediencie, examini et iudicio predictorum et eciam aliorum seniorum, vt supra dixi, **28** ideo clare concluditur ex predicta determinacione illius sancti patris Moysi et aliorum patrum sanctorum, quod omnia sibi reuelata in libris processerunt a Spiritu Sancto et non a dyabolico illusore, **29** et hoc est clarum et manifestum signum apud omnes vere spirituales et doctrina generalis omnium ad euadendum temptaciones et dyabolicas suggestiones et illusiones.

30 Secundum signum visionis diuine, in quo non potest anima decipi, est quando anima tempore, quo videt visionem, sentit se tunc totam repleri et quodammodo dulciter inebriari et inflammari igne infusionis dulcedinis caritatis diuine et quodam sapore interne dulcedinis amoris Dei. **31** Dico enim, quod istam internam caritatem et dulcedinem amoris diuini, quam dyabolus non habet, nullo modo potest eam infundere in anima alicuius, quia nullus dat quod non habet,[16] **32** et ideo concluditur, quod qui talia operatur in anima, Deus est, **33** presertim si tunc illa anima tota roboratur et repletur illuminacione quadam firme credulitatis et obediencie et reuerencie fidei catholice et sancte matris Ecclesie, vt habetur in IIII Libro Celesti, LXXVIII capitulo cum similibus. **34** Probatur eciam hoc pulcre per Hugonem de Sancto Victore in Soliloquio de Arra Anime in fine tocius tractatus, vbi anima loquitur ei sic dicens: **35** *Hoc,* inquit, *vltimum interrogacionis mee suscipias, queso: Quid est illud dulce, quid eius me recordacione tangere solet et tam vehementer atque suauiter afficere, vt iam tota quodammodo a memetipsa alienari et nescio-quo extrahi incipiam?* **36** *Subito immutor. Bene esse incipio vltra quam dicere sufficiam. Exhilaratur consciencia, in obliuionem venit preteritorum dolorum, exultat animus, clarescit intellectus, cor illuminatur, desideria iocundantur,* etc. **37** Cui anime ipsemet Hugo sic pulcre respondens ait: *Vere ille est dilectus tuus qui visitat te,* id est Deus, etc. **38** Et idem dicit beatus Antonius valde late et pulcre docendo discipulos suos discernere visiones bonas ab illusionibus, vt habetur in Vitis Patrum,

28) The iii*de* signe is in the wheche godly vision is knowyn whan the soule beinge 29) in vision bodily or ymaginary and sp*irit*ual felis an intellectual sup*er*natural of [*fol. 253r.*] 1) light of treuþ*e* and than takis trew tokenys of yo thing*es* seen and word*es* and the vnd*er* 2) stonding of it than clerly is openyd . and the treuþ*e* of yat mat*er* is mad opin*n* . this may 3) not be infudid of the deule/in a soule but only of god As thomas seys in s[e]c*un*da s[e]c[un]de ca*pitulo* dep*ro*phecia 4) q.clxxiii*d* where he seis thus. Deulis makis opyn to me*n* ye ying*es* yat they knowe 5) not be yllumyni*n*ge of vndirstondinge . but be su*m* vision ymaginyd . or ell sensibill in 6) speking but not yllumyny*n*g his vndirstonding*e* Therfore clerly it is concludid yat 7) whan ye forseid lady Brigid . shuld take the flood of intellectual light and sup*er*natural 8) in hir visions . yer eu*er* {. .} body expougny*n*g as crist or his moodir or an aungil or 9) su*m* seynt of the whech the si*m*litudis was declarid and expoun*n*yd to hir the v*er*ry tokenys 10) of the visions . as it sheuys in hir bokis. Therfore it folwis yat all hir reuelacou*n*s 11) and scripture of these bokis . was mynistrid of god . the wheche is mighty to werke soche 12) thing*es* and not of the deul illusor to hom it is inpossibil to do soche thing*es.*/as it scheuys 13) be Austyn and Thomais . and all holy fadris and dought[r]is

in primo libro, in legenda beati Antonii, ibi: *Nunc iam ceteras vobis demonum explicabo fallacias,* etc. Et ibi vide plene. **39** Dicit eciam Gregorius in Moralibus, libro XXVIII, capitulo II, quod *cum Deus per semetipsum anime loquitur,* **40** *sola in nobis vis interne inspiracionis aperitur, quia virtus eius intima quadam dulcissima subleuacione cognoscitur,* etc. **41** Et vide hoc clarius in IIII Libro Celesti, LXXVIII capitulo et in vltimo libro, capitulo IIII et in capitulis eiusdem Celestis Libri supra proximo preallegatis cum multis similibus. **42** Ex quibus probatur, quod omnia reuelata beate Brigide, que in istis libris continentur, non ab illusore terribili sed a Spiritu Sancto, consolatore suauissimo, fuerunt ei ministrata, **43** quod patet per istas allegaciones supradictas et per illa consolatoria sentimenta similia, que ipsa senciebat tempore, quo visiones videbat et diuinas locuciones audiebat, vt patet supra per verba eius, que ibi continentur.

44 Tercium signum est, in quo cognoscitur seu discernitur visio diuina ab illusione dyabolica, **45** quando scilicet anima existens in visione siue corporali siue ymaginaria et spirituali sentit influxum intellectualis supernaturalis luminis intelligibilis veritatis **46** et comprehendit tunc significaciones veras illorum visorum et verborum, et aperitur clare tunc intellectus eius ac ostenditur seu manifestatur ei veritas illius materie. **47** Iste enim influxus intellectualis, supernaturalis luminis seu visionis, siue precedat visio corporalis aut ymaginaria siue non, numquam a dyabolo potest infundi in anima, sed solum a Deo, **48** vt ait Thomas de Aquino in secunda secunde, titulo "De prophecia", questione CLXXIII, vbi sic dicit: **49** *Demones,* inquit, *ea, que sciunt, hominibus manifestant non quidem per illuminacionem intellectus sed per aliquam ymaginariam visionem aut eciam sensibiliter colloquendo sed non intellectum illius illuminando. Et in hoc deficit et differt hec prophecia a vera.* **50** Augustinus eciam in libro XII Super Genesim ad Litteram sic ait: *Illuditur autem anima et fallitur in corporali visione,* etc. **51** Et postea subdit: *In visione autem spirituali seu*

Pages 194, 202, 210, and 222 are blank to accomodate the facing pages; the Latin text is considerably longer than the Middle English. These pages, and others with obvious gaps, reflect that textual difference as well as occasional deletions in the Middle English text.

ymaginaria, id est in corporum similitudinibus, que in spiritu videntur, fallitur eciam anima, cum ea, que sic videt, ipsa corpora esse arbitratur, etc. **52** Post hec autem subdit dicens: *At vero in illis intellectualibus visis non fallitur anima,* etc. **53** Et postea subiungit: *Et si videntur futura ita, vt omnino futura noscantur, quorum ymagines presentes iudicentur siue ipsa diuinitus adiuta siue aliquo inter ipsa exponente, quid significent, sicut in Apocalipsi Iohannis exponebatur,* **54** *magna reuelacio est, eciam si forte ignoret ille, cui hec demonstrantur, vtrum e corpore exierit an adhuc sit in corpore, sed, spiritu a sensibus alienato, ista videat.* Vsque hic Augustinus.

55 Sed circa hoc queri potest, que differencia est inter reuelacionem, que fit conficte humano intellectu seu per illusionem in ymaginacione et intellectu hominis et illam, que fit diuinitus per intellectualem visionem. **56** Respondeo secundum Thomam in secunda secunde, questione CLXXIII, articulo II, quod *prophecia seu reuelacio, que fit secundum ymaginacionem et iudicium humane mentis, fit secundum vim intellectualis luminis naturalis,* **57** *sed per donum prophecie diuine confertur aliquid humane menti supra id, quod pertinet ad naturalem facultatem quantum ad vtrumque,* **58** *scilicet quantum ad iudicium per influxum intellectualis luminis et quantum ad accepcionem seu representacionem rerum, que fit per aliquas species.* **59** *Et quantum ad istud secundum potest assimilari reuelacio conficta humanitus aut dyabolica reuelacioni diuine prophecie sed non quantum ad primum.* Vsque hic Thomas de Aquino. **60** Ex quibus patet, quod cum intellectuale lumen supernaturale influitur anime existenti in ymaginaria visione siue non existenti, non a dyabolo esse potest sed a Deo. **61** Concluditur ergo clare, quod cum prefata beata domina in visionibus suis susceperit illum influxum luminis intellectualis et supernaturalis et semper ibi fuit aliquis exponens, vt Christus aut mater eius vel angelus aut aliquis sanctus, **62** a quibus declarabantur et exponebantur ei similitudines ille et verba figuraliter sibi dicta et ostendebantur illi vere

The iiii*te* signe is . in 14) what thing the vision or reuelacou*n* of the good . sprith {fro} differis fro ye illusion of the 15) deul whan yat p*ro*fete or the seer tellis be fore eu*er* trewe thing*es*. And spekis holy misteris 16) and teching*es* and scheuys honest and v*er*tuos man*er*ys And these ar signes yat they ar of god 17) ffor the deule seis su*m* while . trewe in his illusions and su*m*tyme fals . But the trew sprith 18) tellis eu*er* trewe and neu*er* fals. And y*er*fore whan this holy lady brigid . told eu*er* trewe thing*es* 19) and thei be wel vndirstondin/nen {neu*er*} sche seyd <neu*er*> ony. thing*e* fals or lesing' or inhonest 20) but all was trew[y]*at* sche told. Therfore it is clerly concludid yat all these thing*es* 21) were infudid and scheuyd to hir be goddis g*ra*ce and not be the deulis illusiou*n*

significaciones illorum visorum, vt patet in libris suis, **63** sequitur ergo, quod omnes iste sue reuelaciones et scriptura istorum librorum a Deo ministrate sint, qui talia operari potens est, non autem ab illusore, cui hec facere impossibile est, **64** vt supra patet per Augustinum et Thomam, quia in hoc differt visio illusoria a visione diuina, et in hoc omnes sancti patres et doctores concordant.

65 Quartum signum est, in quo differt visio seu reuelacio boni spiritus ab illusione dyabolica, quando scilicet ille propheta seu videns semper vera predicit et catholica misteria et documenta loquitur et honestos ac virtuosos mores indicat. **66** Et hec sunt signa, quod talia a Deo sint, quia dyabolus in illusionibus suis interdum dicit vera, vt decipiat, et aliquando falsa, sed Spiritus Sanctus semper vera et numquam falsa predicit. **67** Quod clare probat Beatus Thomas vbi supra sic dicens: *In aliquibus enim signis discerni potest eciam exterioribus prophecia demonum a prophecia diuina.* **68** Vnde dicit Crisostomus super Matheum, quod *prophetant in spiritu dyaboli, quales sunt diuinatores, sed sic dicernitur, quoniam dyabolus interdum falsa dicit sed Spiritus Sanctus numquam.* **69** Unde dicitur Deutronomii XVIII capitulo: *Si tacita cogitacione responderis: "Quomodo possum intelligere verbum, quod non est locutus Dominus?"* 70 *hoc habebis signum: "Quod in nomine Domini propheta ille predixerit et non euenerit, hoc Dominus non est locutus"* etc. **71** Dicit eciam Augustinus in libro XII Super Genesim ad Litteram, quod *quando aliqui stantes in extasi eleuacionis mentalis, videntes in ymaginaria seu spirituali visione aliqua signa vel ymagines corporum,* **72** *quod si in hoc eos malus arripuerit spiritus, aut demoniacos facit aut arrepticios aut falsos prophetas,* **73** cum autem bonus, facit eos fideles, misteria loquentes aut, accedente diuini luminis intelligencia, veros prophetas aut ad tempus id, quod per eos oportet ostendi, videntes atque narrantes. Hec Augustinus.

The v*te* 22) signe in ye whech visions ar discernyd . mynistred of a good sprith or <of> ylle is the frute 23) and the werkis yat p*ro*cedis fro yo visions or reuelacou*ns*. ffor aftir the gospel . an 24) ylle tre may nat make good frute . *et cetera*/Ye shal know the*m* be yer frute. Therfore it 25) is concludid yat all thes flood*es* has p*ro*cedid fro ye mos[t] pure welle of ye holy gost

74 Et ideo cum ista beata domina semper, si bene intelligantur, vera predixerit, nec in omnibus libris suis aliquid falsum vel mendacium vel inhonestum vel non catholicum dixerit, **75** sed omnia vera annunciauerit et confirmancia fidem catholicam ac dampnancia hereticos et semper virtutes indicauerit, vt patet in isto libro et aliis libris ei reuelatis, **76** ideo concluditur clare, quod omnia ista diuina gracia infusa et ostensa ei sint et non illusione dyabolica.

77 Quintum signum, in quo discernuntur visiones ministrate a bono spiritu vel a malo, est fructus ille et opera, que procedunt ab illis visionibus seu reuelacionibus, **78** quia secundum Euangelium *non potest arbor mala fructus bonos facere,* etc. *A fructibus enim eorum cognoscetis eos.*[17] **79** Nam prophecia vera ordinata et data fuit hominibus ex magna miseracione Dei ad humanorum actuum direccionem et ad regimen agendorum aut ad reuelacionem misteriorum quasi quoddam lumen diuinum, **80** quo homines dirigerentur et instruerentur tam in cognicione fidei quam in omnibus operibus virtuosis secundum quod erat expediens ad salutem electorum. **81** Et diuersificata fuit prophecia semper secundum diuersificacionem temporum et negociorum, sicut ponit Thomas in secunda secunde, titulo "De prophecia", articulo II, capitulo vltimo. **82** Nam dicitur Prouerbiorum XXIX: *Cum defecerit prophecia, dissipabitur populus.*

83 Et ideo quando videmus, quod ex talibus visionibus seu verbis reuelatis mens illuminatur, intellectus et consciencia videntis illustratur et vita eius corrigitur et emendatur, **84** conuertuntur homines viciosi ad virtuosam et religiosam vitam et de guerra et odio ad pacem, de superbia ad humilitatem et obedienciam et de malo ad bonum et hoc in multis personis et diu perseuerat, **85** tunc certissimum signum est, quod tales visiones et reuelaciones, que talem fructum germinauerunt et produxerunt, non a dyabolo sed a Spiritu Sancto pocius processerunt. **86** Que facere dyabolo impossibile est, immo totum contrarium procedit a visionibus seu pocius illusionibus suis. **87** Consueuerunt enim deuiare hominem a fide

26) The vi*te* signe is . yat yes thing*es* be of god and not of the yll sprith . and y*ou* see ye 27) deth or the ende laudabil and v*er*tuos of yat p*er*sone . seinge visions./ffor it is to wet 28) yat sum p*er*sonys has ben disseyued . of visions but radire callid illusions vndir the 29) kende of light/the deule shuld deseyue them . sheuyng*e* <to> the*m* many trew thing*es* and [*fol. 253v.*] 1) and[sic] in y*e* ende shuld deseyue them in oon fals po[yn]t/

catholica, a bonis moribus, a sana doctrina et ab obediencia prelatorum et Sacre Scripture ac eciam a subieccione sancte matris Ecclesie etc. **88** Cum igitur ab istis visionibus et reuelacionibus et verbis istorum librorum reuelatis prefate domine beatissime semper processerunt illa, que Dei sunt, et omnis virtus et mundicia morum et conuersio et emendacio proximorum, reuelacio misteriorum, roboracio fidei, dampnacio hereticorum, increpacio viciorum et prophecia vera futurorum etc, **89** que omnia in libro hoc et in aliis suis libris et per experienciam notoriam et manifestam in multis personis et mundi partibus sunt patencia, **90** ideo concluditur necessario, quod a fonte purissimo et limpidissimo Spiritus Sancti et non a tenebroso lacu fetido illusionis hec omnia flumina processerunt, **91** vt in isto moderno tempore viciorum caligine tenebroso per istam doctrinam sanctam in agendis suis homines instruerentur **92** et sic fugerent a terribili et districta iusticia diuina in hiis libris contenta ad gremium pietatis et misericordie Dei.

93 Sextum signum est, quod hec a Deo sint et non a maligno spiritu, mors seu finis laudabilis et virtuosus persone videntis visiones. **94** Nam sciendum est, quod quando alique persone a visionibus seu pocius illusionibus sub specie lucis longeue decepte fuerunt, ostendendo eis {dyabolus} multa vera, vt in fine in vno falso eas deciperet, **95** communiter semper inuenimus in scriptura sanctorum patrum, quod isti sic delusi in aliquos errores vel morte mala aut subitanea aut sine percepcione sacramentorum in fine ipsorum a dyabolo extincti sunt. **96** Et hoc voluit Deus semper aliis patefacere, vt a similibus illusionibus coloratis doceret eos cauere, **97** sed per contrarium in sanctis suis, qui diuinis visitacionibus seu visionibus in vita eorum consolabantur et illuminabantur, Deus in eorum morte operari solitus est, **98** quia in vita eorum semper eos protegendo direxit ac ipsos multis virtutibus et miraculis adornauit. **99** In morte quoque per aliquam singularem graciam quasi quodam approbacionis indicio eos mirifice clarificauit sicut patet in Iohanne Euangelista et in multis similibus. **100** Sic

The vii*te* signe of agood sprith is 2) clarifieng of meraclis aft*er* the {desh} deth . of the personys seing visions . ffor he yat is illudid 3) be visiou*ns* of the deul on tyl his deth . it is not worthy . yat he be clarified w*ith* godly 4) meraclis aftyr his deth. And for yat this worthi spowse of crist was not illudid {w*ith*} 5) of the deule in hir visiou*ns* in hir liff Therfore aft*er* hir deth she schinyd of crist w*ith* 6) many meruelous meraculys. yat is to sey be resussitacou*n* of many ded bodyes illumynacou*n* 7) of blinde men And helþe of deffmen*n* and be innum*er*abil meruelous kewris of diuers 8) infirmyteis of seke bodyes./yat <the whech he> {she} made cler in liff/aftyr hir deth. he scheuyd to vs 9) more cler The whech all thing*es* ar so opyn and knowin . shewyd and p*re*uyd be awte*n*-tyk 10) docume*ntes* As wel in the kingedom of Swecy as in Rome. and in the kingedom of cecyll[*e*] 11) and in many odir p*er*tes of the word. where

eciam fecit cum ista prefata sponsa sua beatissima ipse bonus Iesus, nam preuenta fuit eius mira superna gracia, quia ordinato progressu ab infimis ascendit ad summa. **101** Fuit enim humilitate sublimis, mortificacione viuida, simplicitate prudens omnique morum honestate conspicua, **102** propter quod ipse eam in vita sua mirandis graciis supernaturalibus extulit et diuinis visionibus et locucionibus ad vtilitatem Ecclesie seraphice decorauit, **103** necnon et in fine vite mortem ei ante predixit et in exitu suo in signum approbacionis eius corporalibus oculis consolatorie se ostendens vt dilectam sponsam ad celestes nupcias ipsius animam dulcissimo amplexu recepit, vt supra dictum est. **104** Et vide hoc clare in vltimo Libro Celesti, capitulo vltimo et in legenda vite eius. **105** Tali enim approbacionis sigillo voluit ipse Deus scripturam istorum librorum, eidem sponse diuinitus reuelatam, quodammodo autenticare et ad vtilitatem Ecclesie et fidelium eam mirifice sigillare, **106** quia ei, cui in vita tociens per propheticam, spiritualem et intellectualem visionem apparuit, ante eius exitum, mortem ei predicendo, se per plus quam propheticam, scilicet corporalem visionem monstrauit.

107 Septimum signum boni spiritus est clarificacio miraculorum post mortem videntis visiones, nam qui vsque ad mortem per visiones a demone illuditur, dignum non est, quod post mortem diuinis miraculis clarificetur. **108** Et quia ista Christi dignissima sponsa a dyabolo in visionibus suis in vita delusa non fuit, **109** ideo post eius exitum multis et mirandis miraculis eam Christus clarificauit, per resuscitacionem scilicet multorum mortuorum et per illuminaciones cecorum et sanaciones surdorum et per innumeras curaciones mirificas de diuersis infirmitatibus infirmorum, vt quam ipse in vita fecerat claram, post mortem nobis ostenderet clariorem. **110** Que omnia in tantum sunt notoria et manifesta et per documenta autentica diuulgata et probata tam in regno Suecie quam in Roma et in regno Sicilie et in aliis multis partibus mundi, **111** vbi ad eius memoriam et reuerenciam a fidelibus ymago eius

as in ye memory and reuerens of trew 12) cristen pepil an ymage of hir is depictid in many chirchis yat nedis noo*n* odir p*ro*bacou*n* 13) ne*n* may not be lauyd in ony thinge. Thes heue*n*ly word*es* of these bokis techis vs to 14) drede god aright/to loue him mekely and desire celestial thing*es* sapiently. Therfore ye 15) yat redis p*re*ue these forseid thing*es* And if 3e finde ony thing odirwise . sey ageyns 16) it boldly. Therfore geue we thanking*es* to ye fadir of m*er*cyes And to god of al co*m*fort 17) and consolacou*n*/ye wheche metys wrecchis w*ith* as many m*er*cyes as ar mis*er*iis in ye 18) word . yat thei fall nat into ye pres[ou]n of desparacou*n* 19) This is the recapitulacou*n* of all the forseyd./vii chapt*er* 20) In recapitulinge the forseid man*er* wise of examinacou*n* {.} doynge or making 21) in p*er*sonys the whech sees visiou*ns* and reuelacou*ns*/I sey breffly . yat ye p*er*sone 22) the whech is foundin very meke in examynacou*n* And namly. if he leue vndir obediens co*n*tinua[l] 23) of a sp*irit*ual fadir to hos discrecou*n* he cast*es* all thing*es* vndir And {.} his mynde is rapt in 24) p*ra*your and felis asingler suetnes of goddis loue/and tha*n* he thus being*e* in ymaginary 25) vision or only intellectual[l] simpilly . felis aflood of a sup*er*natural light and intellectual 26) of god[*des*] treuþe and yan the treu[þ]e . of yat mateer may . be made opyn to him And 27) tellis eu*er* trew thing*es* in his visions . ffro ye whech visou*ns* frute of edifyeng and amending of him self and of his neybouris . alwey p*ro*cedis/ I sey yat soche apersone 29) is not illudid of the deul nen his visions ar not illusory . ne*n* to be disspisid . fforsoþ*e* [*fol. 254r.*] 1) alholly ar godly . and mekely to be reseyued and beleyued and alman*er* of wise to be obeyed 2) and folowyd. As it schewis breffly In/all thing*es* before seid and of the seying*es* of al doctours 3) and holy fadris vp on this mateer diffusly and manyfold wise spekinge/.-//-//

depicta per multas ecclesias inuenitur, quod alia non indigent probacione nec aliqua possunt iam tergiuersacione celari. **112** Hoc eciam mentes omnium ista diuinitus reuelata legencium preparare debet ad faciliorem credulitatis accepcionem et veritatis, quod tanta verba tantaque miracula in istis Celestibus Libris tam seriose contenta non aliam fidem predicant nisi quam Christus predicauit. **113** Non nouum nobis Christum nec eciam antichristum inducunt, sed eundem credendum, amandum feruencius et timendum nos admonent, qui pro nobis passus in cruce fuit. **114** Nichil veritatis, que in Christo est, subtrahunt aut addunt, sed misericordia et iusticia eius ad profectum salutis nostre in eis quam in aliis libris prophetarum diuinitus clarius ostenditur. **115** Docent enim nos verba ista celestia istorum librorum Deum timere recte, diligere pie et desiderare celestia sapienter.

116 Probate igitur vos ista predicta legentes, et si aliter inueneritis, audacter contradicite. Hoc habetur in secundo Libro Celesti, XIIII capitulo in fine. **117** Cedat igitur temeritas suspicionis fallacis spiritus ac detraccio superba et inuida stulti iudicii, et detur locus glorie et gracie Dei, que tanto maior esse dinoscitur, quanto ignorancie et modice fidei nostre videtur incredibilior. **118** Gracias ergo patri misericordiarum et Deo tocius consolacionis agamus, qui in tot senescentis mundi miseriis tot misericordiis occurrit miseris, ne labantur in baratrum desperacionis.

Recapitulacio omnium predictorum.

Capitulum VII.

1 Recapitulando igitur supradictum modum examinis faciendi in personis, que vident visiones et reuelaciones, dico breuiter, quod persona, **2** que in examine reperitur vere humilis et presertim, si viuit sub obediencia patris spiritualis continua, cuius discrecioni omnia subicit, **3** et mens eius in oracione rapta in extasim sentit singularem dulcedinem amoris diuini, **4** et tunc in ymaginaria visione existens aut sola intellectuali simplici sentit influxum supernaturalis luminis intellectualis veritatis diuine, et manifestatur ei tunc veritas illius materie **5** et semper

Pages 194, 202, 210, and 222 are blank to accomodate the facing pages; the Latin text is considerably longer than the Middle English. These pages, and others with obvious gaps, reflect that textual difference as well as occasional deletions in the Middle English text.

vera predicit in visionibus suis, a quibus visionibus fructus edificacionis et emendacionis sui et proximorum semper procedit, **6** dico, quod talis persona non illuditur a dyabolo, nec visiones eius sunt illusorie et despiciende, immo totaliter sunt diuine et humiliter tamquam de manu Dei recipiende et credende ac omnimode obediende et exequende, **7** vt ex omnibus supradictis patet breuiter et ex dictis omnium doctorum et sanctorum patrum super hac materia multifarie diffuse loquencium.

Notes to Middle English and Latin Texts

1. In this transcription abbreviations for words which, in modern English, end in "-tion" and in Middle English, depending on dialect, "-ioun," have been expanded here without the "i": e.g., "examynacoun."
2. *densa . . . tenebrosis* cf. Job 10.21.
3. *incredulitatem et duriciam Pharaonis* Exodus 5.1–12.36, cf. Mark 16.14. *Ventus turbinus* cf. Ezek. 1.4 "*ventus turbinis veniebat ab aquilone*". *scriptum . . . digito Dei* cf. Exodus 31.18.
4. *ventilabrum . . . granum a palea* cf. Matt. 3.12; Luke 3.17.
5. *angelus . . . transformat* cf. 2 Cor. 11.14.
6. *Deus . . . infirma mundi elegit . . . ut confundat sapientes.* 1 Cor. 1.27.
7. *stodstille* dotted for expunction and deleted. This word occurs on the following line about six character spaces to the left, which suggests an eye-slip on the part of the scribe. This may indicate that the scribe was copying from an English text, not translating from the Latin.
8. *Probate . . . sint.* 1 John 4.1 "*probate spiritus si ex Deo sint, quoniam multi pseudoprophettae exierunt in mundum.*"
9. *Gh.* at this point has *sapore,* "wisdom, discernment". It appears that the translator has mistaken this for *sopore,* "slumber, drowsiness".
10. Compare with the *vita* written by Bridget's confessors, Prior Peter and Master Peter. An English translation, with a valuable introduction and notes, is found in Marguerite Tjader Harris, ed., *Birgitta of Sweden, Life and Selected Revelations,* trans. Albert Ryle Kezel (New York, 1990).
11. At this point, *Gh* has *dicens.* The scribe's writing the first two letters of *dicens,* then dotting it for expunction and continuing with *seinge* could indicate that he was copying from a text which had Agnes' speech, and perhaps the preamble to it, in Latin in the English translation. This was not unusual; it lent authority and authenticity to the vernacular text.(See Ian Johnson, "Prologue and Practice: the Middle English Lives of Christ", *The Medieval Translator: The Theory and Practice of Translation in the Middle Ages,* ed. Roger Ellis (Cambridge, 1989), p. 82). However, if this was indeed so, and the scribe decided to translate *all* the Latin, it would suggest that he was literate in Latin and was writing for an audience which was not literate enough to cope with even minimal Latin, possibly an audience of lay women.
12. *Gh* at this point has *seriose* = seriously. It appears that the translator has mistaken this for *series* = in a row, or that s/he has misread an abbreviated form of *seriose.*
13. This interlineated phrase does not appear in *Gh.* The fact that the scribe felt it necessary to extend *man* specifically to include all persons could suggest that he knew himself to be writing for a female audience.
14. *in illo extasi.* For the masculine gender of *extasis* cf. Bridget of Sweden, *Revelaciones* Book VII, ed. B. Bergh (Uppsala, 1967), p. 100
15. See D. Pulignani, ed. "Tres socii," *Miscellanea Franciscana* VII (1898), 4.37.
16. Cf. Prol. Matt. 6 "*nullus dat quod non habet*". See D. Liebs, ed., *Lateinische Rechtsregeln und Rechtssprichtwörter* (Munich, 1982), p. 129 note 40 and p. 132 note 63.
17. Matt. 7.18 and Matt. 7.16.

The French Version of the *Modus tenendi parliamentum* in the Courtenay Cartulary: a Transcription and Introduction

Kathryn Kerby-Fulton and Ruth Horie

The transcription we present here of the *Modus tenendi parliamentum* (a title memorably translated by Galbraith as *How to hold a parliament*) is from London, British Library, MS Additional 49359, one of two extant copies of the French version of this bafflingly quixotic text on parliamentary procedure.[1] Best known in its widely disseminated Latin original, the text's surprisingly idealistic insistence upon the constitutional power of the lower orders of parliament, and upon the importance of public record, has repeatedly astonished and intrigued modern historians, most of whom, however, have ignored its vernacular versions. In fact, both French and English translations survive, and one quickly sees why:

whether in its assertion that petitions in parliament should be heard in the order they are filed "nullo habito respectu ad quorumcumque personas" (XVIII), or its heartwarming insistence that transcripts of the records of parliament should be made available free of charge to those who are unable to pay (XXV), or its amazing assertion that in parliament "two knights . . . have a greater voice in granting and denying [financial aid to the king] than the greatest earl of England, and in the same manner the proctors of the clergy . . . have a greater voice in parliament than the bishop himself" (XXIII), the *Modus* comes across as a text that could hardly have failed to appeal to certain vernacular audiences.[2]

Legal historians have ignored its history as a vernacular text partly because, up till now, the only French version in print has been the textually inferior one published by T. D. Hardy in 1862, from the Finch-Hatton Roll.[3] The copy transcribed here from Additional 49359, the Courtenay Cartulary, is markedly superior, representing a largely faithful and intelligent rendering of the Latin, with fewer errors and omissions. It is, moreover, no mere "lay" text: since French was the language of much parliamentary and civil service reportage in the late fourteenth and early fifteenth centuries, we should not be surprised to discover that the French *Modus* was actually quite politically influential during this period, even in the inner circles of government—in Ireland, in fact, arguably more influential than the Latin version. It is striking that both the extant French copies were owned by politicians active in Irish parliamentary affairs: the copy in the Finch-Hatton roll was owned by Richard O'Hedigan, archbishop of Cashel (1406–40), who was suspected of (and once charged with) manipulating parliamentary matters in Ireland for his own purposes, and who was likely responsible for an audaciously self-serving interpolation into the Latin text of the *Modus* itself, a copy of which was found in the possession of Sir Christopher Preston when he was arrested on charges of sedition in 1418. The *inspeximus* (certified copy) made at the time of the arrest represents the only extant medieval Latin text of the Irish version of the *Modus*; it was copied by the same two Dublin civil servants who wrote a report on the arrest in colorful law French, sporadically peppered with stretches of formulaic Latin.[4] Reading the French of the Preston report one gets a strong sense of the vitality of an office vernacular, and of the political and bureaucratic context in which the French *Modus* came to high-level government attention. The French text printed here from the Courtenay family cartulary has similarly prestigious political connections: it was associated with Philip de Courtenay, who served as the king's lieutenant of Ireland from 1383–85, and who was himself arrested in Ireland in 1390.[5] In the cartulary, the text of the *Modus* appears in the same hand as a list of the charges laid against Roger Mortimer earlier in the century (in 1330), a conjunction that may be explicable by the fact that Courtenay was appointed in 1383 to mop up colonial indignation over the previous lieutenancy, that of the seven-year-old-child, Roger Mortimer (descendant of the Roger judged in 1330).[6] Courtenay apparently wanted a copy of judgments against the earlier Mortimer's "anti-parliamentary" behavior, along with a treatise on parliamentary procedure in order to start his new position, which he must have viewed with all the trepidation of an Englishman venturing among not only the "wild Irish," but into the Byzantine factionalism of colonial Anglo-Ireland. It is, then, not likely simply coincidence that the Mortimer judgments and the *Modus* are in the same hand, and together, in the Courtenay cartulary—nor does the fact that the text was in French rather than Latin imply that the king's new lieutenant was merely a "layman," so to speak, in governmental matters.[7]

The text printed here for the first time is interesting in two further ways: first, it is a witness to the textual importance of the French version of the *Modus.* While Pronay and Taylor, the meticulous recent editors of the three main Latin versions, noted in passing that the Courtenay text is "undoubtedly the better . . . giv[ing] on the whole a full and accurate translation of the Latin original," they, too, like earlier scholars, relied solely on the Finch-Hatton text printed by Hardy to determine the complex relations between what they call the "French" and "Irish" (Latin) textual traditions, and for their conclusion that "[t]here can be no doubt moreover that the Irish version is a compressed form of the French original."[8] But there is no such neat relation between the French text in Courtenay and the Irish version—that is, if one collates the Courtenay text, several of the shared errors upon which Pronay and Taylor's conclusion is based disappear.[9] So this unique textual relationship exists only between the French text of Finch-Hatton and the (earliest) Latin text of the Irish version (the one found on Preston at the time of his arrest)—and this is surely politically, not textually significant: both Preston and O'Hedigan were members of the Ormond affinity during the Lancastrian period. This, moreover, tells us nothing about how the *Modus* was known in *Ricardian* Ireland: for that we need to go to the Courtenay cartulary. The implications of all this, especially when the Courtenay text can be fully collated with a new critical edition of the Latin C text, will change how we understand the complex question of when and how the *Modus* originated, and the fascinating process of its textual development and "contamination."

The text printed here is also significant because it is the earliest extant manuscript of the *Modus*, although, again, because it happens to be a vernacular rather than a Latin text, this has never really been noticed. The copy of the *Modus*, here entitled, "le man(er)e de tenir p(ar)lement," and copied with the Mortimer articles (with the intriguingly vestigial heading, "autres de la ter(r)e Irland," fol. 3r) is written in a hand that can be dated roughly anytime in the mid-fourteenth century,[10] but more likely, given the height of the two-compartment "a," toward the end of the third quarter, rather than earlier. It is, in aspect, a mid-century anglicana formata, but, as Michèle Mulchahey has observed, it lacks some of the characteristic features of that script, especially the anglicana "r." In fact, a closer look at its paleographical features may tell us even more: the Courtenay scribe is actually using, at quite an early date, both the short "r" and the single-compartment "g" of the new *chancellerie royale* hand (first utilized in England by scribes of the Black Prince, and appearing earliest in Lambeth Palace registers beginning in 1375),[11] and this is striking evidence for the possibility that Courtenay may have had at his disposal an active government scribe. Or perhaps, more accurately, a government clerk, quite possibly a shrewd civil servant not unlike Geoffrey Martin, whose bureaucratic work for the appellants of Richard II in 1386 can likewise be connected with early political ownership of the *Modus* (the B recension Latin text).[12] This would give us a likely date for Courtenay's copy of c. 1375–83 (the year he was appointed). We cannot, of course, be certain of this narrow dating, but the *Modus* and the articles against Mortimer are (paleographically speaking) the earliest items in the cartulary, and were certainly assembled with a view to interests in Ireland.[13] And that, given the state of our ignorance about the date and origin of the *Modus* itself, is welcome new evidence.[14]

The transcription symbols follow those in Michelle Brown:[15]

( ) expanded abbreviation
' unexpanded abbreviations or flourishes
\ / cribal insertions between lines
/ end of line
[[ ]] accidental loss of letters
< > doubtful/illegible letters (due to damage to the MS)
⌊ ⌋ textual omissions
\+ + corrupt or obscure text, doubtful readings

Italics indicate rubrics and titles. Orthography, capitalization, and punctuation follow the MS.

University of Victoria

Notes

1. The text takes up fols. 3v-6r. For a detailed discussion of the difficulties the *Modus* poses for modern historians, an analysis of its political history in England and Ireland, and extensive bibliography, see Kathryn Kerby-Fulton and Steven Justice, "Reformist Intellectual Culture in the English and Irish Civil Service: The *Modus tenendi parliamentum* and its Literary Relations," *Traditio* 53 (1998), 149–203. For V. H. Galbraith's views, see his "The *Modus tenendi parliamentum,*" *Journal of the Warburg and Courtauld Institute* 16 (1953), 85.
2. For a list of all the Latin, French and English manuscripts, see Nicholas Pronay and John Taylor, eds., *Parliamentary Texts of the Later Middle Ages* (Oxford, 1980). The quotations, and section numbers, cited above, are from their A Recension edition of the text, pp. 67–79. No modern edition of the English version exists (none, that is, more recent than 1809, when it was reprinted by Sir Walter Scott); see Pronay and Taylor, p. 216.
3. "On the Treatise entitled *Modus Tenendi Parliamentum,*" *Archaeological Journal* 19 (1862), 259–74. The roll is now Northampton Record Society Finch-Hatton 2995.
4. See Jocelyn Otway-Ruthven, "The Background to the Arrest of Sir Christopher Preston in 1418," *Analecta Hibernica* 29 (1980), 73; Pronay and Taylor, *Parliamentary Texts,* pp. 120–22; and Kerby-Fulton and Justice.
5. *C.P.R.* 1388–92, p. 349; Pronay and Taylor, *Parliamentary Texts,* p. 122; and Kerby-Fulton and Justice.
6. On Courtenay, see A. J. Otway-Ruthven, *A History of Medieval Ireland,* 2nd ed. (New York, 1980), pp. 317–18; and for the documents on Courtenay in this paragraph: *C.C.R.*, 1385–89, III, p. 232; *C.P.R.*, 1381–85, p. 88.
7. See the assumption made by Hardy, p. 255.
8. Pronay and Taylor, *Parliamentary Texts,* pp. 215 and 121.
9. Compare the list of these shared errors and omissions in the Irish text (Pronay and Taylor, *Parliamentary Texts,* pp. 128–37) with the corresponding passages in the Courtenay text: for instance, there is no omission of the Latin version's *filios suos milites faciendo* (*Modus,* opening sentence of section XXIII, on aids to the King, omitted from Irish version, section XV), as in Finch-Hatton and the Irish version; and Courtenay does not make the error of which Pronay and Taylor say "alone amongst the medieval versions the French text has the phrase "en lieu appert" . . . translated *aperto loco* in the Irish version" (*Modus,* section XII); Courtenay renders both reasonably accurately. However, the textual relationship of Courtenay to the Latin versions is a complex matter, and scribal reconstruction may have occurred: on this passage, see the possibilities set out in Kerby-Fulton and Justice, note 141. The most significant differences between Hardy's text and Courtenay's are (page numbers in the following list refer to Hardy; "Ct" refers to Courtenay):

   1) "De Clergie," "A parlement somondre . . . priaunt qils voillent estre a soun

parlement'' (p. 266) appears under the heading ''De Sommonz'' in Ct 2) Between ''De Chivalers dez Counteez'' and ''De Burgeys'' (p. 267), Ct has the section ''De Citiseinz'' (fol. 4r); 3) ''Des Cases et Jugementz Doutouses'' (p. 269), last line, ''soit illoeqes adonqes en plein parlement . . . ,'' Ct adds '' . . . et del assent du parlement. . . . '' 4) For ''Lordre'' (p. 269), Ct reads ''Roy.'' 5) ''De la Manere de Parlement'' (p. 270), the last paragraph, ''Le Chauncellere dengliterre . . . bonez excusaciouns'' forms a separate section in Ct, under the heading ''De les Officers le Roye'' (fols. 4v-5r). 6) ''La Comensement del Parlement'' (p. 270), last paragraph, ''Le primer jour . . . procheinement ensuauntz,'' forms a separate section in Ct, under the heading ''De proclamacion du parlement'' (fol. 5r). 7) ''De Lieux et Sessiouns en le Parlement'' (p. 271), second to the last line, ''seerunt lez Chaunceller denglitere,'' Ct adds ''le chief Justice Dengleterre'' (fol. 5v). 8) ''Del Aide le Roy'' (p. 272), the heading in Ct reads ''De demander laide del parlement''; first line, ''pur guerre esteaunt ou pur . . . ,'' in Ct reads '' . . . ses filz afaire Chiualer ou . . . '' (fol. 5v). 9) Same section, (p. 273), line 9, '' . . . chivalers de Countez . . . ,'' Ct adds ''Citeseinz . . . '' 10) ''De lez Transcriptz,'' (p. 273) , line 3, Ct adds ''si noun'' after ''denier.'' 11) ''De lez Degreez'' (p. 273), line 1, ''commenciounri (*sic*)'' reads ''comenceour'' in Ct (fol. 6r). 12) p. 274, line 3, after ''le sisme'' Ct adds ''degree est des Citiseinz et Burgeis et ensi est le parlement de sis degreez. Et fait assauoir qe si ensi soit qe ascuns de . . . '' (fol. 6r).

10. We are grateful to Timothy Haskett and Michèle Mulchahey for examining the manuscript, and giving us their opinions on the hand and the date. Thanks are due also to Barry Beardsmore, who read the transcription and offered suggestions regarding its medieval French.
11. See Malcolm Parkes, *English Cursive Book Hands, 1250–1500* (London, 1979), p. xx, and Charles Johnson and Hilary Jenkinson, *English Court Hand, 1066 to 1500* (1915; repr. New York:, 1967), plates XXVIII- XXX especially.
12. See Kerby-Fulton and Justice, ''The *Modus.*''
13. In the British Library's *Additional Catalogue* (that is, a binder kept in the Students' Room, with loose-leaf paper entries, entitled vol. 33A, 1956–1960/Add MSS 48989–50483/Egerton MSS 3725–3764), the codex is listed as ''Feodary and Chartulary of the Courtenay Family, Earls of Devon, with other miscellaneous material'' and dated ''temp. Edward III-early 15th cent.'' Its contents are in Latin and French, and the main items are listed as follows:

    1) a copy of a grant by William le Spek in 'Wolseres Worthy' (?in Woolfardisworthy, co. Devon) (16 Mar. 1334), early 15th cent., fol. 1r

    2) list of advowsons of the Earl of Devon; French, temp. Edward III, fol. 2r

    3) articles against Roger Mortimer (presented in Parliament 26 Nov. 1330), French, fols. 2v-3r

    4) *Modus tenendi parliamentum*, French, temp. Edward III, after 1330; printed by T. D. Hardy from Finch-Hatton MS 2995, the only other recorded MS of the French version

    5) punishment for breaking homage, early 15th cent., fol. 6v

    6) memorandum of agreement between the Earl of Devon and Philip Courtenay over fees, French, early 15th cent., fol. 6v

    7) list of fees in co. Devon; extracts from rolls of inquisitions for 1252–53,1279–80, 1314–15, temp. Edward III, fols. 7r-23r, 25r-28v

    8) register of fees of the honor of Plympton, temp. Edward III, fols. 24r, 24v, 29r-35r

9) extracts from Assize rolls (1281) and *Placita coram Rege* rolls (1399), temp. Edward III-early 15th cent., fols. 35r-37r
10) register of fees and liberties of Hugh de Courtenay, mainly in co. Devon (compiled 1310–11), temp. Edward III, fols. 38r-53v
11) perambulation of Dartmoor (1239–40), temp. Edward III, fol. 54r
12) genealogical history of the Courtenay family to Hugh of Courtenay (b. 1303), compiled 1335–40, and miscellaneous memoranda, temp. Edward III, fols. 54r-55r
13) mortuary roll of the Earls of Devon to Hugh de Courtenay (d. 1340), and genealogy to Hugh of Courtenay (b. 1303). The date of death is incorrectly given as 1339 in the MS, French, early 15th cent., temp. Edward III, fol. 55v
14) fees of Edward de Courtenay (d. 1419), in co. Cornwall, early 15th cent., fols. 56r-57r
15) copies of miscellaneous documents, inquisitions, Courtenay charters, etc. (incl. pleas, inquisitions, charters, temp. Henry III-20 May 1374), partly French, temp. Edward III-early 15th cent., fols. 58r-73r
16) extent and rental of Crook, in North Tawton, co. Devon (compiled 1315–16), early 15th cent., fols. 74r-78v
17) lists of fees, early 15th cent., fols. 79r-81v
18) copies of deeds and inquisitions (13th cent.-1408/9), late 14th cent.-early 15th cent., fols. 82r-85v
19) extract from memoranda rolls (1343–44), early 15th cent., fols. 87r-89v, 95v
20) accounts (status domus) of Cowick Priory, co. Devon, by Prior William de Estrepeny (13 April 1394), early 15th cent., fol. 92r
21) extracts from 13th-14th cent. statute rolls, partly French, early 15th cent., fol. 92v-95r.
The cartulary has been discussed in G. R. C. Davis, *Medieval cartularies* (1958), no. 1229, and *English Historical Review* 34 (1919), 209–25, as well as in Kerby-Fulton and Justice, "The *Modus.*"

14. For the view that the text originated in the 1380s in Ireland, see G. O. Sayles, "*Modus tenendi parliamentum*: Irish or English?" *England and Ireland in the Later Middle Ages: Essays in Honour of Jocelyn Otway-Ruthven*, ed. James Lydon (Kill Land [County Dublin], 1981), pp. 122–52.
15. Michelle P. Brown, *A Guide to Western Historical Scripts* (Toronto, 1990), p. 6.

The Modus tenendi parliamentum in the Courtenay Cartulary

3v *Cy comence le man(er)e de tenir p(ar)lement.*

[[Icy]] est escript La man<er>e coment le p(ar)lement du Roy Denglet(er)re et <s>es <en>gleys estoit tenutz en temps/

le Roi Edward filz Etheldred le Roi quel man(er)e estoit reherce p(ar) les pl<u>s sages de Roialme deu(a)nt/

William Duk de Normandie Conquerour et Roi Denglet(er)re mesme le Conquerour ceo comand(a)nt/

p(ur) luy p(ro)ue et en sou(n) temps et auxi en temps de ses successours Roiz Denglet(er)re vse. etc./

De Sommonz.

Le sommonz du p(ar)lement doit p(ro)cedere le primer iour de p(ar)lement p(ar) xl. iours. etc./

Au p(ar)lement sommondr(e) et venir deiuont p(ar) resou(n) de lour tenure toutz et chescun Ercheueqe Euesqe/

Abbe Priour et aultres g(ra)untz de Clergie queux teignent p(ar) Countee ou Baronie p(ar) reson de tiel/

man(er)e teinire et nulle meyndres si noun q(e) lo(ur) p(re)sence et venue p(ar) aultre voie q(e) p(ar) lo(ur) tenure soit/

requis si come sil soient du conseil le Roi ou lo(ur) p(re)sence necessarie ou p(ro)fitable au p(ar)lement soi+t+/

dit et a eux le Roi est tenuz mi⌊ni⌋str(ere) lo(ur) custages et despens en venant et demorrant a le p(ar)lement. Et/
ne deiuont tiels meyndres de clergie estre somonez au p(ar)lement mes le Roi soleit enuoier' ses/
briefs a tiels sages priant qils voillent estre a sou(n) p(ar)lement. etc./
De Clergie
It(e)m le Roi soleit enuoier ses sommonz as Ercheuesqes et aultres exemptz p(er)sones si come Abbes/
Priours Deanes et aultres p(er)sones de seinte eglise q'ent Jurisdiccions p(ar) tiels man(ere)s excepcions/
et p(ri)uilegijs de p(ar)tiez qils p(ur) chescun Deaconie et Erchedeaconie Denglet(er)re p(ar) eux mesmes Dea/
⌊n⌋ies et Erchedeaconies ferroient esluz deux sages et couenables p(ro)curatours de lo(ur) p(ro)pre Erche/
deaconie venir et estre a p(ar)lement a respoundre supportez allowez et faire mesme ceo q(e) toutz/
et chescuns des p(er)sones de Denes et Erchideaconies estoient p(er)sonelment et q(e) ceux p(ro)curatours/
vendront oue lo(ur) garrant ouesq(es) les seals de lo(ur) sou(er)eignes double enseals qils custumable/
ment a tiels man(er)s p(ro)curacies sont esluz et enuoiez des queux l(ett)res garantz +lui+ serra deliu(er)e as clercs/
du p(ar)lement a enrouler et lautre demorrera deu(er)s mesmes p(ro)curato(ur)s. Et ensi de soutz cez deux ma/
ners de sommonz +s+oit tut la clergie estre sommonez au p(ar)lement./
De Layes
It(e)m Sommondre et venir deiuont toutz et chescuns Countez et Barons et lo(ur) piers cestassauoir ceux q(e)/
ont t(er)res et rentes al value dun Countee entier cestassauoir vint feez du Chiualers chescun fee a/
compte a vint liuers q(e) font qatre Centz liuers en tot ou la value dun Baronie entier cestassauoir/
trese feez et la tierce p(ar)tie dun fee du Chiualer chescun fee acompte a vint liuers q(e) font en tot/
qatre Centz Marz et nulles meyndres laies ne deiuont estre somonez ne venir au p(ar)lement p(ar) re/
son de lo(ur) tenure si noun q(e) lo(ur) p(re)sence p(ar) aultre cause soit p(ro)fitable ou necessarie au p(ar)lement/

<et>donq(e)s de eux soit estre fait si come il est dit des meyndres de clergie q(ue)ux p(ar) reson de lou<r>/
tenure ne sont tenuz a venir a p(ar)lement. etc./
De Barons de Cink portz
It(e)m le Roi soleit enuoier ses briefs a les gardeinz de Cink portz qil ferroit eslier de cheschun por<t>/
p(ar) mesme le port deux couenables et sages Barons a venir et estre a son p(ar)lement a respoundre/
supportez et alowes et faire mesme ceo q(e) ferroient lo(ur) Barons si come ils mesmes de les Barons/
toutz et chescun p(er)sonelment illeoqes estoient et q(e) tiels Barons viendroient oue lo(ur) garrantz de/
les co(m)munez seals de lo(ur) portz double enseals ensi qils soient a ceo custimablement esluz atto(r)nes/
et enuoietz p(ur) lo(ur) Barons des queux garrantz lun serroit liu(er)e as clers de p(ar)lement et lautre <a>/
remeindre deu(er)s mesmes les Barons des portz eiauntz cunge del p(ar)lement q(a)nt ils deiuont de/
p(ar)tir et donqes soloient auoir le brief de la g(ra)unt seal directe al gardein de les cink portz qil/
ferroit tiels Barons auoir resonables custages et lo(ur) despences de co(mm)i(n)alte de lo(ur) port de le [[primer]]/
io(ur) qils v(er)s l<e> p(ar)lement aleront tanq(e) al io(ur) qils alo(ur) p(ro)pre reuiendr<o>nt et q(e) exp(re)sse mencion fait/
<en> le dit brief de la dem(ur)ge qils ferroient al p(ar)lement et del io(ur) q(e) viendroient et aue<nt> [[conge]]/
a retorner. Et iadis soleit estre fait mencion en le brief q(a)nt tiels Barons <de>[[ueroi]]en<t> p[[ren]]dr<e>/
de tiels com(mun)altez p(ar) le io(ur) cestassauoir ascuns plus et ascuns meyndre[[s]] soleit labi[[lite et]] h<o>nes<t>e/
et regard des p(er)sones. Et ne soleit estre mys p(ur) deux Barons p(ar) le io(ur) ault[[re]] xx. s. [[eant]] reg<ar>[[d]]/
a lo(ur) demorge trauailles et despences et ne soleient tiels despences estre [[mys en certayn]] p(ar) le court/
4r p(ur) ascuns p(er)sones ensi esluz et enuoies p(ur) les co(mm)i(n)altez si noun lo(ur) p(er)sones estoient honestes et soi bien/
eiant en le p(ar)lement. etc./
De Chiualers de Countees
It(e)m le Roi soleit enuoier ses briefs a toutz les viscountes Denglet(er)re qils ferroient [[e]]slire ches/

cun de sou(n) Countee deux Chiualers couenables et honestez et sages a venir a sou(n) p(ar)lement en/
mesme la man(er)e q(e) est dit des Barons de Cink portz et de lo(ur) garantz en mesme la man(er)e einz/
p(ur) les despences de dieux Chiualers dun Counte ne soleit estre mys outre vn marc p(ur) le io(ur)./

De Citeseinz

En mesme la man(er)e soleit et deuoit estre enuoiez as baillifs et p(ro)dhommes ou Maier ou Citeseinz/
Deu(er)wik ou daultres Citees qils p(ur) lo(ur) co(mm)i(n)alte de lo(ur) Citee eslierent deux couenables honestez/
et sages Citeseinz a venir et estre au p(ar)lement en mesme la man(er)e qest dit des Barons de cink/
portz et de Chiualers des Counteez et soloient Citeseinz estre piers et oweles oue Chiualers/
des Countees en despences veiant demorrant et retornant. etc./

De Burgeis

En mesme la man(er)e soleit et deuoit estre enuoiez as baillifs et p(ro)dhommes des Burghes qils de/
soy eslierent deux couenables honestes et sages Burgeis a venir et estre au p(ar)lement le Roi/
en mesme la man(er)e qest dit des Citeseinz einz deux Burgeis ne soloient p(re)ndre p(ur) lour/
despencez p(ur) vn io(ur) outre x. s'. et ascun temps outre d(em)i marc et ceo soleit estre taxe p(ar) le Court/
solonc la q(ua)ntite et poer de les Burgeis et solonc la honeste des p(er)sones enuoietz. etc./

De p(ri)ncipal Clerk du p(ar)lement

Deux Clercz p(ri)ncipals del p(ar)lement Seeront en le my Lieu des Justices q(ue)ux enroilleront co(mm)i(n)es/
plees et bosoignez du p(ar)lement cestassauoir q(e) mesme deux Clercz ne sont subgitz a q(e)conq(e) Justi/
ces et nec ascun Justice Denglet(er)re en p(ar)lement et ne ont p(ar) soy record en p(ar)lement si nou(n) nouelle/
poair a eux soit assigne et done en p(ar)lement p(ar) le Roi et les piers du p(ar)lement si come q(ua)nt ils/
ouesq(es) aultres suitiers du p(ar)lement sont assignes oier et t(er)miner a ceux peticions et querel/
en le p(ar)lement monstrez einz sont mesme deux clercz saunz mesmes subgetz al Roi et sou(n) p(ar)/

lement en co(m)mine si noun serreit vn Justice ou deux assignez a eux examiner et amender/
lo(ur) enrollementz et q(ua)nt les piers du p(ar)lement sont assignez a oier et examiner ascuns peti/
cions especialement p(ar) soy donq(e)s com ils serront dun voillance et dun acord en lo(ur) iugeme(n)t/
en plein p(ar)lement ensi q(e) mesmes deux clercz p(ri)ncipalment enrolleront toutz plees et toutz/
iugementz en le p(ri)ncipal rolle du p(ar)lement et mesmes les rolles liueront al Tresourer/
deuant le p(ar)lement fuit [sic] dep(ar)tiz ensi q(e) en chescun man(er)e mesmes les rolles soient en la may[[n]]/
du Tresourer deuant p(ro)cesse du p(ar)lement ent salue a mesmes les clercs le t(ra)nscript en/
countrerollement ils le voillant auoir. Et mesmes deux Clercs si noun ils soient enaut(re)s/
offices oue le Roi et p(re)ndrent de luy fees ensi qils purront ent honestement viure ils/
p(re)ndront du Roi p(ar) le io(ur) vn marc p(ur) lo(ur) despences p(ar) oweles porcions si noun ils soient a la table/
le Roi ils p(re)ndront outre lo(ur) table forq(e) di' Marc p(ar) le io(ur) p(ar) oweles porcions p(ar) tout le p(ar)lement./

De Cink Clercz du p(ar)lement

Le Roi doit assigner cink Clercs sages et approuez dount. Le p(ri)mer doit Ministrer et seruer as/
Euesqes et le secunde ales p(ro)curato(ur)s de clergie et le tierce as Counteez et Barons le quarte as/
Chiualers de counteez le quinte as Citeseinz et Burgeis et chescun des ditz Clercz si noun il soit/
oue le Roi et p(re)ngne de luy tiel fee ou tiels gages qil ent purroit Honestement viure il p(re)ndra/
du Roi p(ar) le io(ur) deux souldz si noun ils soient a la table le Roi. Et sils soient a la table le/
Roi donq(e)s p(re)ndront xij. d p(ar) le io(ur) q(ue)ux Clercz escriueront les dubitacions et respounces q(ue)ux/
yferront au Roi et le p(ar)lement et serront a lo(ur) conseil en q(e)conq(e) lieu qils eux voudront auoir/
et come ils ne sont ocoupiez eidront les clercs p(ri)ncipals a enroller./

De Casez Jugementz et doutez du p(ar)lement

Come brige ou dure cas de pees ou de guerre auigne en le pialme [sic] ou p(ar) de hors tiel cas soit/
ditz et reherce en escript en plein p(ar)lement et soit trete et dispute illeoq(e)s p(ar)entre les piers du/
4v p(ar)lement et bosoigne soit enuoier p(ur) le Roi ou dep(ar)t le Roi et si le Roi y ne soit a chescun degre/
aleys p(ar) s<oi> et soit tiel cas liu(er)e a lo(ur) clercz en escriptz et en c(er)tein lieu ferront rehercer deuan<t>/
euy tiel caas ensi qils ordeignent et considerent p(ar)entre eux en qele meillo(ur) ou iuste man(er)e p(ro)ce/
dre porront en tiel cas si come ils p(ur) la p(er)sone et les p(er)sones de lo(ur) mesure et p(ur) les p(er)sones deu[[x]]/
p(ur) queux p(er)sones eux sont p(re)sent voudront deuant dieu respoundre et lo(ur) responces et aui/
sementz ferront reportez en escript q(e) toutz lo(ur) respouncez conceils et auisementz ent oiez solonc/
le meillo(ur) et plus fayn conceil soit p(ro)cede et ou nomement la plus greindre p(ar)tie du p(ar)leme(n)t/
se acorde si come il soit p(ar) discorde p(ar)ent(re) le Roi et les aultres g(ra)untz ou p(ar)ent(re) g(ra)untz la pees/
du Roialme du soit enformez ou le poeple en le paijs ensi qil soit auys au Roi et a sou(n) co(n)seil/
q(e) soit en esploit q(e) tiel bosoigne soit trete et amende p(ar) consideracion de toutz les piers de son/
Roialme ou si p(ar) guerre le Roi et le Roialme soient troublez ou si dure caas auigne deuant/
le Chauncell(er) Denglet(er)re ou dure iugement soit a rendre deuant Justices ou autre caas sem-/
blable et si p(ar) auent(ur)e en tiels deliberacions toutz ou nomement la greindre p(ar)tie acorder ne p(ur)ront/
donqe le Counte Seneschal le Counte Constable et le Counte Mareschal ou deux de eux eslirent/
xxv. p(er)sones de toutz piers du Roialme cestassauoir deux Euesqes et treis p(ro)curato(ur)s p(ur) tout la cler-/
gie deux Countes et treis Barons Cink Chiualers de Counteez Cink Citeseinz et Cink Burgeis q(e)/
font xxv. et ils p(ur)ront eslire de lo(ur) mesme xij. et condescendre en eux et ils xij. vj. et condescendre/
en eux et ils vj. vnqore treis et condescendre en eux et ils treis ou plus poy q(e) lo(ur) mesmes ne p(ur)ront/

condescendre si nou(n) p(ar) licence du Roi et si le Roi vorroit consentir ils treis p(ur)rent en deux et de eux/
deux lun poet en lautre condescendre et ensi au derrain esterra son ordinance sur tout le p(ar)leme(n)t/
et ensi condescendant a xxv. p(er)sones tanqe a vn sol p(er)sone si non le greindre nombre acorde/
p(ur)roit et ordeigner a darrein vn soule p(er)sone come il est dit p(ur) toutz ordeignerent quil ouesq(e) soi/
mesmes descorder ne p(ur)roit salue le Roi et son conseil qils tiels ordeinement de puis qils s(er)ront/
en escript examinez et amender p(ur)ront si ceo faire soient et voudroient ensi q(e) ceo soit illeoq(e)s a/
donqes en plein p(ar)lement et del assent du p(ar)lement et ne mye derer le p(ar)lement. etc./

De ley de la deliu(er)aunce et des bosoignes du p(ar)lement.

Les bosoignes p(ur) queux le p(ar)lement est dount estre deliu(er)ez solonc la Kalendarie de le p(ar)lement etc./
solonc lordre des peticions liu(er)ez et affilez null(e) regard eiant a q(e)conq(e) p(er)sone einz qi p(re)m(er)ement soit/
p(re)mys p(re)m(er)ement ferreit en la Kalendarie del p(ar)lement s(er)ront remembrez toutz les bosoignes du p(ar)le/
ment suth' tiel ordre le p(ri)m(er) io(ur) guerre si guerre soit et dautres bosoignes les p(er)sones du Roi et du/
Roigne et de lo(ur) enfantz touchant le secunde io(ur) co(mmun)e bosoignez du Roialme si come de leis a establier/
encontre defaultez de leis origenels iudiciels et executories de puis iugementz renduz q(e) les sou(n)t les/
plus co(mmun)es bosoignes et ceo solonc lordre de filaces des peticions si come il est dit. etc./

De iours et Heures al p(ar)lement.

Le p(ar)lement ne doit estre tenuz en dymenges einz chescun aultre io(ur) hors pris p(ar) toute voie treis io(ur)s/
cestassauoir Le io(ur) de toutz seintz des almes et de la Natiuite de seint Joh(a)n le Baptistre et poet estre/
tenuz et deit chescun io(ur) comencer a la mye Heure le prime a quel Heure le Roi est tenuz estre en/
p(ar)lement et toutz les piers du Roialme et deiuont tenir le p(ar)lement en bien [sic] apert. En aultres/
seintz io(ur)s le p(ar)lement doit comencer al Heure de prime p(ur) diuine seruice. etc./

De la man(er)e du p(ar)lement.
En primes monstre la forme en quele man(er)e et a quel temps chescun sommonz du p(ar)lement doit/
estre fait qi venir deiuont p(ar) sommonz et qi noun secundarie qi p(ar) reson de lo(ur) offices venir/
deiuont et estre sont tenutz p(ar) tout le p(ar)lement sauntz sommonz dont il est a considerer/
q(e) deux p(ri)ncipals Clercs du p(ar)lement esluz p(ar) le Roi et sou(n) conseil et aultres Clercz secundaries/
de q(ue)ux et de lo(ur) offices s(er)ra dit de puis plus especialment. Et le p(ri)ncipal Criour Denglet(er)re/
ouesq(e) ses s/o/usciez Criours et le p(ri)ncipal Huissh(er) Denglet(er)re queux deux offices cest adire/
loffice de Criour et Huissh(er) soloient a vne et a mesme chose app(ar)tenir ceux offic(er)es son<t>/
tenu<z> estre en p(ar)lement le p(ri)m(er) iour. etc./
De les Officers le R<o>y<e>
Le Chauncell(er) Denglet(er)re et tresourer Chamberleins et Barons de Lescheqer Justicez et toutz/
Clercz et Chiualers du Roi Auxi ouesq(e) les s(er)geanz du ley queux sont de conseil le/
5r Roi sont tenuz estre en le p(ar)lement le secunde io(ur) si noun ils eient excusac[[ion]] resonable/
<et>sils ne p(ur)ront y estre donqes deuont enuoier bones excusacions. etc./
De comensement du p(ar)lement
Le Roi serra en my lieu de la greindre Bank et il est tenuz estre p(ri)m(erm)ent en le p(ar)lement/
le vj. io(ur) et soloient les Chauncell(er) Tresourer Barons de Lescheqer et Justicez recorder/
defautz faitz en le p(ar)lement south lordre qensuit. Le p(ri)m(er) io(ur) s(er)ront appellez Burgeys/
et Citeseinz de tout Englet(er)re a quel io(ur) si les Burgeis ne viendront Le Burgh serra/
am(er)cie a C. marz et la Citee a C. li'. le secunde io(ur) s(er)ront appellez les Ch(iuale)rs des Counteez/
de tout Englet(er)re a quel io(ur) sils ne viendront le Countee de qils sont s(er)ra am(er)cie a/
C. li' le tierce io(ur) serront appellez Barons de Cink portz sils ne viendront le Baronie/

de qils sont s(er)ra am(er)cie a C. marz et le Countee a C. li'. et en mesme la man(er)e serra fait deux/
queux sont piers des Counteez et Barons cestassauoir ils qont t(er)-res et rentes al value/
dun Countee ou dune Baronie si come il est auantdit en le title de so(m)monz le qarte/
io(ur) serront appellez les p(ro)curato(ur)s de Clergie et sils ne viendront lo(ur) Euesqe serront am(er)/
ciez p(ur) chescun Erchediaconie q(i) fait defaut a C. marz le quinte serront appellez Deanes/
Priours Abbes Euesqes et a darrein Ercheuesqes et sils ne viendront chescun Ercheuesq(e)/
serra am(er)cie a C. li'. chescun Euesq(e) q(e) tient vne Baronie entier a C. marz et en mesme/
la man(er)e de Abbes Priours et aultres. etc./

De p(ro)clamacion du p(ar)lement.

Le p(ri)m(er) io(ur) doit estre fait p(ro)clamacion p(ri)merement en la sale ou en monstre ou en aultre/
lieu appert ou le p(ar)lement serra tenuz et de puis app(er)tement en la Citee ou en la ville/
q(e) toutz ceux q(e) peticions et querelez deliu(er)er voudront al p(ar)lement qils eux deliu(er)ont/
de le p(ri)m(er) io(ur) de p(ar)lement tanq(e) en Cink io(ur)s p(ro)scheinement ensuantz. etc./

De la p(re)dicacion a P(ar)lement.

Vn Ercheuesq(e) ou Euesqe ou vn g(ra)nt Clerc sage et de beal p(ar)lance esluz p(ar) Lercheuesqe de la/
p(ro)uince en quel le p(ar)lement s(er)ra tenuz doit precher vn de les cink p(ri)m(er)s io(ur)s vn p(ar)lement en/
plein p(ar)lement et en p(re)sence du Roi et ceo q(ua)nt le p(ar)lement s(er)ra p(ur) le greindre p(ar)tie asemblez et/
en sou(n) s(er)moun ensuant declarer declarer [sic] a tout le p(ar)lement qils oue luy Humblement/
dieu supplient et luy honurement p(ur) la pees et t(ra)nquillite du Roi et le Roialme si come/
il serra dit pluis especialment en le title suant de la p(re)dicacion ale p(ar)lement. etc./

De le p(ro)nou(n)cement du p(ar)lement.

De puis la p(re)dica cion doit le Cauncell[[er]] Denglet(er)re oue le chief Justice Denglet(er)re cestassauoir/

celuy q(i) tient plees deuant le Roi ou aultre Justic(e) couenable Honest et de beale p(ar)lance ou/
clercz p(ar) mesmes les Chauncell⌊er⌋ et chief Justice esluz monstrer les causes du p(ar)lement p(ri)m(er)e-/
ment en gen(er)al et de puis en especial esteant et ent fait assauoir q(e) toutz de p(ar)lement q(e)conqes/
ils soient q(ua)nt ils enp(ar)leront escrieront Horspris le Roi ensi q(e) toutz de le p(ar)lement p(ur)ront/
oier celuy q(i) p(ar)le et sil dit obscurement ou bas p(ar)le il dirra autre foitz et p(ar)lera plus en/
haut ou vn aultre p(ar)lera p(ur) luy. etc./

De la p(ar)lance du Roy ap(re)s le p(ro)nou(n)cement.

Le Roi ap(re)s le pronouncement p(ur) le p(ar)lement doit priere Clercz et lays en no(m)i(n)aunt toutz lo(ur)/
degreez cestassauoir Ercheuesq(es) Euesq(es) Abbez Priours Erchedeacones p(ro)curato(ur)s et aut(re)s de/
clergie Countez Barons Chiualers Citeseinz Burgeys et aultres lays qils diligentement stu/
diousement et coerement trauailleront a treter et deliu(er)er bosoignes du p(ar)lement si come ceo/
pluis p(ri)ncipalment estre entendront et senteront p(ri)m(er)ement ala volunte dieu et de puis/
[[al]] <h>ono(ur) et p(ro)fit du Roi et lo(ur) mesmes. etc./

De Labsence de Roy du p(ar)lement.

Le R[[oi]] est tenuz p(ar) toute voie estre p(er)sonelement en le p(ar)lement si noun il soit detenuz/
p(ar) cop(or)al malease et donq(e)s il poet tenir sa Chambre ensi qil ne gist p(ar) de hors la manor/
[[ou]] nomement la vile ou le p(ar)lement est tenuz et donq(e)s doit envoier p(ur) xij. p(er)sones des/
5v greindres et meille(ur)s q(ue)ux font somonez al p(ar)lement cestassauoir deux Euesqes deux Coun-/
tes deux Barons deux Chiualers des Counteez deux Citeseinz et deux Burgeis a veoir/
sa p(er)sone et a tesmoign(er) sou(n) estat et doit en lo(ur) p(re)sence co(m)mettre al Ercheuesq(e) de le lieu le se/
neschal a sou(n) chief Justice qils ensemble et chescun p(ar) soi comenceront et continueront le/
p(ar)lement en sou(n) nou(n) eiant en lo(ur) comission exp(re)sse mencion a ceo de cause de labsence q(e) le/

chose doit seuffez et monest laut(re)s g(ra)ntz et nobles du p(ar)lement ouesq(e) notoir tesmoigne des/
ditz xij. piers et le cause est qar le clamour et murmur soleit estre en p(ar)lement p(ur) labsence/
du Roi qar il est chose p(er)ilouse et damageouse a tout le cominalte del p(ar)lement et auxi le/
Roialme q(ua)nt le Roi fuit absente de le p(ar)lement et ne ceo doit absentir ne poet se non/
seulement en caas suisditz./

De Lieux sossons en le p(ar)lement.

Prim(er)ement si come il est dit se ora le Roi en my lieu de la greindre Bank et en sa p(ar)tie/
dextre s(er)ra Lercheuesq(e) de Canterbury et en sa p(ar)tie senestre s(er)ra Lercheuesq(e) Deu(er)wyk/
et ap(re)s eux ordeinement Euesqes Abbez Priours toute voie p(ar) tiel liu(er)e p(ar)ent(re) les degreez/
suisditz et lo(ur) lieux ensi q(e) nul s(er)ra si nou(n) p(ar)ent(re) ses piers a se veire est tenuz le Senes-/
chal Denglet(er)re si nou(n) le Roi vorroit ceo assign(er) et al pee dextre du Roi serront le/
Chaunceller Denglet(er)re le chief Justice Denglet(er)re et ses co(m)paignons et lo(ur) clercz queux/
sou(n)t du p(ar)lement et a sou(n) pee senestre s(er)ront les Tresourer Chamberleyns et Barons/
de lescheqer Justices de la Bank et lo(ur) Clercz si ascun soit de p(ar)lement./

De Le Huissh(er) en le p(ar)lement.

Le p(ri)ncipal Huissh(er) de le p(ar)lement esterra de deinz le g(ra)nt huis del monstrer sale ou/
autre lieu le p(ar)lement est tenuz et gardera le huis ensi q(e) nul entrera le p(ar)lement si/
nou(n) celuy q(e) viendre doit al p(ar)lement ou s(er)ra appelle appelle [sic] p(ur) bosoigne qil p(ur)suera/
qeu le p(ar)lement et il est bosoigne q(e) celuy Huissh(er) eit conysance des p(er)sones q(ue)ux entrez/
deiuont si q(e) nul soit destourbe de sou(n) entre qi al p(ar)lement estre est tenuz et celuy/
Huissh(er) poet et doit si bosoigne soit au(er)a plusours Huissh(er)s de south' luy. etc./

De le Criour de p(ar)lement.

Le Criour de p(ar)lement esterra p(ar) de hors le huys de p(ar)lement et le Huissh(er) luy mons/
trera ces clamours et le Roi soleit enuoier ses s(er)geantz darmez a estre p(ar) q(ua)nt espace/
p(ar) de hors le Huis del p(ar)lement et a garder le huis ensi q(e) null(e) enp(re)ssiounes ne neise/
ne serront faitz ento(ur) de huis p(ar) q(ue)ux le p(ar)lement purroit estre destorbez sur peyne/
de/prise de/lo(ur) corps[1] qar de droit le huis del p(ar)lement ne doit estre close einz p(ar) Huissh(er)s et/
les sergeantz darmes gardez. etc./
De les p(ar)lantz qesteieront en le p(ar)lement.
Toutz les piers du p(ar)lement seeront et nul esteiera mes q(ua)nt il p(ar)lera ensi q(e) chescun de p(ar)le/
ment luy purra oier et nul entrera la p(ar)lement ne issuera del p(ar)lement si nou(n) p(ar) cel huis/
et toutz les p(ar)lances estoieront a q(e)conq(e) temps qils p(ar)leront ascun chose q(e) doit estre de/
liu(er)e p(ar) le p(ar)lement et la cause est qils s(er)ront oiez de les piers qar toutz les piers sou(n)t Juges et Justices./
De demander laide del p(ar)lement.
Le Roi ne soleit demander aide de son Roialme mais p(ur) guerre esteant ou p(ur) ses filz afaire/
Chiualer ou ses filez amariez et donq(e)s deiuont tiels eides estre demandez en plein p(ar)le/
ment et estre deliu(er)ez en escript a chescun degree de les piers du p(ar)lement et en escript/
estre responez et fait assauoir q(e) a tiels aides estre g(ra)untez il busoigne q(e) toutz piers del/
p(ar)lement se consenteront et fait a entendre q(e) deux Chiualers q(ue)ux sont venuz al/
p(ar)lement p(ur) vne Countee aient plus g(ra)nt voice en le p(ar)lement en g(ra)ntant et contre [[dant]]/
q(e) les plus g(ra)ntz Counteez Denglet(er)re et en mesme la man(er)e les p(ro)curato(ur)s de Clergie dun/
Euesq(e) eiant plus g(ra)nt voice en le p(ar)lement sils toutz soient acordez q(e) leuesq(e) et ceo/

1. actually: de/prise/lo(ur)/de/corps

ein totes choses q(ue)ux al p(ar)lement deiuont estre g(ra)untez faitz ou denyes et ceo appiert/

qar le Roi poet tenir p(ar)lement oue la co(m)i(n)alte de sou(n) Roialme saun Euesqes Coun/

tes et Barons si ensi soit qils soient so(m)monez al p(ar)lement. Et si nul Euesqe/

6r Counte ou Baron a ses so(m)monz viendra qar iadis nestoit Euesq(e) ne Counte ne Baron/

et vnqore a donqes les Rois tenueront lo(ur) p(ar)lement einz en autre man(er)e est encontre qar/

si co(m)i(n)altes de clergie et <l>a<i>ez estoient so(m)monez al p(ar)lement si come de droit ils deu(er)ont et p(ur)/

ascuns c(er)teinz causes venir ne voudreient si come ils discrent q(e) le Roi eux ne gou(er)neroit/

come ils deueroit et assignerent especialement en qeux articles eux ne gou(er)neroit a donq(e)/

le p(ar)lement se+n+oit p(ur) nul et si vnqore ensi s(er)roit q(e) toutz Ercheuesqes Euesqes Countez/

et Barons et toutz lo(ur) piers oue le Roi estoient p(re)sentz (et) p(ur) ceo il est bosoigne q(e) Countez q(e)/

q(e) [sic] deiuont estre g(ra)untez faitz affermez ou denyez p(ar) le p(ar)lement qils soient g(ra)ntez p(ar) la to [sic]/

co(m)i(n)alte del p(ar)lement qel est de treis de greez cestassauoir de p(ro)curato(ur)s de Clergie Ch(iuale)rs/

des Counteez Citeseinz et Burgeis qeux p(re)sentent tout la co(m)i(n)alte Denglet(er)re et ne mye de/

les g(ra)untz qar chescun de eux est p(ur) sa p(ro)pre p(er)sone en le p(ar)lement et ne mye p(ur) ascun aultre./

De le dep(ar)tir du p(ar)lement.

Le p(ar)lement ne doit dep(ar)tir q(ua)nt ascun peticion est pendant nient discusse ou a meynz/

a quel null responce ne soit det(er)minez. Et si le Roi fait la contrarie il est p(er)iurez et nul/

soul de toutz les piers del p(ar)lement puet ne doit dep(ar)tir del p(ar)lement si nou(n) il/

eit conge du Roi et de toutz ses piers et ceo en plein p(ar)lement et q(e) de tiel conge soit fait/

remembrance en les +r+ollez del p(ar)lement. Et si ascun des piers durant le p(ar)lement/

soit a malease si q(e) le p(ar)lement venir ne p(ur)ra a donqes deinz le tierce io(ur) enuoiera ses ex-/

cusato(ur)s al p(ar)lement a qel io(ur) sil ne viendra soient enuoietz a luy deux de ses piers a/
veier et tesmoigner sa maladie et si i soit suspeccion soient ceux deux piers iurez ent/
dient verites et si compiert qil soi feigne soit am(er)cie come p(ur) defaute et sil ne soi feigne/
a donqes il atto(ur)nera ascun suffisant deuant eux a estre p(ur) luy al p(ar)lement sil verroit/
qar si ne poet estre excuse si soit de sayne memorie a le dep(ar)tir del p(ar)lement ensi/
doit estre vse. Prim(erm)ent doit estre demau(n)de et crie en appert en le p(ar)lement ou de/
deinz la palays del p(ar)lement si ysoit ascun qi deliu(er)oit peticion al p(ar)lement a quel/
vnqore ne soit fait respounce et si nul recrie il est a supposer q(e) chescun est fait me-/
dicine ou nomement solonc ceo qil poet estre de droit est respounse et adonqes p(ri)-/
m(er)ement cestassauoir q(ua)nt nulle ysoit qi peticion deuoront celli temps ne recrie nous/
deuo(ns) conge al p(ar)lement. etc./

De les t(ra)nscriptz des recordes en le p(ar)lement.

Les Clercz de p(ar)lement ne deiuoront a nulli transcript ne p(ro)cesse einz ceo deliu(er)eont/
a chescun qi ceo demaunde et p(re)ndrent toutditz p(ur) dix lynes vn dener si nou(n) p(ar) auenture/
y s(er)ra fait foide nou(n) poier en quel cas ils riens ne p(re)ndront les +r+oulles del p(ar)leme(n)t/
contiendront en largesse dis pounz. Et le p(ar)lement s(er)ra tenuz en quel lieu del Roialme/
qil plerra a Roi. etc./

De les degreez de les piers du p(ar)lement.

Le Roi est chief comenceour del p(ar)lement et fin de mesme le p(ar)lement et ensi il nad pier en/
sou(n) degree et le Roi soul est le p(ri)m(er) degree. Le secunde degree est de les Ercheuesqes E-/
uesqes Abbez et Priours p(ar) Baronie tenantz. Le tierce degree est de les p(ro)curato(ur)s de cler-/
gie Le quarte degree est de les Countez Barons et aultres g(ra)ntz et gentils ten(au)ntz al value/

de Countee et Baronie si come il est auantdit en le title des layes. Le quinte degree est/ des Chiualers des Counteez Le sisme degree est des Citeseinz et Burgeis et ensi est le p(ar)le/ ment de sis degreez. Et fait assauoir q(e) si ensi soit q(e) ascuns de Cink degreez ap(re)s le/ Roi soit absent et nient meyns ils tenutz soient p(ar) resonables so(m)monz du p(ar)lement/ garinz nient meyns le p(ar)lement est iugez estre plein. etc.

Name and Place Index

Index of Manuscripts